An Introduction
to
Natural Generative
Phonology

# AN INTRODUCTION
# TO
# NATURAL GENERATIVE
# PHONOLOGY

Joan B. Hooper

*Department of Linguistics*
*State University of New York at Buffalo*
*Buffalo, New York*

Academic Press New York San Francisco London

*A Subsidiary of Harcourt Brace Jovanovich, Publishers*

ACADEMIC PRESS, INC.
111 Fifth Avenue, New York, New York 10003

*United Kingdom Edition published by*
ACADEMIC PRESS, INC. (LONDON) LTD.
24/28 Oval Road, London NW1

Library of Congress Cataloging in Publication Data

Hooper, Joan B.
    An introduction to natural generative phonology.

    Bibliography:     p.
    1.    Grammar, Comparative and general–Phonology.
2.    Generative grammar.    I.    Title.
P217.H6        414            76-2945
ISBN 0–12–354750–4

**To Bill,**
**who is way ahead of his time,**
**and to our Brody**

# Contents

# 8 Morphophonemics in Spanish Verbs 139

## PART II
## NATURAL PHONOLOGICAL STRUCTURE

# 9 Constraints on Phonological Structure 179

# 10 Strength Relations in Syllable Structure 195

# 11 A Strength Scale and Syllable Structure Condition for Spanish 208

# 12

## Further Implications of the Theory of Syllable Structure    227

# 13

## Natural Insertion and Deletion Rules    233

# Preface

Natural generative phonology is based in part on transformational generative theory as developed since the mid-1950s, but there are a number of fundamental differences between the theories that have far-reaching consequences for phonological grammars. The major difference concerns the abstractness of phonological representations and rules. The constraints on natural generative phonology were proposed in 1971 by Theo Vennemann in response to the abstractness problem. Over the past few years a number of linguists have worked actively to examine the consequences of these constraints. The result has been an entirely new theory of the interaction of morphology and phonology. This theory differs both from generative theory as represented in Chomsky and Halle (1968) and traditional American phonemic theory. The major advantage of natural generative theory over previous generative theory is that it gives a realistic representation of linguistic competence by constraining the theory to allow only a small subset of the grammars allowed by the unconstrained theory. The theory requires that phonological rules and representations bear a direct relation to surface linguistic forms; the resulting concrete analyses are to a much greater extent subject to empirical disconfirmation than the abstract analyses of the *Sound Pattern of English* and other works in that vein. Furthermore, the formal devices of natural generative theory are considerably less powerful than those of previous generative theories; consequently they make much stronger claims about the nature of linguistic competence. It should further be noted that the beauty of the constraints originally proposed by Vennemann is that they are not, like most proposed constraints, random attempts at patch-up jobs on a hulking machinery that uncontrollably generates excesses, but a fundamental reformulation of morphophonological theory.

Given the relative power of the two theories, the burden of proof is logically on those who propose the more powerful theory. However, the historical priority of the abstract theory puts a practical demand on the proponents of concreteness to demonstrate the merits of a highly constrained theory. This book is an expansion and revision of an earlier work in which I presented empirical evidence for the more constrained theory. The present book goes far beyond the earlier version in working out and examining the consequences of natural generative theory for the morphophonological analyses of a wide range of data from various languages. It is hoped that the discussion is detailed enough and covers a sufficiently broad range of data to serve as an introduction to this new theory of morphophonology.

As in any theory, certain problems arise, some formal, some empirical. I have tried to uncover, unravel, and resolve as many of these problems as possible; and where more than one solution has been proposed within the framework, I have compared these solutions and argued their relative merit. There is no monolithic agreement among linguists working in the concrete theory, thus what is found in this book is my own interpretation of natural generative theory, which differs in some significant details from other views of the theory. There are also many empirical questions that remain to be answered. These questions arise in the area of morphological analysis and phonological rule naturalness. Hence, the reader will find here a new framework whose general structure is formulated in sufficient detail to be presented as a viable and coherent theory, but which also opens up areas of inquiry that promise to be rich sources of substantive insight into natural language phenomena.

The presentation is largely comparative, since the book is directed toward linguists now working in the area of generative morphophonology, and some acquaintance with contemporary theory is assumed. Of course the force of the argumentation is directed toward showing that natural generative theory makes the correct predictions in a wide range of cases and that the unconstrained theory does not. However, I have not included all the arguments available in the literature in favor of natural generative phonology; for instance, I have not discussed in any detail the principles behind rule inversion (as discussed in Vennemann, 1972c; also in Schuh, 1972; Hyman, 1974) nor have I discussed the uniqueness issue (Vennemann, 1972c). Neither have I marshaled all the arguments against the unconstrained theory, e.g., the methodological arguments developed by Botha (1971). It was simply not possible, due to time and space limitations, to include a discussion of every issue or example relevant to this major theoretical controversy.

The book is organized into two major parts. The first deals primarily with the formal constraints on the theory and their consequences for morphophonological analysis. The topics covered in Chapters 1 through 5 include a general discussion of the abstractness problem, an explanation of the constraints on natural generative phonology, the presentation of empirical evidence supporting extremely concrete analyses, and a discussion of the role of extrinsic rule order (including cyclic rule application) in allowing abstractness. Chapter 6 deals with the theory of historical change that follows from the theory of synchronic grammar and includes a critique of the notion of rule reordering. In Chapter 7 the difficult issue of lexical representations is discussed, and several proposals are evaluated. The proposal adopted here is applied to Spanish data in Chapter 8. The second part of the book deals with substantive phonological issues. In particular I develop here a suggestion for an explanatory theory of syllable structure and a theory of natural insertion and deletion rules.

# Acknowledgments

The development of the ideas presented here has come about through much discussion with other linguists, and I am very grateful to everyone who took the time to share their insights or air their criticisms with me. I am grateful to the students at SUNY Buffalo for their response and support, not to mention their ideas and suggestions, among them in particular, Bernadette Abaurre, Richard Mowrey, William Pagliuca, and Blair Rudes, who very generously gave their time, ideas, and data. Thanks go also to the Chicago Linguistic Society for allowing me to use parts of my article "Rule Morphologization in Natural Generative Phonology," which appeared in the *Proceedings from the Parasession on Natural Phonology*. I would also like to thank Joyce Russell for the patience and care she put into typing the manuscript and its numerous revisions. For reading and commenting on parts of the manuscript in earlier versions, I am grateful to Stephen Anderson, James Harris, Grover Hudson, Paul Schachter, and especially Theo Vennemann. This work has benefited immensely from a long, and sometimes harrowing, correspondence with James Harris, who patiently unloaded mountains of criticism on me, and in so doing forced me to clarify my position and the details of the theory. My greatest debt, of course, is to Theo Venne-mann, who taught me to seek explanations, and who saw how to formulate a new theory at a time when most of us knew only that the old one would not do.

An Introduction
to
Natural Generative
Phonology

# CONCRETENESS
# IN
# MORPHOPHONOLOGY

# 1

# The Abstractness Problem

## 1.1 Generative Phonology

In generative theory, the goal of a descriptive study of language is the construction of a grammar. The grammar is a representation of the knowledge that a native speaker has that enables him to produce and interpret a potentially infinite number of utterances. This knowledge is called "competence." Competence is distinguished from performance in that competence represents the ideal way the speaker would use his language if extralinguistic factors such as memory restrictions and distractions did not interfere (Chomsky, 1964; Chomsky and Halle, 1968). In a generative grammar linguistic competence is formalized in a system of rules that determines the sound–meaning correspondences that a language uses. The grammar, then, is supposed to describe the set of internalized rules a speaker has acquired, which enable him to use his language.

The grammar is organized into components: the semantic component, the syntactic component, and the phonological component. In the present study we will be concerned only with the phonological component and one other part of the grammar, the lexicon.

3

The lexicon contains a list of all the morphemes in the language along with information that characterizes the behavior of each morpheme. This information is semantic, syntactic, and phonological. The phonological information describes the phonological shape of the morpheme in terms of distinctive features. The classificatory distinctive features of the lexicon are binary; i.e., they represent a choice between two opposites, which is stated by a "+" or "−" specification (Halle, 1964). The binary distinctive features used throughout this study are those proposed by Chomsky and Halle (1968), and a familiarity with these features is assumed. (The adoption of this feature system for this study does not imply that it is entirely correct; in fact, in Part II we will be advocating the use of some additional features.)

The phonological shape of a morpheme, as entered in the lexicon, together with surface syntactic information make up the systematic phonemic level. This level is more abstract than the phonetic level; the two are related by the rules that make up the phonological component. The lexical representations of morphemes is not entirely abstract, however, since their representations are stated in terms of distinctive features that have intrinsic phonetic content. It is a requirement of the theory that the phonological representations of the lexicon and the phonetic properties of the morphemes be related in a nonarbitrary way. This requirement is called the Naturalness Condition by Postal (1968).

The phonological component consists of a set of rules (known as phonological rules) that map the systematic phonemic level onto the systematic phonetic level. The phonological rules change the feature values (+'s and −'s) of the segments in certain contexts. Phonological rules apply in sequential order; that is, a rule applies to the input structure A and changes the feature values to obtain a structure B, which in turn is acted on by a second rule to obtain structure C and so on. Each rule may apply only once, and is assigned a particular place in the sequence or is said to be ORDERED with respect to other rules. The theory with this general form will be referred to as transformational generative phonology (abbreviated as TGP).

## 1.2 Abstractness

It is generally agreed that the generative apparatus just described is too powerful; that is, it is capable of describing many systems that are not possible human languages. The long-range goal of theoretical linguistics is to formulate a theory that is just powerful enough to describe correctly all the facts of natural language but, at the same time, is not so powerful that it describes systems or predicts phenomena that never occur in natural language. In keeping with this goal, generative phonology needs to be constrained. One aspect of the theory that needs to be constrained has been discussed under the label of ABSTRACTNESS. The type of abstractness (or its converse, concreteness) that has spawned a controversy is the abstractness of underlying systematic phonemic representations.

While all generative phonologists seem to agree that underlying representations of the phonological form of a morpheme should be specified in features that have intrinsic phonetic content (Postal's Naturalness Condition), there is nothing explicit in the theory that specifies just how different underlying forms may be from surface forms. In a very abstract analysis, underlying forms may be quite different from surface phonetic forms; in a concrete analysis, underlying forms will be very similar if not identical to surface forms. TGP allows both types of analyses, and many analyses ranging from extremely abstract to extremely concrete have been proposed in this framework. A good deal of argumentation has been directed at trying to show that the abstract or the concrete position is correct, and a number of constraints have been proposed to limit abstractness.

Given that the theory of generative phonology needs to be constrained, it is theoretically interesting to formulate the strongest possible constraints on the theory and then to investigate the consequences of these constraints. The purpose of this study is to present and examine a version of generative phonology that places the strongest possible constraints on abstractness in phonological descriptions. We will discuss some particular analyses within this theory and cite independent evidence to support the validity of the claims made by this more constrained theory, the theory of natural generative grammar (Vennemann, 1971; 1972c,e; 1974a,b). Before turning to the constraints on natural generative phonology (abbreviated as NGP), however, we will briefly examine, with two examples, some of the issues in the abstractness controversy.

Consider first an example discussed in Saporta (1965:220–22). In Latin American Spanish a few verbs show an alternation of stem-final /s/ with /sk/. The /s/ appears in all forms except the first singular of the present tense and the present subjunctive, where /sk/ appears. For example, the verb *crecer* 'to grow' illustrates the alternation as shown in (1). The forms with /sk/ are not predictable from the surface phonetic representation of the stem, since there are verbs such as *coser* [koser] 'to sew' that do not alternate. Saporta proposes to differentiate between the verbs such as *crecer*, which have the alternation, and verbs such as

(1)

|  |  | Spelling | Phonetic |
|---|---|---|---|
| Infinitive |  | *crecer* | [kreser] |
| Ind. Sg. | 1 | *crezco* | [kresko] |
|  | 2 | *creces* | [kreses] |
|  | 3 | *crece* | [krese] |
| Subj. Sg. | 1 | *crezca* | [kreska] |

*coser*, which do not, by giving them different systematic phonemic representations. *Crecer* would be /kreθer/, and *coser* would be /koser/. The rule that inserts the /k/ does so only after /θ/, not after /s/:

(2)
$$\emptyset \longrightarrow k / V\theta \underline{\quad} + \left\{ \begin{matrix} o \\ a \end{matrix} \right\}$$

Subsequent to (2) in order of application is a rule that changes /θ/ to /s/ in all cases.

(3)
$$\theta \longrightarrow s$$

A sample derivation:

| kreθo | kreθe | koso | kose | |
|---|---|---|---|---|
| k | — | — | — | rule (2) |
| s | s | — | — | rule (3) |
| [kresko] | [krese] | [koso] | [kose] | |

In Latin American Spanish there is no surface phonetic segment [θ]; there is only one voiceless coronal continuant and it is /s/. There is no evidence at all for an underlying distinction between /s/ and /θ/. Although the orthography reflects this distinction that is found in Castilian, literate Latin American speakers, in attempting to mimic the Castilian dialect, find it almost impossible to correctly distribute the /θ/; the typical result is hypercorrection. In short there is no evidence whatsoever that a distinction between /s/ and /θ/ is a part of the competence of speakers of Latin American Spanish, nor that such a distinction governs the insertion of /k/ in the paradigms of *crecer* and similar verbs.[1]

Analyses of this type have been studied by Kiparsky (1968 [1973]). He calls the putative phenomenon represented by the two rules (2) and (3)

---

[1] In fact, in Castilian, where the /s/–/θ/ distinction is made, the /θ/ does not condition the insertion of /k/, since there is at least one verb *cocer* [koθer] with [θ] that does not undergo /k/-insertion.

"absolute neutralization," because the posited underlying distinction between /s/ and /θ/ in the systematic phonemic representation is marked by the phonological feature, stridency: /s/ is [+strident] and /θ/ is [−strident]. This phonological distinction is used to account for a distinction among verb classes that is totally arbitrary in the synchronic grammar. Since the phonological distinction represented by a difference in stridency is unmotivated in the synchronic grammar, the phonological feature is being used as a DIACRITIC. Kiparsky proposes that the diacritic use of phonological features be limited in order to exclude the questionable analysis represented by rules (2) and (3). To accomplish this end, Kiparsky proposes the Alternation Condition, which has two possible formulations.

The Strong Alternation Condition states that phonological features may NOT be used as diacritics under any circumstances. This condition would exclude Saporta's analysis of the *crecer* verbs and would make it necessary instead to signal the difference between *crecer* and *coser* in some other way. One possibility is to replace the phonological feature Saporta uses with an arbitrary diacritic.

Under this analysis the phonological shape of the verbs *crecer* and *coser* would not give any clue to their different behavior. They would merely be /kreser/ and /koser/. The aberrant characteristics of /kreser/ would be signaled by the diacritic symbol, [+K]; this serves as the trigger for the rule of /k/-insertion, which would also refer to this diacritic:

(4)   Lexical form:   /kres−/
                        [+K]

      Rules:   $\emptyset \longrightarrow k / \text{Vs} \underline{\qquad}]_{\substack{\text{verb} \\ [+K]}} \left\{ \begin{matrix} o \\ a \end{matrix} \right\}$

This analysis captures the fact that the difference between *crecer* and *coser* is an arbitrary morphophonemic difference, not a phonological one. The rule in (4) is similar to the rule given in Harris (1972) for this class of verbs.[2]

Another analysis of these forms that does not involve absolute neutralization is suggested in Foley (1965). Under this analysis, the /k/ is posited in the underlying form /kresk-/ and deleted when it occurs before a front vowel. However, this analysis, like the one in (4), must also contain some morphological information, for the deletion of /k/ between

---

[2] However, in Harris (1972) the underlying form is somewhat different; these differences are not directly relevant to the present discussion.

/s/ and a front vowel may only apply in second and third conjugation. First conjugation forms such as *mascar* 'to chew' and *buscar* 'to look for' retain the /k/ in the present subjunctive, despite a following front vowel: *masque* [maske], first and third singular; *busque* [buske], first and third singular. Therefore if the /k/ is underlying, the deletion rule must be restricted morphologically by the mention of conjugation class.

(5)     Lexical form:   / kres −/
                        [− 1st conj.]

        Rule:   k ⟶ Ø / s ____] $_{\substack{\text{verb} \\ [-\text{1st conj.}]}}$ $\begin{bmatrix} V \\ - \text{back} \end{bmatrix}$

A reference to conjugation class is less arbitrary than a reference to a diacritic such as [ + K], since conjugation class membership is relevant for a number of morphological and morphophonemic rules in Spanish (see Chapter 8). Our purpose here is not to choose between these two latter analyses. (This matter will be taken up in Chapter 7, Section 3.) Our purpose is rather to demonstrate that the Strong Alternation Condition correctly constrains abstractness by excluding the incorrect analyses.

Kiparsky did not, however, advocate the adoption of the Strong Alternation Condition. Instead, a second version of the constraint, the Weak Alternation Condition, was accepted by Kiparsky. The Weak Alternation Condition claims that the diacritic use of phonological features may represent native speaker competence, but that situations described in this way are characteristically unstable and introduce greater complexity into the grammar. By the terms of this condition, then, analyses (4) or (5) would be preferred over the absolute neutralization analysis, but absolute neutralization would still be allowed as a description of a natural language phenomenon. In short, the theory remains virtually unconstrained.[3]

The plausibility of the Alternation Condition is well illustrated by the *crecer* case presented above, and yet even the Strong Alternation Condition is not a sufficient constraint on abstractness in phonological analy-

---

[3] The rejection of the Strong Alternation Condition was based largely on cases in which more than one rule referred to a phonological feature that is used as a diacritic. Kiparsky (1971) has suggested that absolute neutralization be excluded in cases where only ONE rule refers to the phonological diacritic, as in the example in the text, but allowed in cases where several rules use the phonological diacritic. But even in these cases the viability of absolute neutralization has been disputed (see Vennemann, 1974a), and in one case cited by Kiparsky, the analysis of vowels in Spanish, Harris (1969) refrains from using a phonological feature as a diacritic. The case of absolute neutralization proposed in Hyman (1970) is discussed in Section 5.4.

ses. Let us consider another example from Spanish, an analysis proposed by Harris (1969:169).

The lexicon of Modern Spanish contains a large number of vocabulary items borrowed from Latin. When Spanish borrows from Latin, it borrows from its own history; Latin forms bear a phonological relationship to Spanish forms that reflects the phonological history of Spanish. Thus there is a certain regularity between native Spanish forms and the learned forms borrowed from Latin at a later date. Sometimes the difference between the native and learned forms is minimal: *padre* 'father' and *paternal* 'paternal'. In other cases the distance is much greater: *leche* 'milk' and *lactar* 'to lactate'. Yet the phonological relation between these last two is discernible to a linguist, particularly if he knows the history of *leche*. But the existence of a phonological relation between *leche* and *lactar* in a synchronic grammar is questionable, and, if it exists, its status in a synchronic grammar is also questionable.

There are a few other forms that exhibit the alternation between /kt/ and /č/. (Here and elsewhere the symbol [β] is used to represent the voiced labial spirant, as in [oktaβo]. Similarly, [ð] is the interdental voiced spirant and [γ] is the velar.)

(6) *leche*  [leče]  'milk'  *lactar*  [laktar]  'to lactate'
  *láctico*  [laktiko]  'lactic'
 *ocho*  [očo]  'eight'  *octavo*  [oktaβo]  'eighth'
 *noche*  [noče]  'night'  *nocturno*  [nokturno]  'nocturnal'

Harris assumes that a native speaker's competence includes a knowledge of the phonological relationship between these forms. He represents this relationship by giving *leche, ocho,* and *noche* systematic phonemic forms with /kt/: /lakte/, /okto/, and /nokte/. The systematic phonetic forms are then generated by a set of rules that partially recapitulate the historical development of the /kt/ cluster from Vulgar Latin to Modern Spanish:

(7)   /lakte/
   layte  a.  $k \longrightarrow y / \underline{\quad} \left\{ \begin{matrix} t \\ s \end{matrix} \right\}$
   layče  b.  $t \longrightarrow č / y \underline{\quad}$
   leyče  c.  $a \longrightarrow e / \underline{\quad} y$
   leče  d.  $y \longrightarrow \emptyset / \underline{\quad} č$

These rules have scant motivation outside of the derivation of these forms. In fact they are considered by Harris to be minor rules; they apply to *leche* but not to *lactar* and *láctico*. The forms with [č] are marked

[+ S], which serves as a trigger for the application of these rules. There are several reasons for believing that the underlying form /lakte/ for surface [leče] is TOO abstract and does not represent native speaker competence. First, the phonological relation between /kt/ and /č/ is remote, and it is conceivable that some speakers, if not all, will never discover that these forms are phonologically related. But even if the relation is recognized, the history of these forms shows that the relation between them is not likely to be as Harris has claimed.

The Latin word for 'milk' was *lacte*. A series of regular sound changes, approximately represented by the rules in (7), changed the form to [leče]. These were phonetically motivated sound changes, and no relic forms with /kt/ were left to give evidence of the historical rules to the speaker. In other words, the underlying forms with /kt/ were all changed to /č/. There was good reason for this relexicalization: The syllable structure of the language was changing and simplifying. In Latin syllable-final obstruents were common, but through a series of changes in pre-Castilian, all syllable-final consonants, except nasals, liquids, and /s/, are disposed of. For example:

| | | |
|---|---|---|
| lakte $\longrightarrow$ layte | 'milk' | |
| magnu $\longrightarrow$ maynu | 'large, size' | |
| septe $\longrightarrow$ sete | 'seven' | |
| bukka $\longrightarrow$ buka | 'mouth' | |

Other forms also suggest that relexicalization took place. Those from *leche* formed before the re-emergence of *lacte* show no alternation. Thus we have *lechoso* 'milky', *lechero* '(adj.) milk', and *lechar* 'to milk'. The /kt/ does not show up in any of these forms. Furthermore, there is evidence that rule (7) was lost before Latin loan words began to enter Castilian again. In the thirteenth century Latin loan words with /kt/ were modified to be more like Castilian forms, but the change was not /kt/ $\longrightarrow$ /č/, but rather /kt/ $\longrightarrow$ /ut/, as in *acto > auto, tractu > trauto* (Entwhistle 1937:193). These forms show that the rules in (7) did not remain productive.

Much later, the forms *lactar* and *láctico* were borrowed from Latin. Harris's analysis implicitly claims that speakers of Spanish grasped the phonological relationship between the stems /lakt-/ and /leč-/ and changed the underlying form from /leč-/ to /lakt-/, adding the rules in (7) to their grammars at the same time. It is not unreasonable to suppose that borrowed forms have such an influence on the rule system of a language and that phonological relations between native and borrowed forms can be grasped by the speakers. For example, I would not be surprised to learn that speakers of Spanish relate these words:

| *padre* | 'father' | *paternal* | 'paternal' |
| *madre* | 'mother' | *maternal* | 'maternal' |

The difference between these forms is not great, and they exhibit the voiced/voiceless alternation active elsewhere in the language, for example, in verbs:

| *saber* | 'to know' | *sepa* | 'he knows (subj.)' |
| *kaber* | 'to fit' | *kepa* | 'he fits (subj.)' |

On the other hand, it is *not* reasonable to assume that English speakers find a phonological relationship between

| *father* | *paternal* |
| *mother* | *maternal* |

although these forms are phonologically similar and historically related. No linguist would posit rules relating these forms, since there are so few forms that exhibit these alternations and such rules are not phonetically motivated nor productive in English.

A similar conclusion must be drawn for *leche* and *láctico*. In this case there is no evidence that the loan words cause restructuring of the underlying form of a native word, especially since the phonological relation is so distant, and none of the rules relating the forms are productive.

The Strong Alternation Condition does not prevent one from describing *leche* as derived from /lakte/, because, in fact, a diacritic is used ([ + S]) and there is a surface alternation [laktar]/[leče]. Still, it seems desirable to constrain the theory to prevent such excessive abstractness in underlying forms, since there is so little evidence that native speaker competence is correctly represented by an analysis such as (7). It is necessary to place a constraint on the theory that is even stronger than the Strong Alternation Condition.

The next chapter discusses such a constraint.

# 2

# Natural Generative Phonology

Discussions of abstractness in phonological description have been phrased almost entirely in terms of constraints on underlying forms, starting with the Alternation Condition. But the abstractness of underlying forms is not the only issue in the abstractness controversy. Indeed, it may not even be the central issue. There are two other empirical issues that must be settled along with the problem of underlying forms. One of these is the question of what is a linguistic rule and what sort of empirical criteria may be applied to the matter of deciding what is and what is not a rule. The other concerns the nature of alternations and the question of what sort of a relation between forms constitutes an alternation.

Any attempt to constrain generative theory must confront the problem of what is a rule and an alternation, as well as the problem of what is a possible underlying form. In this chapter these problems will be discussed as I outline the theory of natural generative phonology developed by Vennemann (1971; 1972c,e; 1974a) in an attempt to constrain abstractness in phonology.

## 2.1   Rules of the Grammar

Just as we can limit abstractness by placing constraints on possible underlying forms, we can also constrain the theory and limit abstractness by placing constraints on possible rules. In the majority of cases where underlying forms are excessively abstract, the rules needed to derive surface forms will also be very abstract. Take, as an example, Saporta's rule discussed above:

(1) $$\emptyset \longrightarrow k / \theta + \underline{\quad\quad} \left\{ \begin{matrix} a \\ o \end{matrix} \right\}$$

What does it mean to claim that this is a rule of Spanish? As a linguist's rule, it is an hypothesis concerning the form of linguistic generalizations made by native speakers. There is a problem with this rule as an hypothesis, and that is that one of the given elements, $/\theta/$, does not exist. Therefore the hypothesis may not be tested. Looking at the rule from the speaker's point of view, we find that such a rule would be impossible to learn because part of its structural description (SD) does not exist on the surface in Latin American Spanish.

Let us now consider a way to tighten up generative theory so that abstract rules of this type are not allowed. It is not unreasonable to try to restrict the rules of the grammar to generalizations whose predictions are testable and to generalizations that speakers could reasonably formulate, given the surface forms of the language. But even within these limits there would be considerable latitude because opinions will differ about what kinds of generalizations speakers can formulate. Let us try to be more precise and start with the strongest claim we could make concerning what is a possible linguistic rule.

A very strong constraint on rules would be one that does not allow abstract rules at all. It would require that all rules express transparent surface generalizations, generalizations that are true for all surface forms and that, furthermore, express the relation between surface forms in the most direct manner possible. We will call this condition the True Generalization Condition. The True Generalization Condition claims that the rules speakers formulate are based directly on surface forms and that these rules relate one surface form to another, rather than relating underlying to surface form. In Chapter 3, evidence is presented that supports the validity of this constraint. In the present chapter, we will merely examine the consequences of the contraint for a theory of phonology.

Notice that a theory incorporating this condition attributes considerably less abstracting ability to the individual speaker or language learner. This theory at the same time makes STRONGER claims about what is a possible natural language because it restricts considerably the number of possible grammars for any given body of data. For these reasons, it is interesting to consider the consequences of imposing such a restriction on the theory. Consider first the consequences of the True Generalization Condition for the analysis of *crecer* and *coser*. The analysis with underlying /θ/ will be excluded, as it would be if we had placed a constraint on underlying forms, because under the True Generalization Condition no rule could refer to a nonexistent segment. Thus the True Generalization Condition is capable of constraining abstractness by restricting the notion "possible rule."

Another extremely important effect of restricting the concept "possible rule" as it is restricted in NGP is that certain clear rule types emerge, each with their own characteristics (Vennemann, 1971). Further, a rule's type may be determined by merely examining the formal statement of the rule. The types are: phonetically conditioned rules, morphophonemic rules, syllabification rules, morphological spell-out or word-formation rules, and via-rules.

Phonetically conditioned rules are rules describing alternations that take place in environments that are specifiable in purely phonetic terms. "Phonetic terms" refer to phonological features (that have intrinsic phonetic content) and phonological boundaries (that have a necessary and consistent phonetic manifestation). The phonological boundaries are the syllable boundary ($) and the pause boundary. Both of these boundaries are determined by phonetic means. On the other hand, the word boundary (## and #) and the morpheme boundary ( + ) are determined by syntactic and semantic means. These latter boundaries are counted as nonphonetic information. Furthermore, diacritic features, syntactic or morphological categories, and semantic classes are all considered nonphonetic.

Among the rules that contain only phonetic information, which will be designated P-rules, are automatic rules of phonetic detail, such as English aspiration of voiceless stops in syllable-initial position, and automatic neutralizations, such as syllable-final devoicing of obstruents in German. As long as the rule contains only phonetic information, it belongs to this class. It is of no consequence whether the features affected are redundant or contrastive. Among the P-rules are those rules that constitute the "laws of pronunciation" for the language. (These correspond basically to the "natural process" of Stampe (1973a).) Such rules are automatic or unsuppressable, and they usually do not have exceptions (Vennemann, 1971).

There are also phonetically conditioned rules that apply variably. These are the emerging P-rules that have not yet gained generality.

Their application may be blocked by social, morphological, or syntactic factors. For example, Labov (1972) discusses the deletion of syllable-final [t] and [d] in English; this deletion is applied less often when [t] and [d] are the morphological markers of past tense, as in *missed,* than when they are not, as in *mist.* However, as long as the conditioning and motivating environment for the rule is phonetic and the nonphonetic factors BLOCK, but do not condition, the application of the rule, it may be considered a P-rule. This interplay between phonetic and nonphonetic factors is discussed further in Section 6.4.

Morphophonemic rules (MP-rules) change phonological features in environments described in morphosyntactic or lexical terms.[1] These rules must refer to morphological or syntactic categories, such as plural, past, or noun, verb, or the rules refer to arbitrary lexical categories, such as conjugation classes or classes designated arbitrarily by diacritics. For instance, the /k/-insertion rule discussed in Chapter 1, which involved the use of a diacritic to distinguish *crecer* from *coser,* would belong to the class of MP-rules. Similarly, the rule governing the voicing of spirants in certain English plurals (*wife, wives, house,* hou[z]es) is an MP-rule. This English rule contains both lexical information (only a small class of nouns undergo this rule, so these must be lexically marked) and morphological information (the rule applies to plural forms only and not, e.g., to genitives.)

The difference between P-rules and MP-rules is worth emphasizing, because it is one of the most important innovations in NGP and because it makes very strong claims about the nature of language. In TGP no clear distinction is made between rules with phonetic conditioning versus rules with nonphonetic conditioning, because there are not strong constraints (such as the True Generalization Condition) that specify how a rule should be formulated, given the facts of the language. Thus a rule can be formulated in phonetic terms even if it does not correspond directly to the surface phonetic facts. As an example, consider Schane's (1968) analysis of nasalized vowels in French. Schane posits no underlying nasalized vowels; instead, all surface nasalized vowels are derived from sequences of a vowel plus a nasal consonant. The vowel is nasalized if the nasal consonant is in the same syllable, and the consonant is subsequently deleted:

(2)     Nasalization:     $V \longrightarrow [+\text{nasal}]/\underline{\hspace{1.5em}} [+\text{nasal}] \begin{Bmatrix} \# \\ C \end{Bmatrix}$

(3)     Nasal deletion:     $\begin{bmatrix} C \\ +\text{nasal} \end{bmatrix} \longrightarrow \emptyset / \begin{bmatrix} V \\ +\text{nasal} \end{bmatrix} \underline{\hspace{1.5em}}$

[1] The conception of MP-rules presented here will be altered when we discuss underlying representations in detail in Chapters 7 and 8. Until that point, we will assume the definition of MP-rules given here.

Thus *un bon frere* is realized as [æ̃ bɔ̃ frɛr], where underlying /bɔn/ becomes [bɔ̃]. If the nasal consonant is followed by a vowel, no nasalization takes place: *un bon ami* is realized as [æ̃bɔnami].

Given the True Generalization Condition, the nasalization rule could not be formulated as a P-rule. The reason is that there are cases of vowel plus nasal consonant followed by a consonant that do not undergo the rule; e.g., the feminine form *bonne* in a phrase such as *une bonne soeur* is realized as [bɔn] even though a consonant follows: [ynbɔnsœr]. Schane excludes the feminine form from undergoing the nasalization rule by giving it an underlying final vowel /bɔnə/, so that at the point at which nasalization applies, the /n/ is followed by a vowel. But, for NGP, the existence of phonetic [bɔnsœr] means that the rules given above as (2) and (3) do not express true generalizations about French.

In NGP a rule expressed in phonetic terms must actually correspond to the physical details of articulation. These physical details are quite regular; thus an alternation is considered to be phonetically motivated only if it always takes place when the phonetic motivation is present on the surface. If an alternation fails to take place when the phonetic environment is present (as in [bɔnsœr]), or takes place when the phonetic condition is NOT present (as in [bɔ̃frer]), then it cannot be associated with a phonetic environment but must be associated with something else in the language, e.g., a particular morpheme, a syntactic category, etc. Such an alternation will be described in an MP-rule. The claim is that phonetic alternations are actually caused by the phonetic environment and that speakers construct phonetic generalizations only when these are regular and transparent. In other cases nonphonetic generalizations are constructed. Tranel (1974b) and Picard (1974) have shown that this claim is correct for the French example just discussed, and other evidence for the validity of this claim is presented in the next chapter.

P-rules, then, describe the way the surface contrastive features will be manifested in a phonetic environment. In addition, a causal relation between the phonetic environment and the structural change of the rule is postulated. Thus P-rules describe processes governed by the physical properties of the vocal tract.[2] Obviously, these processes are not random and totally language-specific, but rather their form and content can be predicted on universal principles. Thus it is further claimed that

---

[2] Some linguists might want to add perceptual factors to those motivating P-rules. There is evidence that acoustic and perceptual factors may play a role in historical reanalysis, but I am not convinced that such factors may motivate the P-rules of a language. More evidence bearing on these matters needs to be assessed.

all P-rules are natural rules. This claim is subject to empirical disconfirmation (see Section 7.4).

MP-rules, on the other hand, take part in the sound–meaning correspondence of a language and are therefore language-specific. They are apt to be phonologically quite arbitrary (e.g., they may be inverted phonetic rules; see Vennemann, 1972e), and they are likely to have exceptions. There are also differences between P-rules and MP-rules in the way they behave historically. These will be discussed in Chapter 6.

We have now discussed phonetically conditioned and morphologically conditioned alternations. What about putative alternations of the type discussed above between *leche* and *lactar*, *noche* and *nocturno*? For this type of relation, Vennemann (1972e) has proposed a type of lexical rule, known as the via-rule.

In Chapter 1 we saw evidence that casts doubt on the contention that *leche* has as its underlying form /lakte/. In NGP we can express the phonological relationship between *leche* and *lactar* (assuming that one exists) without having to make the indefensible claim that one form is derived from the other. Since the rules Harris gives (7a–d) to derive [leče] from /lakte/ are not productive (after all, they do not apply to *láctico, octavo,* and *nocturno*) and since they do not represent any regular derivational relation (for instance, we cannot claim that /kt/ is for verbs because there is also the verb *lechar* 'to milk'), in an NGP the relation between these forms is expressed lexically in a via-rule. Both *leche* /leče/ and *lactar* /laktar/ are entered in the lexicon, and the two entries contain a special statement to the effect that they are related to one another by a rule of the following form:

(4) $\qquad\qquad\qquad$ kt $\longleftrightarrow$ č

Since each individual lexical entry must be marked as related to another individual item, it is possible in an NGP for a particular native speaker to grasp the phonological relation between *ocho* and *octavo*, *noche* and *nocturno*, but not between *leche* and *lactar*. In this case the former pairs are marked as related by via-rule (4), but the latter pair are not marked as related by via-rule. Similarly, it is possible that some native speakers of Spanish do not have the via-rule (4) in their grammars at all.[3]

A comment concerning rules with word boundaries in their SDs is necessary here. If a rule contains a word boundary but no other non-phonetic information, it will be considered a sandhi rule. Sandhi rules constitute a class that is intermediate between P-rules and MP-rules.

---

[3] The difference between MP-rules and via-rules is discussed in Chapter 4, where further justification for via-rules is given.

On the one hand, the word boundary functioning in a sandhi rule must be considered a syntactic boundary because it is determined arbitrarily by the syntax and semantics and not by the phonology. On the other hand, the word boundary resembles a phonological boundary because it always has the potential to coincide with a syllable boundary—the beginnings and ends of words may also be the beginnings and ends of syllables, respectively. Furthermore, where a word begins and ends, there also an utterance may begin and end. A word boundary is potentially a pause boundary. This intimate connection between word boundaries and phonological boundaries may explain why sandhi rules often behave like P-rules: They may be productive and regular and, furthermore, unsuppressable (see Section 7.2 and Vennemann, 1974b).

The remaining types of rules are similar to rules needed in any theory of morphophonology. These are morphological spell-out rules, word-formation rules, and syllabification rules. Morphological spell-out rules give a phonological shape to abstract morphemes (e.g., English: plural⟶ + z + ; Spanish: past participle⟶ + do + ; etc.). In principle these rules operate in NGP as they do in TGP, except that in NGP it is not necessarily considered desirable to have only ONE underlying phonologically representation for each morpheme (see discussion in Chapter 8). Word-formation rules specify the order and type of morphological elements that constitute a word. Syllabification rules assign syllable boundaries ($) to the phonological string; syllabification rules can, and often do, reapply in the course of a derivation. Their exact nature will be discussed in detail in Part II, but throughout Part I we will assume the model of syllabification proposed in Hooper (1972c) and Vennemann (1972d).

## 2.2 The No-Ordering Condition

Now that we have discussed rules in NGP, let us consider briefly the manner in which rules apply. In TGP rules apply in a sequential order; each rule applies to the output of a preceding rule, and it applies only at a fixed position in the order. Vennemann (1971; 1972c) recognized that this type of extrinsic rule ordering allows abstract analyses, and that if rules are not restricted to applying only once, and in a fixed order, certain abstract analyses would not be allowed. Vennemann proposed that rules apply sequentially (one applying to the output of another), but that they be allowed to apply more than once and not in a fixed order but, rather, a rule will apply to any form that meets the structural description of the rule.

The No-Ordering Condition is an implementational principle that tells how rules will be applied to forms, but it also serves as a constraint against certain types of abstractness. Notice, for example, that in Saporta's analysis of *crecer*, the two rules he postulates must apply in a fixed order:

(5) $$\varnothing \longrightarrow k / V\theta \underline{\hspace{1cm}} + \begin{Bmatrix} o \\ a \end{Bmatrix}$$

(6) $$\theta \longrightarrow s$$

If (6) applies before (5) has a chance to apply, the wrong result will be obtained: Rule (6) will wipe out all occurrences of /θ/, and rule (5) will have no forms to apply to. The first person singular form of *crecer* will be incorrectly generated as *[kreso]. Saporta's analysis, then, can not be formulated with the No-Ordering Condition.

The No-Ordering Condition effectively eliminates this and many other cases of absolute neutralization. It also eliminates a number of other abstract relations among rules, as we will see in Chapter 5. However, the No-Ordering Condition does not entirely eliminate abstractness from generative phonology. It is possible to formulate very abstract analyses in which all rules are INTRINSICALLY ordered. A case in point is Harris's derivation of *leche* [leče] from /lakte/, discussed in Chapter 1.

The rules Harris posits are the following, in their order of application.

(7)        /lakte/

layte    a.    $k \longrightarrow y / \underline{\hspace{1cm}} \begin{Bmatrix} t \\ s \end{Bmatrix}$

layče    b.    $t \longrightarrow \check{c} / y \underline{\hspace{1cm}}$

leyče    c.    $a \longrightarrow e / \underline{\hspace{1cm}} y$

leče     d.    $y \longrightarrow \varnothing / \underline{\hspace{1cm}} \check{c}$

Notice that (a) and (b) are intrinsically ordered: (b) cannot apply until (a) has applied, because (a) creates the /y/ that is a necessary part of the SD of (b). Similarly, (c) cannot apply until (a) has created the /y/, since it is also the conditioning factor in (c). Rule (d) is intrinsically ordered after both (a) and (b), because (a) creates the /y/ and (b) creates the /č/ of the SD of (d). The only extrinsic relation is between (c) and (d), since if (d) applied first, the /y/ would be deleted and (c) could not apply. This can easily be remedied by stating (d) as

(d')        $$y \longrightarrow \varnothing / \begin{bmatrix} V \\ -\text{low} \end{bmatrix} \underline{\hspace{1cm}} \check{c}$$

Now (d') cannot apply until (c) has applied. The entire derivation proceeds without the use of extrinsic rule order.

Thus the No-Ordering Condition alone cannot succeed in limiting all types of abstractness; a more substantive condition, such as the True Generalization Condition, is also needed. However, the No-Ordering Condition and the True Generalization Condition are closely related. This relationship will be explored in greater detail in Chapter 5, where we will see an example showing that the True Generalization Condition will be ineffective without the No-Ordering Condition.

## 2.3 Underlying Forms

We have now seen that constraints on abstractness may be imposed by radically constraining the notion "possible rule." As we mentioned above, we can also constrain abstractness by placing conditions on underlying forms, by placing a limit on how great the difference may be between underlying and surface forms. The issue of underlying lexical representations is more difficult to resolve than the issue of rules because the evidence for lexical representations is less accessible. In most cases we can decide if a rule as expressed is a true generalization by examining surface forms and by observing what rules a speaker applies in pronouncing nonsense or borrowed forms. We also have evidence from linguistic change concerning the generalizations speakers formulate. (Such evidence is discussed in the next chapter.) Underlying forms, however, are never directly accessible. They are accessible only through the rules of the grammar. We cannot compel informants to speak in underlying forms. For this reason I have chosen to express the major constraint on abstractness as the True Generalization Condition, a condition on rules, rather than a condition on underlying forms. (Although, as NGP was originally formulated by Vennemann (1971), the major constraint was a condition on underlying forms. This will be discussed in Chapter 7.) We have already seen that the True Generalization Condition has definite consequences for underlying representations, for if there are no abstract rules, there is certainly no point in having any abstract phonological segments or features. The relation between underlying representations and surface representations is quite direct: No phonological features appear in the lexical representations of a morpheme except those that occur in some surface representation of that morpheme. As for the details of lexical representation, several proposals have been made, all of which are compatible with the general principles of NGP (Vennemann, 1974b; Hudson, 1974a, 1975b; Hooper, 1975; Rudes, 1975). These proposals will be discussed in Chapter 7. For our present purposes I will outline my own conception of lexical representations.

First, we must distinguish between nonalternating morphemes (which have only one surface allomorph) and alternating morphemes (which have two or more allomorphs). Nonalternating morphemes will be effected only by P-rules. They may be entered in the lexicon in a form identical to their phonetic form, except that the features predicted by P-rules are removed, i.e., remain unspecified. (For example, English /p/ in [pʰɪn] must be specified as [−voice] but needs no specification for aspiration: the /p/ in [spɪn] may be left unspecified for the feature [voice].)

There are several types of alternating morphemes, just as there are several types of rules that govern alternations. Phonetic alternations are of two types: nonneutralizing and neutralizing. The first type involves a feature that is always predictable for a given segment. For example, in Spanish, the feature [∓ continuant] is always predictable for voiced obstruents: After a pause or after a homoarticulate consonant with occlusion (e.g., nasal consonants) the obstruent is [−continuant]; otherwise it is [+continuant]. Thus *dedo* 'finger' will appear phonetically with an initial stop or spirant, depending on the environment: [undeðo] 'a finger' or [siŋkoðeðos] 'five fingers'. The lexical representation of voiced obstruents may be left blank for the feature [continuant]. If the phonetic alternation involves a neutralization, the nonneutralized value of the feature must occur in the lexical representation. For example, in English /t/ and /d/ between a stressed syllabic and an unstressed syllabic both become a flap. Both *writing* and *riding* have a medial flap, but in other forms of these morphemes, e.g., *write* and *ride*, a voicing contrast appears. Thus in the underlying forms, the final segments of these morphemes must be specified as [−voice] and [+voice], respectively.

MP-rules govern alternations between contrastive features in nonphonetic environments, as in the alternation between [kres-] and [kresk-]. There are several ways of representing the underlying forms of morphemes that have nonphonetic alternations. One constraint is necessary in this framework: The underlying forms must contain only feature values that actually occur in the surface allomorphs. In Chapters 7 and 8 we will discuss such underlying representations in detail. In the meantime we will assume that one of the surface allomorphs is chosen as an underlying form, and the other allomorphs are generated from this one by MP-rules. Alternations governed by via-rules, as we mentioned above, are considered nongenerative: All variants are listed in the lexicon in a form identical to the surface form, except that predictable feature values remain unspecified.

## 2.4 Comparing Two Theories

I have outlined briefly the theory of natural generative phonology. NGP and TGP make essentially the same claims as regards the expression of phonetically motivated processes. The difference between the theories lies in the derivation of morphophonemic alternations. It will become clear in the next chapter that the alternations that NGP would describe directly as a function of morphological and lexical categories TGP describes as the result of abstract phonological representations and ordered rules.

The question is which description best represents the internalized grammar of the native speaker: Which description has psychological reality? There is some independent evidence that bears on the choice between the descriptions predicted by each theory. Linguistic changes often provide insight into the way the grammar is internalized. We know that some linguistic changes come about with the transmission of the language to a new generation. We also know from observing children learning their native language that there is a tendency to generalize rules and obliterate exceptions. Thus we find children forcing English suppletive paradigms into regular patterns and producing *foots, goed,* and so on. This tendency is one of the strong forces behind change in the system of rules. In cases where there is more than one interpretation of the synchronic data, we can determine what the strongest pattern is by observing the direction of the changes in the system. In the next chapter I will examine two different aspects of Spanish phonology. For each I will compare the proposed TGP analysis to the NGP analysis and discuss the evidence from linguistic change that bears on the choice between alternate analyses.

# 3

# Empirical Evidence for Concreteness in Morphophonemic Descriptions

## 3.1 Verb Stress in Spanish

In this section we will examine the stress pattern for verbs in Spanish.[1] First we will examine an analysis of verb stress in the TGP framework, a proposal made by Harris (1969).[2] This analysis will be compared to the NGP analysis of the same data. Upon examining previous and on-going changes in the system, we will see that the generalizations expressed in the NGP analysis represent the generalizations internalized by the speakers of Spanish.

The paradigms in (1) represent the complete conjugation of a Spanish verb (except that the perfect tenses, which are combinations of a conjugated auxiliary and the past participle, are omitted). The stress pat-

[1] A complete discussion of stress in Spanish in the NGP framework is found in Hooper and Terrell (1976).

[2] Since I first proposed this analysis in Hooper (1973), Harris has revised his treatment of verb stress in Spanish (see Harris, 1974). While Harris no longer supports the position discussed here, it is still a possible analysis in the TGP framework and will serve as a basis of comparison of the claims made by the two theories. Harris's more recent analysis is critiqued in Hooper and Terrell (1976).

tern is regular for all verbs. Monosyllabic verbs are, of course, stressed on their only syllable. (The verbs are in standard orthography.)

(1)

| a. Nonfinite | b. Present Indicative | c. Present Subjunctive | |
|---|---|---|---|
| 'to love' | *ámo* | *áme* | Sg.1 |
| *amár* | *ámas* | *ámes* | 2 |
| *amándo* | *áma* | *áme* | 3 |
| *amádo* | *amámos* | *amémos* | Pl.1 |
| | *amáis* | *améis* | 2 |
| | *áman* | *ámen* | 3 |
| d. Preterite | e. Imperfect Indicative | f. Imperfect Subjunctive | |
| *amé* | *amába* | *amára* | Sg.1 |
| *amáste* | *amábas* | *amáras* | 2 |
| *amó* | *amába* | *amára* | 3 |
| *amámos* | *amábamos* | *amáramos* | Pl.1 |
| *amásteis* | *amábais* | *amárais* | 2 |
| *amáron* | *amában* | *amáran* | 3 |
| g. Future | | h. Conditional | |
| *amaré* | | *amaría* | Sg.1 |
| *amarás* | | *amarías* | 2 |
| *amará* | | *amaría* | 3 |
| *amarémos* | | *amaríamos* | Pl.1 |
| *amaréis* | | *amaríais* | 2 |
| *amarán* | | *amarían* | 3 |

In the TGP framework, Harris (1969) proposes to account for verb stress by a rule that stresses the penultimate syllable (if there is one) of all verb forms except the first and second plural of the imperfect indicative and subjunctive. The rule is formalized as follows:

(2)
$$V \longrightarrow [\text{1stress}] / \underline{\quad} (([-\overset{ba,\ ra}{\text{perf.}}])C_0 V)C_0 \#]_{verb}$$

This rule has three expansions. On the first expansion all of the SD is present. The feature [ − perfective] stands for the imperfect morphemes *-ba* and *ra* (see (1e) and (1f)). This first expansion places the stress one syllable before the imperfect marker, if a vowel follows this marker. This first expansion, then, applies only to the first and second plural of the imperfect:

amábamos     amáramos
amábais      amárais

In the second expansion the imperfect morpheme does not appear:

$$/\_\_\_C_0VC_0\#]_{verb}$$

This expansion assigns stress to all penultimate vowels. The third expansion

$$/\_\_\_C_0\#]_{verb}$$

assigns stress to monosyllable forms.

This rule basically claims that all verbs except first and second plural imperfect are stressed on the penultimate syllable; I will refer to it as a penultimate stress rule. On the surface there are forms that have stress on the last syllable. In these cases penultimate stress exists only on a more abstract level. Harris's analysis for these cases should be explained. (i) The infinitive, *amar*, has a final vowel *e* in the underlying form, which is deleted AFTER stress assignment. (ii) The preterite forms *amé* and *amó* are derived from /am + a + I/ and /am + a + U/, respectively. The penultimate vowel is stressed, then altered, and the final vowel is deleted. Notice that in this case of deletion, and in the case in (i), the deletion rule must be extrinsically ordered to FOLLOW the stress rule in order for stress to be placed correctly. In both cases, this means that although the rule claims stress is penultimate, these surface forms do not have penultimate stress. (iii) The future and conditional forms are derived in Harris's analysis from infinitives followed by an auxiliary verb. Harris claims that the person/number endings on the future and conditional forms are associated with the present and imperfect forms of *haber*, which are

(3)

|        | Present | Imperfect |
|--------|---------|-----------|
| Sg.1   | é       | abía      |
| 2      | ás      | abías     |
| 3      | á       | abía      |
| Pl.1   | émos    | abíamos   |
| 2      | ábeis   | abíais    |
| 3      | án      | abían     |

(The medial /b/ is phonetically spirantized to [β].) The syntactic proposal is that the future be derived from the structure underlying the construction illustrated by the following sentence:

> *Ha de estar aquí ahora.*
> 'He's probably here now.'

Harris's semantic argument is that there is one meaning of the *haber de* plus infinitive construction that is synonymous with one meaning of the future construction. That is, the future *estará aquí ahora* can mean 'He's probably here now'. Both constructions also have other meanings, so that the semantic correspondence is less than perfect. Furthermore, the phonological correspondence is also less than perfect. For the conditional (and the second plural of the future) the /ab/ of *haber* must be deleted. Harris does not attack this particular problem. The evaluation of Harris's semantic argument is left to the interested reader; suffice it to say that such a dubious relationship would not be drawn in NGP. In NGP the future and conditional forms are analyzed as stem plus inflection. Later in the chapter I will give a rule for assigning stress to the future and conditional forms under that analysis.

To complete the explanation of Harris's analysis, he treats the future and conditional forms as a combination of two separate words: infinitive and auxiliary. Stress is assigned to both words: [[amáre]á]. The infinitive is stressed on the penultimate as explained above, and stress is assigned to the single syllable of the auxiliary (or to the penultimate, as in /émos/, or the conditional forms, /ía/, etc.). Later a general rule removes all but the rightmost stress, leaving the stress on the auxiliary: [amará].

Harris's rule of verb stress claims that stress in verbs is for the most part penultimate, with the imperfect forms exhibiting exceptions to this rule in the first and second person plural. For the infinitive and the first and third singular of the preterite, his analysis claims that at some abstract level even these forms are penultimately stressed.

This particular analysis of verb stress is not available in NGP because Harris's stress rule is not a true generalization about surface forms, and the analysis relies on rule order to give a systematic account of apparent exceptions. In NGP one cannot claim that *amár, amé,* and *amó* receive stress by a penultimate stress rule. In NGP it would be rather complicated to try to predict stress on the basis of a rule that counts syllables from the end of the word, and, in fact, the paradigms in (1) show that we actually do not want to. Looking again at (1), the most striking point about stress in the verb forms is NOT the fact that the majority of forms have penultimate stress, but rather that for each tense (except present) all persons have stress on the same syllable in relation to the stem. In the imperfect, the first and second plural forms are not a special case because they do not have penultimate stress. Rather their antepenultimate stress is just what makes them regular: The stress in that form falls on the same vowel, the theme vowel, as does the stress in all other person number forms. (The theme vowel is the vowel that identifies the conjugation class of the verb.) Historical evidence supports this view. In Latin and in Spanish for many centuries the first and second person plural of the imperfect was stressed on the penultimate vowel. The stress shifted back one syllable in order that the stress of the entire paradigm be regular, i.e., stressed on the same vowel, the theme vowel. The survival of Latin stress would have given the following pattern:

(4)

| Indicative | Subjunctive |
| --- | --- |
| amába | amára |
| amábas | amáras |
| amába | amára |
| amabámos | amarámos |
| amabáis | amaráis |
| amában | amáran |

But in the modern forms the stress occurs on the theme vowel for the entire paradigm. It is also worthwhile to note that although Harris's rule treats these two paradigms together with the feature [ − perfective], it is not clear that the past subjunctive is indeed an imperfect, since no subjunctive forms exist that correspond to the preterite indicative and in fact the past subjunctive may be used with a preterite meaning, that of completed action, which is certainly not semantically [ − perfective].[3]

It is also significant that stress has a morphological function in the verb forms. Each tense has a characteristic position for its stress. The present tense forms have stress on the stem vowel, the past forms have stress on the theme vowel, and the future forms have stress on the first vowel after the future marker. Notice also that stress is distinctive in the verb forms. Only stress differentiates these pairs:

| | | | |
| --- | --- | --- | --- |
| ámo | 'I love' | amó | 'he loved' |
| áme | '$\left\{{I \atop he}\right\}$ love (subj)' | amé | 'I loved' |
| amára | '$\left\{{I \atop he}\right\}$ loved (subj)' | amará | 'he will love' |
| amáran | 'they loved (subj)' | amarán | 'they will love' |

The TGP analysis claims that stress contrasts such as these are just accidental products of the abstract derivation. In Harris's analysis, the only tense or mood that has any consequences for the stress is the imperfect.

[3] This point is made in Reyes (1972).

To summarize, then, a description of verb stress in Spanish should account for the following facts:

(i) Stress is not determined by counting syllables from the end of the word.

(ii) Forms stressed on the ultimate or antepenultimate are regular in their paradigms (i.e., first and second plural imperfect are NOT special).

(iii) Each tense stresses a certain vowel in all person/numbers (but the first and second plural of the present are an exception).

(iv) Stress is actually one of the markers of tense and mood.

As it happens, once extrinsic rule order is removed and the True Generalization Condition imposed, any reasonable account of (1) will have to be consistent with the facts listed above. In this analysis the only conditioning factor for the assignment of stress in verbs is the tense/aspect of the verb.

In NGP the verb stress rule assigns stress to the verb forms as they appear on the surface. It has several parts. Starting with the past tenses, we see that the stress falls on the first vowel after the stem in all past forms and all nonfinite forms. Stress can be predicted on these forms by the following rule:

(5) $$V \longrightarrow [+\text{stress}] / ]_{\substack{\text{stem} \\ \text{verb}}} X \underline{\hspace{1cm}} + \begin{Bmatrix} [+\text{past}] \\ [-\text{finite}] \end{Bmatrix}$$

where X contains no [+ syll] segments. The variable in this rule is necessary for the few cases in which the first syllabic element after the stem is preceded by a glide that is not part of the stem; e.g., in second and third conjugation forms, the third singular of the preterite has the person/number suffix /yo/, as in *comió* [komyó] and *vivió* [biβyó]. In order for the first syllabic after the verb stem to be stressed, the glide must be skipped. Where the theme vowel is a diphthong, as in *comieron* [komyéron], third person plural preterite, and *comiendo* [komyéndo], present progressive, the stress is assigned before the diphthong is formed. In Chapter 8 the rules for verb stress are integrated with the morphological rules.

The future and conditional forms all receive stress on the first V of the person/number ending, i.e., the V following the marker of subsequence, /r/.

(6) $$V \longrightarrow [+\text{stress}] / [\text{subsequent}] + \underline{\hspace{1cm}}$$

Again, refer to Chapter 8 for the details of verb morphology in Spanish.

These two rules, (5) and (6), assign stress to all verb forms except the present indicative and subjunctive. The stress on present tense forms is not as regular as the stress for the other tenses; the present tense has retained its historical penultimate stress. There are at least two ways a rule could be formulated to predict stress on the present forms. The rule could place stress on the penultimate syllable in present tense:

(7) $$V \longrightarrow [+\text{stress}] / \underline{\qquad} C_0 V C_0 \#]_{\text{verb} \atop [+\text{present}]}$$

Or a rule could be formulated that is analogous to the other two stress rules. That is, the rule could identify a particular V, the stem V, as receiving stress, and the first and second persons plural could be taken as exceptions to this general rule. The last vowel of the stem is considered the stem V. It is possible that this vowel is marked in the lexicon as the stem V. However, I do not know of any other morphological process that requires the stem V to be identified. Therefore it is preferable to formulate the rule so that the last V of the stem is stressed; this, of course, is necessary because polysyllabic stems do exist.

(8) $$V \longrightarrow [+\text{stress}] / \underline{\qquad} C_0]_{\text{verb stem} \atop [+\text{present}]}$$

Except: first and second persons plural; these forms are stressed by rule (5).

Rules (7) and (8) make different claims about the way speakers of Spanish view verb stress, but both rules are completely consistent with the principles of NGP. Rule (8) seems undesirable because it has exceptions. On the other hand, rule (8) is of the same form as the rules for assigning stress in the other tense/aspect paradigms, while rule (7) claims that stress in present tense is viewed as a process quite different from stress for all other verb forms. Rule (7) associates stress with the end of the word, while rule (8) associates stress with a location in relation to the internal composition of the verb form.

In terms of the generally accepted evaluation procedure, rules without exceptions are more highly valued than rules with exceptions, if both account for the same data. By this reasonable standard, rule (7) would be chosen to account for stress in the present tense. But there are indications that speakers do not utilize this reasonable simplicity criterion.

We have already seen that historically a penultimate rule for the imperfect was given up in favor of a rule that stressed the theme vowel. Thus the stress on the first and second plural was retracted, resulting in a regular paradigm (see (4) above).

Similarly, an analogous stress shift occurs in the present tense in many dialects of Spanish. For the present subjunctive, the penultimate rule has been (or is being) abandoned in favor of a rule that stresses the stem vowel in all persons. In Chicano Spanish (Bowen, 1952; Reyes, 1972) the subjunctive forms in all conjugations have undergone the stress shift:

(9)

| First Conjugation | Second Conjugation | Third Conjugation |
|---|---|---|
| *amar* 'to love' | *comer* 'to eat' | *vivir* 'to live' |
| *áme* | *cóma* | *víva* |
| *ámes* | *cómas* | *vívas* |
| *áme* | *cóma* | *víva* |
| *ámemos* | *cómamos* | *vívamos* |
| *(ámeis)* | (*cómais*) | (*vívais*) |
| *ámen* | *cóman* | *vívan* |

(In Chicano the second plural form is not used.) In Andalusian this stress shift has affected only the second and third conjugations (Mondéjar, 1970), and in this dialect, in which the second plural is used, the stress is shifted on this form also.

Now consider what this change tells us about the internalized grammar of the native speaker. As I mentioned above, it is well known that a change of this type comes about as a generalization of a preexisting rule. In the terms of Vennemann (1972a), the motivation for this change in stress is Humboldt's Universal, which states that "suppletion is undesirable, uniformity of linguistic symbolization is desirable: both roots and grammatical markers should be unique and constant" (Vennemann, 1972a). Harris (1973a) has also described the stress shift as a case of "paradigm uniformity." What the stress shift means is that the present tense is marked by a characteristic stress: stress on the last V of the stem. The stress shift has occurred in an attempt to reduce suppletion and fulfill the demands of Humboldt's Universal. The stress shift shows that the first and second plural forms are (or were) regarded as suppletive, exceptions to the general rule. Thus independent evidence shows that rule (8) represents a real native speaker analysis of present tense stress, since first and second plural stress has to have been analyzed as exceptional BEFORE the actual stress on these forms was retracted.

NGP did not give us a unique analysis for present tense verb stress when we considered only the verb forms for standard Spanish. This means that NGP is not yet a perfect theory of grammar. The theory did, however, give a unique description of the stress in past, nonfinite, and future/conditional forms. For these cases NGP claims that verb stress is morphologized. On the basis of this information then, we could predict that present tense verb stress will also be morphologized, and the dialectal evidence bears out this prediction. Notice that the TGP penultimate stress rule cannot make these predictions, because in fact if the verb stress were truly regarded as penultimate, these changes would not occur. According to Harris's rule (2), before the first stress shift, the imperfect stress shift, the stress was completely penultimate on an abstract level (as the preterite forms show). The imperfect stress shift added a complication, a special case to be included in the rule. But on the basis of the original rule, there was absolutely no way to predict this development. Similarly, the present tense stress shift must be regarded in TGP as additional complication of the rule,[4] and this complication is also not predictable from the TGP rule.

This case illustrates clearly the empirical consequences of the difference between TGP and NGP. Notice that in NGP, in order to explain the imperfect stress shift and the present stress shift, it must be the case that speakers had already analyzed stress as morphological before the two stress changes took place. This means that they were placing stress by tense/aspect AT THE TIME WHEN STRESS WAS STILL PREDICTABLE BY THE PENULTIMATE STRESS RULE. That is, they preferred the morphological analysis to the phonological analysis, because in some tenses (especially the preterite) the phonological analysis was becoming too abstract or opaque. NGP claims, then, that speakers do not make use of rule order and abstract underlying forms to maintain a phonological analysis; NGP claims that speakers will consistently choose the analysis that identifies phonological phenomena with morphological phenomena. The reason is that the function of grammar is to associate meaning with sound. Speakers prefer to consider phonological variations meaningful rather than predictable and meaningless. This preference accounts for the morphologization of phonological rules, and the verb stress in Spanish serves as an excellent illustration of this process. Since we have evidence that verb stress is indeed morphologized, this case offers strong support for the claims of natural generative phonology.

[4] Reyes (1972) takes Harris's rule as basic and formulates a stress rule for Chicano verbs as follows (p. 35):

$$V \longrightarrow [\text{1stress}] / \underline{\hspace{1cm}} \left( \left( \left\{ \begin{matrix} +\text{ba}+ \\ +\text{ra}+ \\ \text{pres.} \\ \text{subj.} \end{matrix} \right\} \right) C_0 V \right) C_0 \#$$

This rule illustrates the additional complexity mentioned in the text.

## 3.2 Morphophonemic Developments in Andalusian Spanish

In order to show that the case examined in the previous section is not an isolated example of the choice of a morphological analysis of an alternation over an abstract phonological analysis, I will present another example of a similar phenomenon in this section.

According to Navarro Tomás (1957), there is a tendency for Spanish vowels to have at least two variants each, an open and close varient. The general conditioning factor for this phonetic variation is the shape of the syllable; close vowels are found in free syllables, and open vowels are found in checked syllables. (A checked syllable ends in a consonant, a free syllable ends in a vowel.)

In many dialects of Spanish, especially those spoken in some parts of America and southern Spain, a syllable-final /s/ is weakened to aspiration, [h], or lost entirely. This process has serious consequences for the morphology in these dialects, since noun plurals are formed by adding a word-final /s/, and second person singular of several verb tenses ends in an /s/. The combination of vowel-laxing and /s/-deletion produces noun singular/plural pairs such as the following:

(10)

| Orthography | Standard | Dialectal |
|---|---|---|
| *clase* | [klase] | [klase] |
| *clases* | [klasẹs] | [klasẹ] |
| *pan* | [pan] | [pan] |
| *panes* | [panẹs] | [panẹ] |

(The open vowel is indicated by the cedilla.) One dialect that reportedly has pairs such as these is Uruguayan. For this dialect Saporta (1965:223) proposes the following two rules:

(11)          Vowel laxing: e $\longrightarrow$ ẹ / ____C$

(where $ stands for syllable boundary. For the assignment of syllable boundaries, see Hooper (1972c) and Part II of the present work.)

(12)          S-deletion: s $\longrightarrow$ Ø / ____$

In Saporta's analysis pluralization proceeds as in the standard dialect: /s/ is added to a stem-final V, /es/ to a stem-final C. Rules (11) and (12) apply to such plural forms. They must be extrinsically ordered with respect to one another, (11) applying before (12). If (12) were to apply first, the /s/ that conditions the laxing of /e/ in plurals would be deleted. The SD of (11) would not be met, and an incorrect plural, [klase] or [pane], would result.

The theory of NGP claims that a description of the data in (10) by the extrinsically ordered rules (11) and (12) does not represent an account of native speaker competence. NGP claims that natural languages do not function in the way that this analysis implies. Given the True Generalization Condition, the phonetic motivation for a phonological rule must be observable from the surface. NGP claims that native speakers do not reconstruct a pluralization rule with /s/ and the two rules (11) and (12) for the pairs in (10). Given that two phonetically motivated rules such as (11) and (12) are interacting in a language, NGP predicts that one of the following two situations will result:

(i) First, both rules will retain their phonetic motivation and remain productive, applying in intrinsic order. The distribution of open and close vowels would continue to be governed by syllable shape: open V's in checked syllables, close V's in free syllables. With the deletion of word-final /s/, new free syllables are created; and the V's in these syllables, like the V's in all free syllables, are close, not open.

(ii) The second possibility predicted by NGP is that with the loss of the plural marker, /s/, the rule of V-laxing becomes morphologized. The plural morpheme is restructured: an open V, /ẹ/, marks plural instead of the /s/.

Rules (11) and (12) are interacting in many dialects of Spanish. In the dialects of Andalusia, the situation has stabilized with rather interesting results.[5] In these dialects we find data exemplifying both of the predictions made by NGP. We do NOT find a stabilized situation such as that illustrated in (10). Rather we find that the dialects have changed as a result of the interaction of the two rules and that the changes have proceeded in two directions. In the dialects of western Andalusia the developments follow the path described in (i) above, and in the eastern dialects the developments follow (ii).[6] Let us examine each situation in detail.

Mondéjar (1970) has described the development of the verb system in the Andalusian dialects. Second person singular of the present tense

---

[5] Saporta's source, Vasquez (1953), indicates that in Uruguay the situation is still variable and describes it as similar to the Andalusian dialects to be discussed in the text, but notes that in Uruguay the changes have not advanced as far as they have in Andalusia.

[6] The theoretical significance of these dialects is also discussed briefly in Norman (1973).

(and most other tenses as well) is signaled in standard Spanish by the morpheme /−s/:

(13)    Orthography: *comer* 'to eat'
            Sg. 1 *como*         Pl. 1 *comemos*
                2 *comes*               2 *comeis*
                3 *come*                3 *comen*

Without the /s/ the second singular form would be identical to the third singular form. Given the rule of V-laxing, *comes* would be [komęs]. In western Andalusia, when the /s/ is dropped, the open V does not remain; rather, a close V appears, and the distinction between the second and third singular is lost: *comes* [kome], *come* [kome]. In this dialect the phonetically motivated rule of V-laxing remains productive, but it does not apply when its SD is not met by the surface forms.

The situation in this dialect would be described in NGP as follows: The /s/-deletion rule causes restructuring of any lexical items that previously contained /s/, including the plural morpheme and the second person singular morpheme for most tenses. The rule governing the openness of V's remains productive.

This example shows that in one dialect in which a situation describable by abstract rules and extrinsic rule order potentially exists, the potential is not realized. Instead, the situation adjusts so that the phonetically motivated rule applies only in cases where SD is met on the surface.

In eastern Andalusia the adjustment takes the path of morphologization. We can assume that the rule of V-laxing was productive here in the recent past, affecting all V's in checked syllables. The rule of /s/-deletion is actually a weakening of /s/, whose end result is either aspiration, [h], or Ø (Alonso et al., 1950). Considering noun and adjective singular and plurals again, there would be pairs such as the following[7] (V-laxing affects all V's):

(14)

| Orthography | | Singular | Plural |
|---|---|---|---|
| *pedazo* | 'piece' | [peðaθo] | [peðaθǫʰ] |
| *cabeza* | 'head' | [kaβeθa] | [kaβeθąʰ][8] |
| *fin* | 'end' | [fįn] | [finęʰ] |

---

[7] To my knowledge these forms are not actually documented for this dialect. For the purpose of exposition I have made the very plausible assumption that such a stage existed. This stage certainly exists in other dialects, notably the Uruguayan dialect Vasquez describes.

[8] The open and close variants of the non-low V's are as in many languages. The open

At this point the plural is marked by aspiration and an open word-final V.

It would be quite reasonable to describe these data with a TGP analysis, similar to Saporta's (1965), and say that the plural marker is underlying /s/ and that the rules of V-laxing and /s/-aspiration are both productive. These rules would not have to be extrinsically ordered as long as there is some degree of aspiration present on the surface. There is evidence that a rule of /s/-aspiration is present in the language; pairs such as the following exist:

(15)

| | Orthography | Singular | Plural |
|---|---|---|---|
| *voz* | 'voice' | [bo̞ʰ] | [bose̞ʰ] |
| *tos* | 'cough' | [to̞ʰ] | [tose̞ʰ] |

In these forms the stem-final /s/ is aspirated in the singular but not in the plural. If new words entered the language, any syllable-final /s/'s would be aspirated. This TGP analysis, then, is quite defensible.

The NGP analysis would be similar as long as the phonetic conditioning, the [s] or [h], is consistently present. But when the final consonant is deleted, this analysis cannot be maintained in NGP as it can in TGP. NGP claims that if V-laxing takes place in the absence of aspiration (its phonetic motivation), the rule must be an MP-rule. The existence of plurals such as [peða̞θo̞] and [kaβeθa̞] are evidence that V-laxing has a morphological rather than a phonetic environment. That is, V-laxing takes place in the plural. A plural morpheme /e̞/ is added to forms that end in consonants, and this vowel is lax also, e.g., [fin], [fine̞]. For forms ending in vowels, the plural is marked by rule (16). (The difference in open and close V's will be described as a difference in tenseness: Close V's are [+tense], open V's are [−tense].)

(16)         $V \longrightarrow [-\text{tense}] / \begin{bmatrix} \overline{\phantom{xx}} \\ +\text{plural} \end{bmatrix} (h) \ \#\#$

Similarly, V-laxing in the second singular of the verb would be conditioned morphologically.

There are, then, two possible ways to describe the interaction of the rules of aspiration and V-laxing. Even though the TGP analysis is quite reasonable in that it does not require extreme degrees of abstractness,

---

variant of the low V, [a̞], cannot be phonetically lower or more open than /a/. Instead the low V that occurs in the plural is fronted and lengthened (Alonso et al, 1950).

we find in contemporary eastern Andalusian strong indications that the process of V-laxing has become morphologized. Interestingly enough, the rule morphologization has occurred while the phonetic motivation for V-laxing (the word-final [h]) still appears optionally in the language.

The vowels of the dialect of Granada, which is located in the eastern half of Andalusia, have been studied carefully in Alonso et al. (1950). The data presented by these authors show clearly that the conditioning for V-laxing is quite different in the Granada dialect than in Castilian. In the Granada dialect the shape of the syllable is of no significance to V-laxing. The distinction between open and close V's is governed entirely by morphological category. For nouns and adjectives, the singular has close V's and the plural open V's. This distinction does not appear only in word-final V's; the stressed V (and in some cases even the unstressed V's) of the noun or adjective also alternate. The following are phonetic transcriptions of singular/plural pairs as given in Alonso et al. (1950). (Irrevelant details have been regularized in some cases. Aspiration seems to be variable.)

(17)

| Orthography | Singular | Plural | Gloss |
|---|---|---|---|
| *pedazo* | [peðáθo] | [pẹdą́θọ] | 'piece' |
| *alto* | [álto] | [ą́ltọʰ] | 'tall' |
| *cabeza* | [kaβéθa] | [kạβẹ́θạ] | 'head' |
| *selva* | [sélva] | [sẹ́lvạ] | 'forest' |
| *lobo* | [lóβo] | [lọ́βọʰ] | 'wolf' |
| *tonto* | [tónto] | [tọ́ntọ] | 'stupid' |
| *piso* | [píso] | [pịsọʰ] | 'floor' |
| *fin* | [fíŋ] | [fịnẹʰ] | 'end' |
| *grupo* | [grúpo] | [grúpọʰ] | 'group' |

The forms in (17) show the development of a vowel harmony system.[9] The stressed V agrees with the word-final V in openness, or tenseness. The alternation occurs in both free and checked syllables.

The data in (17) do not alone show that V-laxing has become an MP-rule, since the alternations in the stressed syllables are predictable by a phonetically motivated rule from the quality of the final V. The important question is still how the quality of the final V is predicted. The forms in (17) do show that the open word-final V of the plural cannot be generated by a general rule of V-laxing in checked syllables as in Castil-

---

[9] The data of Alonso et al. show that the vowel harmony is extremely regular for all but the high V's. In checked syllables /i/ only sometimes laxes and /u/ never does. These fine points will be ignored in the text.

ian, since open V's are not restricted to checked syllables nor do all checked syllables contain open V's.

We might consider the possibility that the plural V is laxed because it occurs before an underlying /s/, or aspiration. But there are forms that show that this is not the correct generalization either. In Castilian the forms for the days of the week are invariant: *el martes* is 'Tuesday' and *los martes* is 'on Tuesdays'. The plural is not marked on the noun. In Granada the plural of *martes* is marked. The singular has a close V [marte] and the plural an open V, [mạrtẹ]. The /s/ or [h] cannot condition the opening of the V for, if it did, the singular of *martes* would be identical to the plural.

It is clear that the V alternation in word-final position must be predicted on the basis of the number of the noun or adjective. Only in this way can the most general statement about the alternation be made. This approach also explains an additional fact about this dialect. Alonso et al. (1950) note that the difference between the two varieties of each V is much greater in the Granada dialect than in Castilian. The close V's are very tense, the open V's are very lax. This is characteristic of phonetic distinctions that have semantic significance (cf. the principle of maximal differentiation and functional yield in Martinet (1952)). In Castilian the V's do not have to be carefully distinguished, because the distinctions between them are never phonemic or significant. In the Granada dialect, however, the tenseness distinction carries semantic information, and it is important that the two V types be distinguished. Since our analysis relates the vowel tenseness to the meaning, this fact is directly explained.

The vowel harmony system also shows that the V tenseness is associated with singular or plural. The development of the vowel harmony system is both a generalization of this morphological association and an attempt to maximally differentiate between singular and plural. That is, the difference between the pairs [e, ẹ, o, ọ, a, ạ, i, ị, u, ụ] is small compared to their semantic function. Vowel harmony reinforces the distinction by spreading it to the other vowels, thus maximizing the phonetic difference between singular and plural pairs.

Before formalizing the MP-rules for this dialect, one important point needs to be emphasized. This highly developed morphological use of V tenseness evolved before the phonetic motivation for the original V tenseness rule was completely lost. In the transcriptions of Alonso et al., syllable final /s/ never occurs, but syllable-final and word-final [h] occurs in about one-half of the forms that etymologically contained /s/. While the phonetic conditioning for laxing was optionally present, the fact that it was not systematically present led the speakers to assign a morphological function to the open V's. This case, like the verb stress case discussed in the previous section, supports the strong claims of NGP that the phonetic motivation for a phonological rule must be systematically observable on the surface. If the phonetic motivation for an alternation is lost or obscured on the surface, the alternation itself will be lost (as in the western Andalusian dialects), or the alternation will assume morphological significance (as in the eastern dialects). Of course it is not possible to find independent evidence that chooses between analyses in all cases. However, the fact that NGP makes stronger claims about natural language, and the fact that these claims are supported where independent evidence exists, make NGP a more highly valued theory of grammar.

It seems worthwhile to examine the details of this very interesting morphophonemic phenomenon in the Granada dialect and to propose a formal analysis of the vowel alternations in that dialect. We have already seen evidence that the tenseness of the word-final V is determined morphologically. Now we must ask if the tenseness of the other V's in the word is also determined morphologically or if the V harmony is a phonetically motivated agreement with the word-final V.

The evidence indicates that the V harmony is also conditioned morphologically and is not a mere phonetically motivated agreement. There are some singular nouns that have open V's: *tos* [tǫ] 'cough', *sol* [sǫl] 'sun', and *Rafael* [rafaęl] 'Rafael'. The monosyllables do not affect the argument here except to illustrate that underlying open V's occur in Granadense.[10] The form for *Rafael* shows that harmony is not a phonetically motivated agreement with the final V. If it were, the phonetic form for *Rafael*, although singular, would have all open V's.

For nouns and adjectives, the laxing of V's should be accomplished by a morphological rule that states that a noun or adjective marked for plural will have all open vowels.

(18)         $V \longrightarrow [-\text{tense}] / X \underline{\hspace{2em}} X\#]_{\text{noun, adjective}}^{[+\text{plural}]}$

Rule (18) laxes all the V's of the stem and also laxes the final V. Rule (18), like all rules of NGP, may apply to the same form iteratively as long as a

---

[10] There is no hint in Alonso et al. as to why some singular forms retain the open vowel. However, there are very few such forms. In addition to the three forms mentioned in the text, four more appear in the word list (of approximately 200 words): *miel* [myę́ʰ] 'honey', *mies* [myę́ʰ] 'grain', *color* [kǫlǫ́ʳ] 'color', and *portier* [portyę́ʳ] 'door curtain'. It appears that only stressed mid vowels are retained as open in singulars, only before etymological /l/, /r/ and /s/, and furthermore, only in final syllables. Still, there are exceptions: *clavel* 'pink' is listed with a close vowel, [klave⁽ˡ⁾].

part of that structure meets the rule's structural description. Rule (18) applies once for every V in a [+plural] form. Only the presence of a word boundary (##) blocks the harmonizing process. For nouns that end in consonants, the vowel /E/ is added as part of the pluralization process.

In Granada the V harmony phenomenon is also observable in verbs. For instance, the present tense forms of the verb *correr* 'to run' are:

(19)

| | Standard | Orthography | Granada |
|---|---|---|---|
| Sg. 1 | | corro | [kóro] |
| 2 | | corres | [kǫrę̧] |
| 3 | | corre | [kóre] |
| Pl. 1 | | corremos | [kǫrę́mǫ] |
| 2 | | correis | [kǫrę́i] |
| 3 | | corren | [kórẽ] |

Notice that the second singular and plural and the first plural have open V's in the stem as well as the desinence. The second and third persons singular are distinguished solely by the tenseness of the V's. Comparing the standard forms, we see that, as with the nouns and adjectives, the presence of open V's is traceable to an original word-final /s/. However, we know that the tenseness distinction is morphologized and cannot be attributed to an underlying /s/, because the irregular verb *ser* 'to be' has a third singular form that ends in /s/ in the standard dialect: *es* [es]. But in the Granada dialect this form has a close V. The form is simple [e] 'he is', never *[ę̧ʰ]. This means that the close V is associated with the third singular, not with an etymological or underlying /s/.

To account for (19), we posit underlying tense V's in the stem, add the inflectional endings in the usual manner, and apply a rule of V laxing, rule (20).

(20) $\qquad$ V $\longrightarrow$ [−tense] / X $\underline{\qquad}$ X#] $\left[ \left\{ \begin{smallmatrix} \text{verb} \\ \text{[2nd person]} \\ \text{[1st plural]} \end{smallmatrix} \right\} \right]$

Rule (20), like rule (18), laxes every V in a word of a certain morphological category, in this case the second singular and plural and the first singular. Because NGP requires identity between lexical and surface forms of nonalternating morphemes, the present inflectional endings for second conjugation verbs are /o, ę, e, ęmǫ, ęi, ẽ/. Rule (20) applies vacuously to the forms of the second singular and plural and the first plural.

There is one other interesting occurrence of V harmony that this analysis is designed to account for. In Spanish, clitic pronouns occur before a finite verb form but immediately follow a nonfinite verb form. In the orthography the clitic pronouns that follow the nonfinite verb are written attached to the verb. The verb + clitic structure is considered to be one word, since it is stressed as one word, i.e., the clitics are always unstressed.

(21)             a.  *Lo vi*
                 it I saw
                 'I saw it'
             b.  *Quiero verlo.*
                 I want see it
                 'I want to see it.'
             c.  *Quiero verlos.*
                 I want see them
                 'I want to see them.'

In Granada vowel harmony affects the nonfinite verb (Alonso et al., 1950). If the clitic pronoun is singular, the V's of the infinitive are tense: *verlo* [berlo], *hacerlo* 'to do it' [aθerlo]. If the clitic is plural, the V's of the infinitive are lax: *verlos* [bɛrlǫ], *hacerlos* 'to make them' [aθɛrlǫ]. This phenomenon seems anomalous if we have conceived of the V harmony as affecting only plural in nouns. Clearly there is no semantic sense in which one can say that an infinitive is plural if it has a plural object pronoun (particularly since the infinitive is invariant when the object is a full NP, even if it is plural). This case seems to show that V harmony affects a whole word if that word has the plural morpheme (for nouns and adjectives) at its end.

Rule (18) is formulated to account for this case of harmony, if we assume that the verb + clitic structure is as follows:

$$[\# \text{ ver } [ \# \text{ los } \#]_N \# ]_V$$

The harmony is only blocked by ##, which marks the boundaries between words. The fact that the clitic is a noun triggers the V harmony.

Vowel harmony in Granada, then, is predicted by morphological categories. This case is interesting theoretically because the rule of V-laxing became morphologized before the aspiration [h] was completely deleted. The V-laxing rule was interpreted as morphological at a time when V-laxing was still describable as phonological in TGP. NGP predicts this morphological interpretation with the No-Ordering Condition and the True Generalization Condition. (Of course, NGP could not predict the development of the vowel harmony system. Linguistic science is a long way from being able to predict the development of phenomena of this nature.)

In this chapter we have examined two cases that strongly motivate a concrete approach to morphophonological description. A number of other examples that point to a concrete grammar will be discussed in Chapters 4 through 8, as we examine in detail particular aspects of the theory of natural generative phonology.

# 4

# Cyclic
# Rule
# Application

We have now discussed a number of ways that abstract phonology is used to describe morphophonemic alternations. One more device of abstract phonology should be discussed. This is the cyclic application of rules. In TGP it is claimed that some phonological rules apply in cycles in the following manner. Phonological strings are analyzed into syntactic constituents; the constituent breaks are symbolized with brackets: [[[x]y]z]. When phonological rules apply cyclically, they apply first to the material in the innermost brackets. In our example this would be only $x$. The innermost brackets are then removed, and the phonological rules apply to the material in the second set of brackets, which are now the innermost brackets: [[xy]z]. This is $xy$. On the third cycle the brackets around $xy$ are removed, and the rules apply to the string $xyz$. The cyclic application of phonological rules is an extremely powerful device, and it has been used to describe several different types of morphophonemic phenomena. In this chapter I will examine one analysis that uses the phonological cycle and show how the same data may be accounted for in NGP using less powerful devices.

## 4.1 The TGP Analysis

In Harris (1969:125–27) the stress rule is regarded as applying cyclically. Harris notes that word pairs such as the following are related by a rule of diphthongization (where the spelling *ie* = [ye] and *ue* = [we]):

(1)  *diéstro* 'skillful'            *destréza* 'skill'
     *muéble* '(piece of) furniture'   *mobláje* '(set of) furniture'
     *viéjo* 'old'                  *vejéz* 'old age'

The rule of diphthongization is stated with stress as the conditioning factor:

(2)
$$\begin{bmatrix} e \\ o \end{bmatrix} \longrightarrow \begin{bmatrix} ye \\ we \end{bmatrix} / \begin{bmatrix} \overline{\phantom{xxx}} \\ +\text{stress} \\ +D \end{bmatrix}$$

where [+D] is a diacritic distinguishing vowels that diphthongize from those that do not. In Harris's final version of this rule he actually uses the feature [−tense] instead of [+D], although he indicates that the decision to use a phonological feature is somewhat arbitrary. In NGP no such arbitrary decisions need to be made, since NGP prohibits the diacritic use of a phonological feature. We will, with Harris, use /E/ to represent a [+D] vowel, and /e/ for the [−D] vowel. This putative tenseness distinction is NOT the same as the one discussed in Chapter 3. The distinction under discussion here is the historical distinction between the Latin long and short vowels. This historical distinction in tenseness is no longer observable on the surface, and it does NOT coincide with the tenseness distinction related to syllable shape. In fact, Harris claims that the free/checked syllable vowel alternation does not exist in Mexican Spanish, the dialect he is describing.

Consider also a regular present tense paradigm, where the vowel of the stem diphthongizes when stressed.

(3)              *podér* 'to be able'    *sentír* 'to feel'
      Sg. 1    *puédo*                *siénto*
          2    *puédes*               *siéntes*
          3    *puéde*                *siénte*
      Pl. 1    *podémos*              *sentímos*
          3    *puéden*               *siénten*

Now there are a few verbs that have diphthongs in the stem whether or not the stem is stressed: Consider *adiestrar* 'to become skillful' (cf. *destreza* and *diestro* in (1) above).

(4)    Sg. 1  *adiéstro*
          2  *adiéstras*
          3  *adiéstra*
     Pl. 1  *adiestrámos*
          3  *adiéstran*

Two other verbs of this type are *amueblar* 'to furnish' (cf. *mueble* and *moblaje*) and *aviejar* 'to grow old' (cf. *viejo* and *vejez*).

Harris accounts for the (to him) unexpected form *adiestrámos* as follows. The verb is formed from the stem that underlies *diestro* and *destreza*, i.e., /dEstr-/ (where E = [e, +D]). The stress rule is the only rule that applies cyclically; it applies in two cycles, first to the monosyllabic form in the innermost brackets and the second cycle to the penultima. After diphthongization applies, all stress except the rightmost are erased.

(5)    [$_V$# a [$_A$#dEstr #$_A$]a + mos #]$_V$      First Cycle
          É                                          stress

                                                     Second Cycle
                   á                                 stress
       [$_V$# a #dÉstr# á + mos#]$_V$
             yé                                       diphthongization
       [adyestrámos]                                  erase stress

Harris would also use the cyclic stress assignment to account for the following unstressed diphthongs in (6). The (a) column exhibits the unstressed diphthong, (b) shows the stressed diphthong, and (c) shows a related form with a monophthong when unstressed. The morpheme *-isimo* means 'very', and *-ito* is a diminutive.

(6)

|       | (a)                        | (b)                | (c)                     |
| ----- | -------------------------- | ------------------ | ----------------------- |
|       | *buenísimo* 'very good'    | *bueno* 'good'     | *bondad* 'goodness'     |
|       | *fuertísimo* 'very strong' | *fuerte* 'strong'  | *fortaleza* 'strength'  |
|       | *viejito* 'little old man' | *viejo* 'old'      | *vejez* 'old age'       |
|       | *pueblito* 'little village'| *pueblo* 'village' | *población* 'population' |

One example of how the cycle works in these cases should suffice. Consider *pueblito:*

(7)           [# [# pObl #<sub>N</sub>] ito #]<sub>N</sub>     First Cycle
                Ó                      stress

                                     Second Cycle
                      í                 stress
           wé                    diphthongization
        [pweblíto]            erase stress

The forms in (6c) do not have diphthongized stem vowels because their morphological structure is such that stress is assigned to them only once:

                 [pObla + sion]
                        ó       stress
              [poblasyón]

We should note carefully the claims made by the cyclic analysis. This analysis states that diphthongization is conditioned by the phonetic factor of stress. It also claims that stress can condition diphthongization on some abstract level in a position in which stress is never phonetically realized. There is no independent evidence for cyclic application of rules, and there is no independent justification for the different morphological structure of, for example, *pueblito* and *población*. The cycle and the posited constituent structure of these forms do only one job: They solve the problem they were created to solve. The phonological cycle is such a strong device that one would hope that the postulation of its existence were based on empirical evidence. But in fact there is no empirical data that can be brought to bear on the question of the existence or nonexistence of the phonological cycle. The most we can do is show that the cycle is not necessary, because all the relevant data can be handled by simpler mechanisms.

## 4.2 The NGP Analysis

Given the True Generalization Condition, we would not claim that diphthongization is always conditioned by stress; because there are forms such as *pueblíto, buenísimo,* and *adiestrár,* which show that the diphthongs occur in the absence of stress. These forms show that the effect of stress (the diphthong) has been lexicalized. If stress were the conditioning factor in these forms, the absence of stress would also mean the absence of diphthongization, and instead of *pueblito,* etc., we would find *\*poblito, \*vejito, \*bonisimo,* etc.

Let us distinguish productive morphology from lexicalized morphology.[1] Words containing lexicalized morphemes are entered in the lexicon as separate items. A word derived by productive processes is not listed in the lexicon. One criterion used to decide whether a suffix is productive or lexical is the meaning. If the meaning of the stem plus suffix is entirely predictable from the combination of the meaning of the stem with the meaning of the suffix, then the suffixation is productive. For instance, in English and Spanish the plural morpheme has a consistent semantic effect on the noun it attaches to. It is not necessary to list all singular and plural forms in the lexicon, because the semantic and phonological shape may be derived by rule. The suffixes *-ito* and *-ísimo* in Spanish also have this characteristic. The diminutive *-ito* may be attached to a noun to produce the meaning 'little (noun)'. The superlative *-ísimo* may be attached to an adjective to produce the meaning 'very (adjective)'.

Bear in mind, however, that the same suffixes may appear on words with unpredictable meaning, as in *bonito* 'pretty', which is etymologically from *bon-* 'good' plus the diminutive suffix. The existence of such words does not detract from the productivity of the suffix, since productivity is determined by the ability of the affix to produce new forms with predictable meaning and phonological shape (Thompson, 1974).

The suffixes listed in (6c), *-dad*, *-ez(a)*, and *-ción*, are lexicalized suffixes. When these suffixes are attached to a stem the meanings are not all predictable. It may be the case that one meaning is predictable, but words formed from these suffixes usually have other nonpredictable semantic readings as well. This is because the combination of morphemes has been used enough as a unit to take on meaning all its own, and the suffix itself is restricted enough in occurrence that its exact meaning has been obscured. For instance, *vejez* means 'old age' or 'oldness' as predicted by the combination *vej-* 'old' and *ez* meaning 'state of' or 'quality of'. But *vejez* also has a meaning not directly derivable from *vej* + *ez*. This meaning is 'platitude, boring repetition'. Similarly, *población* means, as predicted by the combination of morphemes, 'population', since one reading of *pueblo* is 'people', and 'village', since one reading of *pueblo* is 'village'. But the nonpredictable meaning of *población* is 'city'.

The second criterion for distinguishing productive from lexicalized morphology is the ability to combine with any form of the appropriate category. Productive suffixes such as *-ito* and *-ísimo* can be added to practically any noun and adjective, respectively. The suffixes *-ez(a)* and *-dad* have limits on their distribution that are arbitrary. These suffixes

---

[1] A similar distinction is discussed in Thompson (1974) from a semantic point of view.

have similar meanings; they both form nouns from adjectives. But there is no synchronically discernible reason why there exists *vejez* but not *\*vejedad, bondad* but not *\*boneza*.

The final criterion involves phonological shape. Productive suffixes tend to be more constant, and if they have allomorphs, these are in some way predictable. Consider as an example the regular English plural forms that vary but are predictable on phonological grounds. The Spanish lexicalized suffixes we have been discussing vary unpredictably Thus there is *fortaleza* but not *\*fortalez, vejez* but not *\*vejeza*.

Because natural languages are forever changing and evolving, the difference between productive and lexicalized morphology is not always absolutely clear. As is well known, these processes must always begin as productive processes, usually by compounding two words, such as the English *god-like* or, more recently, *sit-in*. Even some lexicalized suffixes have limited productivity. When lexicalized morphemes are used productively, it is done on the basis of a pattern with other forms, not by morphological rule and derivation. It is possible to make up a new word in English using a suffix such as *-ation* or *-ity*, but these differ sharply from the truly productive suffixes such as *-ness* and *-like*. As an example, compare *-ity* with *-ness*, since they both have the same use. There are synonyms such as *grammaticality* and *grammaticalness, productivity* and *productiveness*. In many cases where the form with *-ness* has only the meaning that is the sum of the stem plus *-ness,* the form in *-ity* has been extended to some special meaning: *localness, locality, technicalness, technicality*. These examples show that *-ness* should be considered productive while *-ity* is not.

Returning to Spanish morphology, we have shown that, on the basis of the criterian presented above, the forms in (6c) are lexicalized, while the forms in (6a) are generated by productive morphological process. Thus *población* is listed in the lexicon, as is *pueblo*. We know that *pueblo* has a diphthong in its lexical form, because a form derived directly from it, *pueblito,* has a diphthong even though the stem vowel is unstressed. This indicates that the effect of stress, the diphthong, has been lexicalized.

The underlying forms in NGP differ from those in TGP in the following way: In TGP *pueblo, población,* and *pueblito* are derived from the same stem, /pObl-/; in NGP the stem of *población* is /pobl-/, but the stem for *pueblo* and *pueblito* is /pwebl-/. The meaning similarity and the phonological similarity of the two stems /pobl-/ and /pwebl-/ are expressed in via-rules.

A phonological via-rule expresses a lexical relation. The lexical entry for *población* contains morphological, syntactic, and semantic information, in addition to via-rule information of the form [rel m via x] (Vennemann, 1972e), which is interpreted as "related to the lexical item *m* (in this case *pueblo*) via-rule *x*" (in this case, diphthongization). Here the rule specified by the via feature is not only a via-rule, but also a morphophonemic rule that functions in the verb paradigms.[2] It is stated as (8).

$$(8) \qquad \begin{bmatrix} e \\ o \end{bmatrix} \longrightarrow \begin{bmatrix} ye \\ we \end{bmatrix} / \begin{bmatrix} +\text{stress} \\ +\text{verb} \\ +D \end{bmatrix}$$

As a via-rule, the part of the SD that follows the slash line is ignored. As far as I know, via-rules do not have conditioning environments. The arrow in (8) reads "is rewritten as" when (8) is an MP-rule, but as a via-rule the arrow means "is related to." In this sense a via-rule implies no directionality and could as well be written with the arrow pointing in both directions.

We see, then, that the monophthong/diphthong alternations in the verb paradigms of (3) are a different type of relation than the alternations in the adjective and noun forms of (6b) and (6c). The verbal inflections are all productive. The person/number forms are generated directly from the verb stem by adding inflectional endings and rewriting the stem vowel as a diphthong under the appropriate conditions. But as *pueblito* and *adiestrar* demonstrate, the noun and adjective forms such as *pueblo* and *diestro* have been restructured to contain diphthongs. Productive morphophonemic alternations, such as those in the verb paradigm, are generated by morphophonemic rule; lexicalized alternations, such as those involving nouns and adjectives, are expressed in a via-rule.

The cyclic analysis and the noncyclic analysis account for the same data. The cyclic analysis expresses the generalization that diphthongization is always conditioned by stress. Our analysis does not make such a generalization for nouns and adjectives, because surface forms show that there is no such generalization.[3] The advocate of the cycle would

---

[2] The notation for MP-rules will be revised in Chapters 7 and 8.

[3] Notice further that there are occurrences of the diphthongs in question in forms where these diphthongs cannot be derived from underlying mid vowels, both stressed—e.g., *ciéncia* 'science', *diéta* 'diet', *juéves* 'Friday'—and unstressed—e.g., *cuestión* 'question', *piedád* 'piety', *bienál* 'biennial'. Thus it cannot be said that we are giving up the more subtle generalization that all words with unstressed diphthongs are derived productively from forms with stressed diphthongs.

claim that it is absurd to give up the generalization that stress conditions diphthongization because of a few exceptions such as *pueblito*. In NGP it is claimed that such exceptions cannot ever arise until the speakers have begun to give up that generalization. The alternation must be morphologized or lexicalized BEFORE any exceptions develop.

It is not possible to discuss here all proposed analyses using cyclic rule application. Neither is it necessary, because the strongest analyses using cyclic rule application involve the cyclic application of stress rules and are exactly analogous to the case discussed here (Brame 1974).[4] All languages have productive morphological processes that form new words on the basis of existing forms. When new words are formed by productive processes, the surface phonetic shape of the word is used. Thus *viejito* is formed from [byex-] not from /bEx-/. Since the surface form is used, in an abstract grammar it appears that phonological rules have applied to the stem used. To get these rules to apply to the new word, the cycle must be used in some cases, such as the one discussed here. Brame (1974:55) makes the following observation: "What stands out about each of the earlier examples of cyclic application of stress is the fact that the string constituting the first cycle itself shows up elsewhere as an independent phonetic word." On the basis of this observation, Brame proposes to restrict cyclic rule application to cases in which the material to which the first cycle of rules applies exists elsewhere in the language as an independent word.[5] To do so he must identify these strings both phonetically and semantically in much the way we have in this chapter. In other words, all the cases of cyclic rule application considered valid by Brame have the same characteristics as the case discussed here. And all of these cases can be accounted for quite naturally without the cycle by making two quite plausible assumptions: (i) Words whose meaning and phonetic shape are not fully predictable must be entered in the lexicon (indeed no one has ever shown how we are to avoid listing such words in the lexicon); and (ii) the lexical representation is identical to the phonetic representation except that all phonetically predictable redundancies have been removed (e.g., the

---

[4] The evidence for cyclic application where segmental phonology, rather than stress, is involved is considerably weaker. See for example Kaye and Piggott (1973) and the reply to them in Truitner and Dunnigan (1975). The rules discussed in these articles are clearly MP-rules; if they were formulated more restrictively, cyclic application would not be necessary.

[5] Notice that this restriction would not quite work for the Spanish examples discussed, since the innermost strings, /bEx-/ of *viejito* and /mObl-/ of *amueblar*, etc., are stems rather than words; they lack gender markers or theme vowels.

underlying form of *viejo* is /byex-/, not/bEx-/). With these two constraints cyclic rule application is simply unnecessary.

## 4.3 Diphthongization in Chicano

Diphthongization in Chicano dialects presents a somewhat different situation in some verb paradigms, and this situation demonstrates rather conclusively that a theory of grammar must be able to account for relations between words with a device such as the via-rule.

The first conjugation verbs that in standard Spanish have an alternation between *ue* and *o* do not alternate in Chicano Spanish. The diphthong is found in every form (Reyes, 1972). A few forms will illustrate the difference.

(9)

|  |  | Standard | Chicano |
|---|---|---|---|
|  | Infinitive | *contár* | *cuentár* |
| Present | Sg. 1 | *cuénto* | *cuénto* |
|  | Pl. 1 | *contámos* | *cuentámos* |
| Preterite | Sg. 1 | *conté* | *cuenté* |
| Imperfect | Sg. 1 | *contába* | *cuentába* |

(Notice that in the Chicano verb, as in the standard forms cited above, stress does NOT condition diphthongization.)

Both Reyes (1972) and Harris (1973b) observe that the Chicano verbs could be accounted for with underlying forms containing diphthongs. In other words, the underlying forms for these verbs have been restructured. However, both authors also point out that if the underlying verbs contain diphthongs, it would be impossible in TGP to state the relation between the verbs and the nouns that are related to the verbs. For instance, related to *cuentar* 'to count' is the phrase *al contado* 'in cash'; related to *sueltar* 'to loosen' is *soltura* 'looseness'; *vuelar* 'to fly' is related to *volador* 'flier' (Reyes, 1972). Reyes (a native speaker of this dialect) states that such relations are "to obvious to deny" (p. 38).

In TGP the only way to capture phonological relatedness is to arrange for the two related forms to be derived from the same underlying forms. Thus Reyes and Harris must posit an underlying lax /O/ for the verb *cuentar* and add to the diphthongization rule a special case that diphthongizes all /O/'s in the first conjugation verbs. The word *contado* is derived from the same stem.

The TGP analysis claims, in effect, that the relation between *cuentar* and *al contado* is exactly the same kind of relation as exists between the infinitive of a verb and one of its finite forms, say *pensar* 'to think' and *pienso* 'I think'. There are several facts that go against this implied claim. First is the fact that ALL forms of the verb contain diphthongs. If the underlying form contained an /O/, one would expect that the /O/ would show up in at least a few forms. The other, more compelling argument is that a phrase such as *al contado* is a set phrase or idiom; there are no productive rules that derive such phrases, and its meaning does not equal the sum of its parts. *Al* is a contraction of *a* + *el* meaning literally 'to the'. *Contado* is a past participle form, 'counted'. I can see no automatic semantic relation between this and 'in cash'. Clearly *al contado* must be listed in the lexicon as a phrase.

It is just this type of relation that is expressed in NGP by via-rules. In NGP it is possible to give the most natural treatment of the verbs, that is, to say that the underlying stem contains a diphthong, and still draw the obvious relation between the verbs and the other words (nouns and adjectives) or phrases. The underlying stem for *cuentar* is /kwent-/. (Notice that NGP REQUIRES that the diphthong be present in the underlying form.) Related words or phrases are listed separately. Each related lexical entry contains the via-rule information: /kwent-/ is related to *al contado* via the diphthongization rule (rule (8) of the previous section).

## 4.4   The Power of the Theories

The theory of NGP is less powerful than the theory of TGP. In all the examples discussed so far, we have seen that several solutions to each problem are available in TGP. But in NGP the range of solutions is quite narrow, and, we have claimed, the solution suggested by the principles of NGP is the solution that best expresses what the speakers know about the data. Thus not only does NGP make strong claims about natural language, it appears to make the correct claims.

NGP has discarded extrinsic rule order and abstract underlying representations and added another device, the via-rule. The distinction between phonological rules, morphophonemic rules, and via-rules is claimed to be both necessary and empirically motivated. NGP claims that speakers do not internalize linguistic processes in phonological terms made abstract by the depth given the derivation by rule ordering, but rather that speakers understand such processes as morphophonological or lexical relations. The evidence presented above supports the claim that via-rules represent one type of phonological relation possible in natural language, while extrinsically ordered rules do not. We have also seen evidence that speakers learn quite easily to associate phonological alternations with morphological categories. This is because speakers have access only to the surface data of the language, and they must construct simple, plausible hypotheses on the basis of the data they have. In many cases the morphological association of sound to meaning is more obvious than a purely phonetic association, and in these cases we often find independent evidence that speakers have internalized rules of grammar that depend on morphological categories rather than abstract phonology.

# 5

# Rule
# Order

One of the basic principles of generative phonology is the principle that allows extrinsic ordering of grammatical rules. Since this principle has been widely accepted and generally applied in phonological analyses, it is necessary to examine in some detail the consequences of this principle and the consequences of the No-Ordering Condition, which excludes extrinsic rule order. To this end I will discuss the various ordering relations, feeding, bleeding, counter-feeding, and counter-bleeding, and examine the consequences of the relations for particular analyses. In addition, I will show what sort of analysis NGP predicts for each case. The purpose here is not necessarily to argue that NGP predicts a better analysis in each case (although in many cases it is obvious that this is true), but merely to demonstrate what the analysis would be like. In order to show that NGP is superior to TGP it would be necessary to find independent evidence that NGP can explain but TGP cannot. We have seen in Chapter 3 that such evidence is available in some cases. In this chapter we will concentrate on showing that reasonable analyses of a wide range of data are available in a theory that does not use extrinsic rule order.

## 5.1  Feeding Order

Rules are intrinsically ordered if the only factor involved in determining when and where the rules apply is the information given in the SD. Rules are extrinsically ordered if an ordering statement prevents the rule from applying to a form that meets its SD.

Feeding order is intrinsic order. Rule A is said to feed rule B just in case rule A creates new input to rule B, i.e., creates forms that meet the SD of rule B. Rule B then applies to these forms on the basis of the SD and is not prevented from applying to any form that meets its SD. For instance, Brazilian Portuguese has a palatalization process affecting /t,d/ before high front vowels, palatalizing these segments to [č, ǰ]. This process is completely regular and productive: [t,d] NEVER OCCUR before [i].[1]

(1)       *gatinho*      [gačiɲu]   'small cat'
          cf. *gato*     [gatu]     'cat'

          *tipo*         [čipu]     'type'

          *dedinho*      [deǰiɲu]   'finger (dim.)'
          cf. *dedo*     [dedu]     'finger'

          *diferente*    [ǰiferẽči] 'different'

These forms are from the andante speech style. Also apparent in these forms is a rule raising unstressed mid vowels to high vowels. Unstressed mid vowels still occur in the slowest style of speech, largo, but are raised in andante. Compare the following forms:

(2)       largo          andante

          [mɔhte]        [mɔhči]    'death'
          [onde]         [onǰi]     'where'
          [behnadɛte]    [behnadɛči] 'Bernadette'

Notice that the raising of the vowel creates the environment for palatalization and that palatalization does indeed take place. The derivation of [mɔhči] would proceed as follows.

(3)                    / mɔhte /    (underlying
                          i         raising
                          č         palatalization
                   [mɔhči]          (phonetic

In this derivation, raising FEEDS palatalization in the sense that raising creates new input to palatalization. This is an intrinsic order because it is

---

[1] I am grateful to Bernadette Abaurre for supplying these examples.

determined by the rules themselves; palatalization CANNOT apply to
/mɔhte/ before raising does because the SD of palatalization is not met
until raising has applied.

This example also illustrates why rules are applied SEQUENTIALLY
rather than SIMULTANEOUSLY. In simultaneous rule application, all rules
apply to underlying forms directly; in sequential application, a rule applies to the output of some other rule. If we allowed only simultaneous
application, it would not be possible to derive [mɔhči] from /mɔhte/ by
the rules as given; since palatalization would be required to apply only
to the underlying form /mɔhte/, but in this form the SD of palatalization
is not met. The only way that the two rules can apply to /mɔhte/ to give
the correct results is sequentially, palatalization applying to the output
of raising. Of course, it is possible to state the rules in such a way that a
simultaneous application will give the correct results. The palatalization
rule would have to apply before unstressed mid-front vowels, as well as
before stressed or unstressed high-front vowels. Under this formulation, the SD of the raising rule is written into the palatalization rule resulting in a loss of economy and, worse, a rule that violates the True
Generalization Condition, since there is no surface evidence for palatalization before mid-vowels.

It should also be mentioned in the discussion of intrinsic orders that
some extrinsic orders are necessary only because of the notation chosen
for the expression of the rules. In such cases there are two rules, both
valid generalizations, but they are stated in such a way that one must be
extrinsically ordered before the other. Consider, for instance, English
vowel nasalization. A word such as *can't*, derived from *can* /kæn/, may
be pronounced [kæ̃t] in my own speech. To derive this form, two rules
may be posited:

(4) $\qquad$ V $\longrightarrow$ [+nasal] / $\_\_\_$ [+nasal] Co$^\$$

(5) $\qquad \begin{bmatrix} -\text{syll} \\ +\text{nasal} \end{bmatrix} \longrightarrow \emptyset / \_\_\_ [-\text{voice}]^\$$

Rule (4) must apply before rule (5) because (5) deletes the conditioning
environment for (4). But these rules can also be stated in such a way that
they are intrinsically ordered. An additional restriction may be placed
on the SD of rule (5) so that the preceding vowel is nasalized:

(6) $\qquad \begin{bmatrix} -\text{syll} \\ +\text{nasal} \end{bmatrix} \longrightarrow \emptyset / [+\text{nasal}] \_\_\_ [-\text{voice}]^\$$

The additional feature in rule (6) adds explanatory value to the rule
since it explains the deletion and states a universal condition: that a
nasal consonant deletes only after nasalizing the preceding vowel, oth-

erwise important information would be lost. (In some languages, after nasal consonant deletion, the nasality of the vowel is also lost.)

Vennemann (1971), in making a similar point, discusses the following case. In colloquial German the infinitive suffix /−n/, as in /ze: +n/ [ze:n] 'to see' and /fa:r+n/ [fa:rn] 'to go', becomes syllabic after obstruents: /hof + n/[hofn̥] 'to hope'. Furthermore, after stops, the suffix assimilates the point of articulation features of the stop, and the latter is reduced to glottal stop:

(7) /kip + n/ 'to turn     /bit + n/ 'to ask'     /šik + n/ 'to send'
    over'
    kipn̥                    bitn̥                  šikn̥   syllabification
    kipm̥                    bitn̥                  šikŋ    nasal assimilation
    kiʔm̥                    biʔn̥                  šiʔŋ    stop reduction

Nasal assimilation and stop reduction may be formulated as follows:

(8)
$$\begin{bmatrix} +\text{nasal} \\ +\text{syll} \end{bmatrix} \longrightarrow [\alpha \text{ Point}]/ \begin{bmatrix} -\text{cont} \\ \alpha \text{ Point} \end{bmatrix} \underline{\hspace{1cm}}$$

(where [α Point] is used as an abbreviation for agreement in the features such as coronal, anterior, etc.)

(9)
$$\begin{bmatrix} -\text{cont} \\ -\text{nasal} \\ -\text{voice} \end{bmatrix} \longrightarrow ʔ/\underline{\hspace{1cm}} \begin{bmatrix} +\text{nasal} \\ +\text{syll} \end{bmatrix}$$

Rules (8) and (9) must be extrinsically ordered because (8) must assimilate the nasal to the stop BEFORE it is reduced to [ʔ]; otherwise the contrast between [m, n, and ŋ] could not be derived.

The necessity of extrinsic ordering in this case is a consequence of the formal statement of the rules. Vennemann proposes that if stop reduction is modified slightly, the rules will be intrinsically ordered. The modification required is the condition that the stop may reduce to [ʔ] only if the following nasal agrees in point of articulation:

(10)
$$\begin{bmatrix} -\text{cont} \\ -\text{nasal} \\ -\text{voice} \\ \alpha \text{ Point} \end{bmatrix} \longrightarrow ʔ/\underline{\hspace{1cm}} \begin{bmatrix} -\text{nasal} \\ +\text{syll} \\ \alpha \text{ Point} \end{bmatrix}$$

In this formulation, stop reduction cannot apply until nasal assimilation has applied. Rule (10) is somewhat less simple than rule (9); but, Vennemann argues, it is more explanatory, since it states explicitly that the point of articulation information must be transferred to the nasal consonant before the stop is reduced. In the process of reducing /p, t, k/ to [ʔ], no information is lost, since the point of articulation features are now apparent from the nasal.[2]

In this case, and many similar cases, one could make a more radical reformulation by positing one rule rather than two. The claim is that what appears as two operations is one and the same operation. The forms in (7) could be generated by (11).

(11)
$$
\begin{bmatrix} -\text{son} \\ -\text{cont} \\ -\text{voice} \\ \alpha \text{ Point} \end{bmatrix}
\begin{bmatrix} +\text{nasal} \\ +\text{syll} \end{bmatrix}
\Longrightarrow
\text{ʔ}
\begin{bmatrix} +\text{nasal} \\ +\text{syll} \\ \alpha \text{ Point} \end{bmatrix}
$$

Mowrey (1975) has suggested an explanation for this phenomenon as a single process. Rather than viewing the nasal as progressively assimilating, we could view the nasality as encroaching regressively on the voiceless stop, changing it to a nasal segment with the same point of articulation. The glottal stop then develops as the last vestige of the voiceless stop. In this view there is really only one process rather than two. If this view is correct, then there will be no stage at which [kipm̩] and [sikn̩] occur phonetically. English is similar; we have the casual pronunciations of *open* as [owpn̩] and [owʔm̩], but never *[owpm̩].

A reformulation that improves the rules is possible when the rules in question are true generalizations about surface forms. Reformulations are also possible for other proposed rules, but if the rules are not true generalizations, reformulations to avoid rule order will lead to more and more ad hoc rules.

## 5.2  Disjunctive Ordering

There is a certain type of ordering relation among subparts of rules that appears to be valid and, in fact, indispensable for phonological descriptions. This is the disjunctive ordering relation. If the subparts of a rule are disjunctively ordered, then the application of one subpart to a form precludes the application of any other subpart to that form. Disjunctive ordering expresses a complementary relation among the subparts of rules. For example, the disjunctive relation exists in rules that

---

[2] In the vowel nasalization case, a single rule of the form VN$^S \longrightarrow$ Ṽ is often possible. In English this rule would be complex, since the nasal consonant only deletes before voiceless consonants, but not at the end of the syllable (e.g., *can, render*) or before a voiced obstruent (e.g., *canned, sand*).

predict the values of completely redundant phonetic features. In some dialects of English, the feature [nasal] is wholly predictable for vowels: Vowels followed by nasal consonants in the same syllable are [ + nasal], all others are [ − nasal]. The complementary distribution of nasality may be expressed as follows:

(12)     $V \longrightarrow$ $\begin{cases} [+\text{nasal}] / \underline{\phantom{xx}} [+\text{nasal}] \ C_0 \ \$ & \text{(a)} \\ [-\text{nasal}] \qquad\quad \text{elsewhere} & \text{(b)} \end{cases}$

Subpart (b) affects only those forms not affected by the preceding subpart; thus it will not change any [ + nasal] vowels back to [ − nasal].

The alternative to the disjunctive ordering format for a rule such as (12) would be to specify the environment for [ − nasal] vowels:

(13)     $V \longrightarrow$ $\begin{cases} [+\text{nasal}] / \underline{\phantom{xx}} [+\text{nasal}] \ C_0 \ \$ & \text{(a)} \\ [-\text{nasal}] / \underline{\phantom{xx}} \begin{cases} \$ \\ [-\text{nasal}] \end{cases} & \text{(b)} \end{cases}$

The format of (12) has advantages over (13) in addition to its greater simplicity. Rule (13) makes it appear that [ − nasal] is conditioned by its environment, just as [ + nasal] is. We know, however, that [ − nasal] is not a conditioned value, but rather the natural or unmarked value for the feature when no environmental conditions are affecting it. The statement in (12) captures this fact, while (13) misses it entirely. Furthermore, the statement in (13) makes it appear accidental that the (a) and (b) environments are complementary. The statement in (12) expresses exactly this fact. Thus the disjunctive ordering format is quite appropriate for phonetic rules of this type.

Disjunctive ordering has also been used in the representation of other rules: for example, stress rules. Consider the Latin stress rule, which stressed the antepenultimate syllable if the penultimate was weak:

(14)     $S \longrightarrow [+\text{stress}] / \underline{\phantom{xx}} \begin{bmatrix} S \\ \text{weak} \end{bmatrix} S \# ]$

e.g., *família* 'family', *inútīlis* 'useless'; or stressed the penultimate syllable if it was strong, e.g., *portĕntum* 'portent', *tribū́nus* 'tribune'. There is no need, given rule (14), to make a strong syllable a condition on penultimate stress; we can merely say, stress the penultimate syllable elsewhere and collapse the two subparts by parentheses notation:

(15)     $S \longrightarrow [+\text{stress}] / \underline{\phantom{xx}} ( \begin{bmatrix} S \\ \text{weak} \end{bmatrix} ) S \# ]$

The two subparts must be disjunctively ordered so that the second part will not assign penultimate stress to forms already carrying antepenultimate stress. In this case disjunctive ordering makes it possible to represent in a natural way the fact that each syllable had only one stress.

The only problem with disjunctive ordering is the theoretical problem of predicting which rules will have disjunctively ordered subparts and which will not. Several principles have been proposed, i.e., Anderson (1974), Sanders's Proper Inclusion Precedence (Sanders, 1974), and Kiparsky's Elsewhere Condition (Kiparsky, 1973a). There has been some discussion about the correctness of these principles, but all proposals concerning disjunctive ordering have maintained that the environments of the subparts be complementary and that the more specific rules PRECEDE the more general rules. (The most general rule will be the "elsewhere case.") We will use these general principles in determining the domain of disjunctive ordering.

## 5.3   Counter-Feeding Order

If there are two rules A and B such that the output of A meets the SD of B (that is, A feeds B), the feeding relationship can be prevented by ordering rule B before rule A. Such an ordering relation is a counter-feeding order. Since rule B can apply only once, it cannot act on the output of rule A, even though the forms meet its SD. The consequences of counter-feeding order become clear when we examine an analysis using this type of order. The example involves velar softening in Spanish and is taken from Harris (1969:163 ff).

In Spanish there are alterations between /k/ and /s/, and /g/ and /x/:

(16)

| k | s | | g | x | |
|---|---|---|---|---|---|
| api[k]al | ápi[s]e | 'apical, apex' | fonólogo | fonolo[x]ía | 'phonologist, phonology' |
| produ[k]ción | produ[s]ir | 'production, to produce' | laringólogo | larin[x]e | 'laryngologist, larynx' |
| vo[k]al | vo[s] | 'vocal, voice' | | | |

In addition, underlying [g] gives [k] by devoicing and [x] by velar softening in the following forms:

(17)

| | *k* | *x* | |
|---|---|---|---|
| | *prote*[k]*tor* | *prote*[x]*er* | 'protector, to protect' |
| | *prote*[k]*ción* | | 'protection' |
| | *dire*[k]*tor* | *diri*[x]*ir* | 'director, to direct' |
| | *dire*[k]*ción* | | 'direction' |

Harris sets up an underlying velar in the stems of all of these forms and derives the [s] and [x] by a very general rule of velar softening. (Harris actually breaks the rule up into several stages, but we will ignore those details here.)

(18)
$$\begin{bmatrix} k \\ g \end{bmatrix} \longrightarrow \begin{bmatrix} s \\ x \end{bmatrix} / \underline{\hspace{1cm}} \begin{bmatrix} V \\ -\text{back} \end{bmatrix}$$

It is important to note that this rule is stated in purely phonological terms and is considered to be quite general.

There are, however, a number of forms that do not undergo the rule; in fact velars before front vowels in modern Spanish are quite common:

(19) *que* [ke] 'what, that'  *águila* [agila] 'eagle'
 *quien* [kyen] 'who'  *guerra* [gerra] 'war'
 *quitar* [kitar] 'to remove'  *guión* [gyon] 'cross'
 *quejar* [kexar] 'to complain'  *guisa* [gisa] 'manner'
 *kilo* [kilo] 'kilo'  *guia* [gia] 'guide'

In order to maintain a totally general velar softening rule, the forms above must somehow be prevented from undergoing it. Harris accomplishes this by positing underlying /k$^w$/ and /g$^w$/ for velars that do not undergo velar softening: e.g., *que* /k$^w$e/, *quitar* /k$^w$itare/, *kilo* /k$^w$ilo/, *aguila* /ag$^w$ila/, *guerra* /g$^w$erra/, etc. Then there must be a rule that delabializes underlying labiovelars before front vowels. (The labialization remains before /a/: *cuando* [kwando] 'when', *cual* [kwal] 'which', *tregua* [tregwa] 'respite'.) Delabialization is effected in two stages. The first makes the labialization into a labial glide:

(20)
$$\begin{bmatrix} -\text{sonor} \\ +\text{round} \end{bmatrix} \varnothing \Longrightarrow [-\text{round}] \ w$$

Thus /k$^w$e/ → /kwe/. This rule is needed (according to Harris, p. 155) because underlying /k$^w$/ and /g$^w$/, as in *cuando* and *tregua*, give the same PHONETIC representation as [kw] and [gw] derived from /kO/ and /gO/ by diphthongization: /kOnto/ → /kwento/, /agOra/ → /agwera/.

The second stage merely deletes the round glide if a non-back vowel follows.

(21)

$$w \longrightarrow \emptyset / \begin{bmatrix} -\text{sonor} \\ +\text{back} \end{bmatrix} \underline{\hspace{1cm}} \begin{bmatrix} V \\ -\text{back} \end{bmatrix}$$

There are two uses of counter-feeding order in this analysis, both of them quite typical. First notice that delabialization (rules (20) and (21)) produces new sequences of velars followed by front vowels and thus potentially feeds velar softening. We do not want delabialization to feed velar softening, however, since the labiovelars were set up expressly for blocking velar softening. Thus velar softening must be ordered BEFORE delabialization so that it may not be allowed to apply to the output of delabialization. The order that produces the correct results is a counter-feeding order.

(22) Counter-feeding

| /apik + e/ | /kʷe/ | /laring + e/ | /gʷerra/ | |
|------------|-------|--------------|----------|--|
| apise | —— | larinxe | —— | velar softening |
| —— | kwe | —— | gwerra | delabialization (a) |
| —— | kØe | —— | gØerra | delabialization (b) |
| [ápise] | [ke] | [laríŋxe] | [gér̃a] | |

(23) Feeding

| /apik + e/ | /kʷe/ | /laring + e/ | /gʷerra/ | |
|------------|-------|--------------|----------|--|
| —— | kwe | —— | gwerra | delabialization (a) |
| —— | kØe | —— | gØerra | delabialization (b) |
| apise | se | larinxe | xerra | velar softening |
| [ápise] | *[se] | [laríŋxe] | *[xér̃a] | |

What does counter-feeding order do? In this instance, because counter-feeding order was used, it is possible to posit abstract segments /kʷ/ and /gʷ/ that never appear in surface forms. If counter-feeding order were not allowed, these segments could not block velar softening as they were intended to because velar softening would apply to the output of delabialization, producing the incorrect output as in (23) above. Thus one of the typical consequences of counter-feeding order is that it allows the analyst to posit abstract underlying segments.

Another typical consequence of counter-feeding order is that it allows rules to be stated in maximally general form and in completely phonological terms, even when the surface forms show that the rule is not totally general. Thus velar softening is stated as a general rule of Spanish, applying in a particular phonological environment, even though there are many surface instances of this environment where the rule does not apply, e.g., [ke], [agila], etc. In formal statement, velar softening is not differentiated from the very general rules of the language, such as intervocalic spirantization.

Similar consequences result from the second use of counter-feeding order in this analysis. This time the rules involved are delabialization and diphthongization. Diphthongization changes specially marked /o/'s ([o, +D], represented as /O/) to [we] when stressed. Thus *contár* /kOntár/ 'to tell, to count' has a first singular *cuénto* [kwénto]. Since the round glide shows up phonetically in *cuénto*, this form must be exempted from delabialization. This is accomplished by counter-feeding order. Delabialization must apply before diphthongization, which would produce new input to delabialization:

(24)          Counter-feeding
             /kOnto/   /kʷe/
             ——      kwe   delabialization (a)
             ——      kØe   delabialization (b)
             kwento  ——   diphthongization
             [kwento]  [ke]

(25)          Feeding
             /kOnto/   /kʷe/
             kwento  ——   diphthongization
             ——      kwe   delabialization (a)
             kØento  kØe   delabialization (b)
             *[kento]  [ke]

In this case the primary consequence of counter-feeding order is that it allows the maximally general statement of delabialization. If delabialization were to apply after diphthongization, it would have to be restricted so as not to affect /kw/ and /gw/ sequences deriving from diphthongization.

For both velar softening and delabialization, the use of counter-feeding order allows the rules to be stated in their most general form even though surface evidence shows the rules to be restricted. In the theory of phonology in which this analysis was formulated (Chomsky and Halle, 1968), grammars containing optimally general statements are highly valued, and grammars having restricted rules or exceptional forms are less highly valued.

In NGP general statements are also highly valued, but such statements are allowed only when they accurately reflect the surface facts of the language. Counter-feeding order is not allowed in NGP precisely because counter-feeding order allows the use of rules that are not true

generalizations. How, then, would the rules of velar softening and delabialization be formulated in NGP? First observe that the only forms that
have alternations of /k/ and /s/ and /g/ and /x/ are forms related by nonproductive derivational morphology: *ápice, apical,* etc. Productive derivational morphemes do not cause velar softening:

(26)        *rico  riquísimo*    [rikísimo]   'rich,' 'very rich'
              *largo  larguito*    [largíto]    'long,' 'longish'

(The distinction between lexicalized morphology and productive morphology is fully discussed in Chapter 4.) Verb forms do not undergo
velar softening. In *markar,* the /k/ occurs in all forms (e.g., [marka]
present indicative [marke] present subjunctive); in *proteger,* the /x/
occurs in all forms (e.g., [protexe] present indicative, [protexa] present
subjunctive). (Two verbs, *decir* and *hacer,* have an alternation of /s/ with
/g/, but these verbs are irregular.)

Since the alternation described by velar softening only occurs in
forms related by derivational morphology, this relation may be expressed by a via-rule. All the forms in (16) and (17) are listed in the lexicon separately; they are not all derived from the same stem. The relation between the stem-final consonants is expressed in a via-rule:

(27)                 $\begin{bmatrix} k \\ g \end{bmatrix} \longleftrightarrow \begin{bmatrix} s \\ x \end{bmatrix}$

The via-rule is included in the lexical entry along with other information about the item.

Delabialization will be treated similarly, although there are so few
forms related by delabialization that it is conceivable that the relation
may not even exist. The forms Harris lists (p. 157) are

(28)    *li*[kw]*ar*      'liquify'       *li*[ki]*idar*     'liquidate'
        *e*[kw]*ación*   'equation'    *e*[k]*ivalente*   'equivalent'
        *ye*[gw]*a*        'mare'        *e*[k]*itación*    'horseback'
        [kw]*al*         'which'       [k]*e*          'what'
        [kw]*ando*      'when'        [k]*ien*        'who'

Thus velar softening and delabialization are treated as minor relations,
not as general rules. There is no need to posit abstract segments such as
/kʷ/ and /gʷ/.

The cases of counter-feeding order discussed here are typical:
Counter-feeding order allows a rule to be formulated as very general
even if there are many surface forms that it does not apply to, and

counter-feeding order allows surface exceptions to a rule to appear unexceptional. Further, abstract underlying forms are usually needed in this type of analysis, for the second rule of the pair ordered in a counter-feeding relation acts on abstract underlying forms, e.g., in the analyses just discussed, labiovelars in Spanish. Disallowing counter-feeding order disallows a certain type of abstractness, and it also excludes the possibility of formulating rules as very general when in fact they are not.

## 5.4 Counter-Bleeding Order

If there are two rules A and B such that the application of A destroys some (or all) of the environments to which B is applicable, these rules in the order A, B are in bleeding order. The same rules applying in the order B, A are in counter-bleeding order. That is, counter-bleeding order allows the application of rule B in environments that rule A will destroy later in the derivation.[3] As with counter-feeding order, the use of counter-bleeding order allows abstractness in phonological descriptions and the formulation of dubious generalizations.

Counter-bleeding order is always involved in cases of absolute neutralization. The example discussed in Chapter 2, in which the difference between *crecer* ([kresko], [kreses], etc.) and *coser* ([kweso], [kweses]) was accounted for with an underlying distinction between /s/ and /θ/, used rules ordered in counter-bleeding order. The rule that neutralized the contrast between /s/ and /θ/ would destroy all cases where /k/ should be inserted if /k/ is to be inserted only after /θ/. Thus the order K-insertion, $\theta \rightarrow$ s, is a counter-bleeding order, and this order is absolutely essential to this analysis. We have already shown that a reanalysis of these data using morphological information is straightforward and well motivated.

Another interesting and celebrated analysis using counter-bleeding order and absolute neutralization was proposed by Hyman (1970) for Nupe. On the surface, Nupe has a series of plain, palatalized, [Cʸ] and labialized [Cʷ] consonants. The palatalized and labialized consonants are largely predictable. Front vowels are always preceded by palatalized consonants: [ēgʸī] 'child', [ēgʸē] 'beer'. Round vowels are always preceded by labialized consonants: [ēgʷū̄] 'mud', [egʷó] 'grass'. The surface contrast between plain, palatalized, and labialized consonants

---

[3] In all cases of counter-bleeding order, the conditioned variant produced by a rule shows up in surface forms where the conditioning context is not present.

occurs only before [a]: [ēgā] 'stranger', [ēgʸà] 'blood', [ēgʷā] 'hand'.

Hyman proposes that the underlying structure of Nupe has three phonologically distinct low vowels, a front vowel /ɛ/, a back rounded vowel /ɔ/, and a back unrounded vowel /a/. The former two vowels cause palatalization and labialization, respectively, and then are neutralized to [a]. Hyman's analysis, then, contains the following three underlying forms, /ēgā/ 'stranger', (ēgɛ̀/ 'blood', (ēgɔ̀/ 'hand', and the following two assimilation rules:

Palatalization Rule (PR):

$$(29) \quad [+\text{cons}] \longrightarrow \begin{bmatrix} -\text{back} \\ +\text{high} \end{bmatrix} / \underline{\quad} \begin{bmatrix} V \\ -\text{back} \end{bmatrix} \qquad (C \longrightarrow C^y / \underline{\quad} \begin{Bmatrix} i \\ e \\ \epsilon \end{Bmatrix})$$

Labialization Rule (LR):

$$(30) [+\text{cons}] \longrightarrow \begin{bmatrix} +\text{round} \\ +\text{high} \end{bmatrix} / \underline{\quad} \begin{bmatrix} V \\ +\text{round} \end{bmatrix} \qquad (C \longrightarrow C^w / \underline{\quad} \begin{Bmatrix} u \\ o \\ \mathfrak{o} \end{Bmatrix})$$

In addition, there is a rule of absolute neutralization (AN):

$$\begin{bmatrix} V \\ +\text{low} \end{bmatrix} \longrightarrow \begin{bmatrix} -\text{round} \\ +\text{back} \end{bmatrix} \quad (\epsilon, \mathfrak{o} \longrightarrow a)$$

The derivation of 'blood' and 'hand' will proceed as follows.

(31)  /ēgɔ̀/  /ēgɛ̀/
      ─────  ēgʸɛ  Palatalization Rule
      ēgʷɔ   ─────  Labialization Rule
      [ēgʷā]  [ēgʸà]  Absolute Neutralization

Notice the use of counter-bleeding order: AN must apply after PR and LR, and not before. If AN applied before the assimilation rules, the palatalized and labialized consonants before low vowels could not be derived. Hyman presents several arguments in favor of his analysis. In the following paragraphs I will summarize the relevant arguments; in the next section I will present the NGP analysis and compare arguments for and against the two analyses.

First, Hyman argues that if the surface contrastive occurrences of $C^y$ and $C^w$ (or Cy and Cw) were underlying phonemes, these phonemes would have a very restricted distribution: They occur only before the low vowel /a/. Thus they would violate otherwise valid morpheme structure conditions that state that all Nupe consonant phonemes are neither palatalized nor labialized. In his analysis, since all occurrences of C$^y$ and C$^w$ are derived by rule, the underlying phonemic structure is simplified and there are no oddities of distribution.

In favor of underlying /ɛ/ and /ɔ/, Hyman argues that the occurrences of [a] that derive from these abstract segments ACT AS THOUGH they are [−back] and [+round], respectively, not just with regard to PR and LR, but also with regard to the reduplication rule. Reduplication is used to nominalize monomorphemic verbs. The reduplicated syllable consists of a copy of the stem-initial consonant plus a high vowel. The vowel is [i] if the stem vowel is /i/ or /e/, and [u] if the stem vowel is [u] or [o].

(32)    /gí/ 'to eat'        ⟶ [g$^y$īg$^y$í] 'eating'
        /gē/ 'to be good'    ⟶ [g$^y$īg$^y$e] 'goodness'
        /gú/ 'to puncture'   ⟶ [g$^w$ūg$^w$ú] 'puncturing'
        /gò/ 'to receive'    ⟶ [g$^w$ūg$^w$ò] 'receiving'

If the stem vowel is [a], the reduplicated vowel is either [i] or [u]. It is [u] in just those cases where Hyman posits /ɔ/ as the underlying stem vowel, i.e., in those stems that have labialized initial consonants. Thus the underlying abstract /ɔ/ accounts for both the reduplicated vowel and the labialized consonant.

(33)    /tɔ́/ 'to trim'       ⟶ [t$^w$ūt$^w$á] 'trimming'     *t is missing?*
        /tɛ́/ 'to be mild'    ⟶ [t$^y$īt$^y$á] 'mildness'      t$^y$it$^y$á
        /tá/ 'to tell'       ⟶ [t$^y$īá] 'telling'           t$^y$itá

The reduplication rule copies the roundness of the underlying stem vowel before the AN rule applies. Reduplication is stated as follows:

(34)    RED ⟶ C$_1$ $\begin{bmatrix} +\text{high} \\ \alpha\text{round} \\ \alpha\text{back} \\ 2\text{tone} \end{bmatrix}$ / ___ C$_1$ $\begin{bmatrix} V \\ \alpha\text{round} \end{bmatrix}$

Hyman further argues that the rule of AN is productive and applies in loan word adaptations. The following are examples of nativized Yoruba loans.

(35)    Yor. [kɛ̀kɛ́]____Nupe [k$^y$àk$^y$á] 'bicycle'
        Yor. [ɛ̀gbɛ̀]____Nupe [ègb$^y$à] (a Yoruba town)
        Yor. [tɔ̄rɛ̄]____Nupe [t$^w$ār$^y$ā] 'to give a gift'
        Yor. [kɔbɔ́]____Nupe [k$^w$áb$^w$à] 'penny'

Hyman says

> a Nupe speaker will consistently 'nativize' [Cɔ] as [Cʷa] and [Cɛ] as [Cʸa].
> This is also sometimes perceptible in the way Nupes attempt to speak Yoruba,
> which has /ɔ/ and /ɛ/. What this means, in the case of /ɔ/, for instance, is that the
> Nupe 'perceives' the two features [ + round] and [ + low] and that he identifies
> /ɔ/ with the class [ + round] already represented in his language by /u/ and /o/; he
> accordingly labializes the preceding consonant of the incoming word. Also,
> since Nupe has only one [ + low] vowel (which can be long or nasalized, how-
> ever), /ɔ/ merges (absolutely neutralizes) with /a/, and the distinction between
> the two is lost (except insofar as the preceding labialization accompanies the [a]
> derived from /ɔ/). It is as if the Nupes do a feature analysis in these terms, apply
> LR in the case /ɔ/ and PR in the case of /ɛ/, and then simplify the three-way oppo-
> sition in [+low] vowels [Hyman (1970)].

Hyman's characterization of the borrowing phenomenon is probably
correct, but, as we shall see below, it does not imply the abstract rules
he posits do exist in Nupe. We will return to this point after we examine
the NGP solution to this problem.

First observe that Hyman's analysis is not allowed in NGP. This case
is interesting because it shows why both the No-Ordering Condition
and the True Generalization Condition are needed in NGP. Notice that
all of Hyman's rules are true generalizations about surface forms in
Nupe. PR and LR express true generalizations because all C's before
front vowels are palatalized and all C's before round vowels are labialized. The fact that Cʸ and Cʷ also occur before back and unrounded
vowels does not affect the status of this generalization. The rule of AN
is also a true generalization, since it is a fact that in surface phonetic
representation all low vowels are back and unrounded. The analysis is
disallowed because it makes use of extrinsic role order; specifically, it is
counter-bleeding order that allows this abstractness, as pointed out
above and by Vennemann (1974a).

Hyman (1973a) has shown that the AN rule can be modified so that it
will be INTRINSICALLY ordered with respect to PR and LR. This is done
by allowing the neutralization only in the environment of palatalized or
labialized C's:

(36) $\begin{bmatrix} \epsilon \\ \mathfrak{c} \end{bmatrix} \longrightarrow a / \begin{Bmatrix} C^y \\ C^w \end{Bmatrix} \underline{\quad} \quad \left( [+ \text{high} ] \right)$

(37) $\begin{bmatrix} V \\ +\text{low} \end{bmatrix} \longrightarrow \begin{bmatrix} +\text{back} \\ -\text{round} \end{bmatrix} / \begin{bmatrix} C \\ +\text{round} \\ -\text{back} \end{bmatrix} \underline{\quad}$ ?

Extrinsic rule order is circumvented by this reformulation, but the analysis is still disallowed in NGP because the AN rule is not a true generalization about Nupe. Low vowels are back and unround everywhere, not just after $C^y$ and $C^w$. Thus the original AN rule is the correct constraint on low vowels, but if it is not ordered, Hyman's analysis is not possible.

The NGP analysis of the Nupe situation will contain the rules Hyman formulates as PR, LR, and the original AN rule, but will contain different underlying forms. The AN rule in the NGP analysis is a rule specifying the predictable features for low vowels. Thus the only low vowel will be /a/, and its archisegmental representation may be blank for back and round. As for the consonants, palatalization and labialization are entirely predictable and need not be specified before non-low vowels. However, before /a/ there will be a three-way underlying contrast between $C^y$, $C^w$, and C. Thus, consonants occurring before /a/ must be specified for [high], [back], or [round].

Such a system has the asymmetrical distribution of contrastive features that Hyman argues against; however, the facts of the language require such an asymmetry in the underlying features. While it is true that languages often show a remarkable symmetry in both contrastive and noncontrastive features, such a symmetry is never absolute. Skewed distributions are quite common, and no one has ever proposed that symmetry be a condition on the distribution of contrastive features. Thus I would argue that we should posit a symmetrical system only where the language exhibits symmetry. (See Clayton (1975) for similar arguments.)

Notice also that Hyman's solution and the one required by NGP use the same number of contrastive features. A form such as [ēg$^w$ā] must have a contrastive marking of [+round]. In Hyman's analysis the marking is on the vowel; in the concrete analysis it is on the consonant.

Reduplication in the concrete analysis must take a slightly different form. For a form such as [t$^w$á] 'to trim', [t$^w$ūt$^w$á] 'trimming', the backness and roundness of the reduplicated vowel cannot be traced to the stem vowel, since there are also forms such as [t$^y$á], [t$^y$īt$^y$á] 'mildness' and [tá], [t$^y$ītá] 'telling'. But the necessary feature is still present in the stem. It is merely located on the consonant rather than the vowel. Since this is so, it is possible to make the reduplication rule sensitive to the features of the consonant rather than the vowel, as shown in (38). The reduplicated vowel will be [u] if the stem consonant is [+round], [i] otherwise.

Consider now the borrowing evidence Hyman cites. I agree with Hyman that loan word adaptation is a good test for the productivity of phonological rules. If a phonetically conditioned rule is truly alive, it

(38)

$$\text{RED} \longrightarrow C_1 \begin{bmatrix} V \\ +\text{high} \\ \alpha\text{round} \\ \alpha\text{back} \\ 2\text{tone} \end{bmatrix} \quad / \underline{\hspace{1em}} \begin{bmatrix} C_1 \\ \alpha\text{round} \end{bmatrix}$$

will apply to borrowed words. But the entire process of loan word adaptation cannot be attributed to the phonological rules of the language. In their nativization changes are made in words that are not the result of the application of phonological rules. Hyman's explanation of the adaptation, that the features of the Yoruba vowel are conserved, the roundness and backness on the consonant and the lowness on the vowel, is surely correct. However, the same type of adaptation can and does take place in languages that do not have the rules Nupe has. For example, as Kiparsky (1973b) points out, Japanese adapts English words such as *cap* [kæp] very much as Nupe adapts Yoruba words such as [kɛkɛ]. The frontness is given over to the consonant, the lowness retained on the vowel. The result is Japanese [kʸappu] 'cap', also [kya-puten] 'captain', [kyanjii] 'candy'. The process is exactly parallel to the Nupe case, yet Japanese has no underlying /æ/. If the adaptation of English loan words in Japanese can be accounted for without positing underlying /ɛ/ and ɔ/, the possibility is also open for Nupe.

We have seen, then, that the NGP analysis without extrinsic rule order or abstract underlying segments can account for all the facts of Nupe that Hyman cites. There remains an additional fact about Nupe that is easily accounted for in the NGP analysis but impossible to account for under the abstract analysis. This is the fact that the palatalization and labialization on consonants before [a] is obligatory, strong, and stable, while the palatalization and labialization on consonants before the non-low vowels is considerably weaker and variable (Smith, 1967). The reason for the difference is that before [a] the palatalization and labialization are contrastive, while in other cases they are predicted by rule (Schane, 1971). There is no way to account for this difference in Hyman's analysis, since all cases of palatalization and labialization are derived by the same rule. In the NGP analysis, the description of this difference is quite straightforward. Palatalization and labialization before /a/ is strong and constant because these features are underlying and contrastive in this context. Before the other vowels however, Cʸ and Cʷ are derived by a phonetically conditioned rule that is subject to variability as are many phonetically conditioned rules. See also Hudson (1975a) for further discussion.

We see, then, that counter-bleeding order and the abstractness it allows do not lead in this case to the best analysis of the data. NGP allows only one analysis of the Nupe data, and, as I have tried to show, this is the analysis that best fits the facts of Nupe. In a theory that has the additional powerful devices of extrinsic rule order and abstract underlying forms, several analyses are allowed (see Harm's (1973) analysis and Hyman's (1973a) reply) but none of these accounts as simply for the full range of the facts.

## 5.5   Bleeding Order

Although bleeding order was assumed by Kiparsky (1968) to be the marked order, we will see in this section that bleeding order was wrongly accused. In terms of abstractness and opacity, bleeding order is not the consistent culprit that counter-feeding and counter-bleeding order were found to be. There are, however, some proposed cases of bleeding order that would not be allowed under the strong constraints of NGP, in particular, cases in which the rules do not express true generalizations about surface forms. These analyses would be reformulated along the lines suggested for other extrinsic orders. In other cases, however, both rules express true generalizations and yet must still apply in bleeding order, an extrinsic order, to obtain the correct results. We will discuss the latter type of case in this section. We will see that all cases of this sort have well-defined characteristics and that the problem presented by these cases is simply a formal problem, which is easily solved.

Kenstowicz and Kisseberth (1973) first observed that some bleeding orders are "unmarked." In these cases, both of the rules involved represent true generalizations about surface phonetic forms and in order for these rules to apply so that their outputs are transparent, they must apply in bleeding order. Further, in each of these cases, the second rule (the rule that is bled) is a P-rule, i.e., a surface transparent, phonetically conditioned rule. The first rule changes the phonetic conditions so that the second rule is not applicable. We know what type of rule the second rule is; what we need to determine is the characteristics of the first rule. Kenstowicz and Kisseberth (1973) claim that the first rule is always a rule that alters syllable structure. The following example is a typical case.

In Lithuanian there is a voicing assimilation rule that produces a phonetically conditioned alternation in some prefixes:

(39)  *ap +arti*      'plough'      *aparti*      'finish ploughing'
      *dirpti*      'work'      *abdirpti*      'work through'
      *gyventi*      'live'      *abgyventi*      'inhabit'
  *at +eiti*      'go'      *ateiti*      'arrive'
      *gimti*      'be born'      *adgimti*      'be born again'

In cases where the prefix ends in a C that is homorganic with the C the stem begins with, vowel epenthesis occurs in order to break up the potential geminate cluster:

(40)       *puti*      'rot'      *apiputi*      'to grow rotten'
        *teisti*      'judge'      *atiteisti*      'to adjudicate'
        *duoti*      'give'      *atiduoti*      'to give back'
        *bekti*      'run'      *apibekti*      'to run around'

The ordering problem here occurs with the last two forms of (40). There should be a stage after prefixation at which the SD of the voicing assimilation rule is met, e.g., where the forms are /at + duoti/ and /ap + bekti/. If the voicing assimilation rule applies at this stage, prior to epenthesis, the incorrect forms, *[adiduoti] and *[abibekti], would result. Thus the voicing assimilation rule cannot be allowed to apply freely. One possibility is to modify the SD of the voicing assimilation rule so that it does not apply to homorganic sequences. But this solution is ad hoc and unexplanatory: The voicing assimilation skips /at + duoti/ and /ap + bekti/, not because the stops are homorganic, but rather because these stops will not be contiguous on the surface. Voicing assimilation skips these forms precisely because epenthesis is going to apply to them. This is exactly what the bleeding order relation between epenthesis and voicing assimilation suggests. Voicing assimilation does not apply to homorganic sequences because another rule takes care of them.

This order is natural or unmarked because it allows voicing assimilation to apply only to consonant sequences that occur phonetically.[4] Since P-rules represent the rules of pronunciation, there is absolutely no reason why such rules should apply to strings that are not going to be pronounced. Since the second rule (the bled rule) is always a P-rule in these cases, the only problem is to find some way to keep P-rules from applying to strings that are not sequentially well-formed. Kenstowicz and Kisseberth suggest that syllable structure rules should

---

[4] In discussing the naturalness or markedness of rule order, I assume, with Kiparsky (1971) and in accord with the principles of NGP and the evidence cited throughout this book, that the most natural, and in fact the only, rule order is the transparent rule order. See Section 5.6.

apply before phonetic rules. This suggestion is certainly reasonable, since there is no point in applying phonetic rules to syllables that are not well-formed C and V sequences; but it is not always obvious which rules are syllable structure rules and which are not, as I pointed out in Hooper (1975). In this case it is not obvious that epenthesis is a syllable structure rule; while it breaks up geminate clusters, these clusters transcend two syllables. Furthermore, there is a degemination rule in Lithuanian that has the same function. What is to prevent it from applying before epenthesis?

More destructive of Kenstowicz and Kisseberth's hypothesis regarding syllable structure rules is a case of an unmarked bleeding order in which the first rule has nothing whatever to do with syllable structure. This is a well-known case discussed by Kiparsky (1968) involving the German umlaut rule, which is an MP-rule, and a P-rule of back vowel lowering before dentals, palatals, and /r/.

(41)     Umlaut:    $V \longrightarrow [-back] / \begin{bmatrix} \text{morphological} \\ \text{information} \end{bmatrix}$

(42)     Lowering:   $\begin{bmatrix} V \\ -\text{high} \\ +\text{back} \end{bmatrix} \longrightarrow [+\text{low}] / \underline{\quad} \begin{bmatrix} +\text{cons} \\ +\text{coronal} \\ -\text{lateral} \end{bmatrix}$

In the Schaffhausen dialect of Northern Switzerland the singular form [bɔdə) 'floor' is affected by lowering, but the plural form [bödə] is not. Given an underlying form /bodə/, umlaut must apply first to the plural, bleeding lowering:

(43)                    Singular   Plural
                        /bodə/     /bodə/
                        ———        bödə      umlaut
                        bɔdə       ———       lowering
                        [bɔdə]     [bödə]    phonetic

If lowering applies first, the incorrect form *[bɔ̈də] would be derived. (The Kesswil dialect, which has [bɔ̈də] for the plural, is discussed in Section 6.3.)

Neither of these rules has anything to do with syllable structure, yet this is clearly another case of an unmarked bleeding order. Since lowering affects only back vowels, there is no reason for it to apply to an umlauted vowel. In fact, the phonetic motivation for the lowering is the position of the back of the tongue for the consonants in question. Lowering could not apply to front vowels in the environment of these consonants because the front of the tongue would be high in anticipation of coronal consonants (Vennemann, 1972b:876–877, 879–880). Therefore, lowering should certainly not apply to a vowel that will surface as a front vowel.

Another example of an unmarked bleeding order is the usual analysis of the English plural. The underlying form is taken to be $+z+$. To derive the plurals of nouns ending in sibilants, a vowel must be inserted: *kisses* [kɪsɨz], *coaches* [kowčɨz], *wishes* [wɪšɨz]. To derive the plurals of nouns ending in voiceless consonants (other than sibilants), a rule of devoicing applies: *cops* [kaps], *chiefs* [čiyfs], *socks* [saks]. For all other nouns the plural is [z]. The rule of devoicing is clearly a P-rule and, furthermore, a very general rule of English: All tautosyllabic obstruent clusters in English agree in voicing, the second obstruent assimilating to the first:

(44)     $[-son] \longrightarrow [-voi]/[-voi]$____ in the same syllable

In order to obtain the desired results, it is necessary to apply the vowel insertion rule before the devoicing rule. If the rules apply in the other order, an underlying form such as /kɪs + z/ will be acted on by devoicing, giving /kɪs + s/ and, with vowel insertion, *[kɪsɨs]. As in the other cases of unmarked bleeding orders, the P-rule should not apply because the phonetic structure to which it appears to apply will be altered before reaching the surface.

What all of these cases have in common is an intermediate stage of derivation in which unacceptable sequences of allomorphs are strung together, e.g., /kis + z/. The problem arises if a P-rule applies to the unacceptable string. This is basically a notational or formal problem because there is no reason to expect P-rules that are basically laws of pronunciation to apply to structures that will never be pronounced. One way to prevent the application of P-rules to ill-formed structures is to derive allomorphs in such a way that there are no intermediate stages of representation containing ill-formed structures. It happens that this is the automatic consequence of the model of lexical representation to be adopted in Chapter 7 for other reasons, the model proposed in Hudson (1975b). The arguments for choosing Hudson's model over other alternatives are given in Section 7.3 and Section 8.5; for the present, I will briefly outline the model to demonstrate that it solves the problem of unmarked bleeding orders.

In the problem cases discussed above, the lexical representation of the morpheme in question is ONE of the surface allomorphs. The problem arises when the basic allomorph appears in a position that on the surface is occupied by a different allomorph. In Hudson's model, one surface allomorph is not chosen for the lexical representation, rather the lexical representation is an archisegmental representation of all the surface allomorphs. Thus the vowel that appears in the English plural morpheme in [kɪsɨz] is contained in the lexical entry for the plural morpheme as an optional element. The lexical representation for plural is informally, $/ \left\{ \begin{matrix} I \\ \varnothing \end{matrix} \right\}$ z/. This representation is added to nouns, and a rule applies to correctly distribute the allomorphs. The rule states that /I/ occurs after sibilants and does not occur elsewhere. This rule is roughly equivalent to the epenthesis rule of the other analysis, except that it does not INSERT the vowel so that there will never be a stage at which the SD of the devoicing rule is presented erroneously.

When Hudson's model is explained in greater detail in Chapters 7 and 8, it will be quite clear that the problem of unmarked bleeding orders is merely a pseudoproblem that is solved as soon as we settle on the correct formalisms for representing morphemes in the lexicon.

## 5.6 Universal Principles Determining Extrinsic Rule Order

Two empirical arguments for imposing an order of the application of phonological rules have been developed since the beginning of generative phonology. The first is that related dialects may be described as having the same rules but applied in a different order (Halle, 1962). The second is that some historical changes may be described as changes in the order of application of two rules (Kiparsky, 1965). These descriptive techniques will be discussed in the next chapter. A third, formal argument is given in Halle (1962). Halle argues that phonological grammars may be simplified significantly if rules are ordered. More recently, however, Koutsoudas, Sanders, and Noll (1974) have observed that all extrinsic ordering statements are language-specific and therefore must be assigned a cost in terms of a particular grammar. If extrinsic ordering is a universal phenomenon, then there must be some universal principles that predict language-specific ordering relations. If this is the case, then ordering statements will not be assigned a cost to the particular grammar.

In the past several years there have been several proposals that attempt to replace all language-particular rule ordering statements by a few universal principles. In this section we will discuss three of these proposals: the Koutsoudas, Sanders, and Noll (1974) proposal (hereafter referred to as the KSN proposal), the theory of local ordering (Anderson, 1974), and the minimization of opacity (Kiparsky, 1971; Kisseberth, 1973). It is important to note all of these proposals are made with the idea of keeping all other parts of the theory intact. The intent of these proposals is to eliminate entirely or reduce the number of language-particular ordering statements. Extrinsic rule order will still be allowed, but it will be largely predicted on universal principles. It should also be noted that the proper use of the simplicity criterion depends upon the development of the proper notational devices, and the choice of notational devices must be empirically justified. Thus universal ordering principles should be empirically based.

KSN propose that all rules be ordered according to two principles. The first and most general principle states that "every rule is applied to every structure to which it is applicable" (p. 6). This appears to be similar to the No-Ordering Condition of NGP. However, there is one very significant difference: KSN allow rules to apply simultaneously. Thus, if there is an underlying form that meets the structural description of two rules, these two rules apply at the same time. But rules may also apply sequentially if one rule creates input into another rule; that is, rules are allowed to apply in feeding order.

The consequence of allowing simultaneous application is that counter-bleeding order is allowed. For example, as KSN show, if we take Saporta's rules of K-insertion and stridency neutralization discussed in Chapters 1 and 2:

$$(45) \qquad \emptyset \longrightarrow k / V\theta\underline{\qquad} \begin{Bmatrix} o \\ a \end{Bmatrix}$$

$$(46) \qquad \theta \longrightarrow s$$

and apply them simultaneously to the underlying form /kreθ-/, we obtain the desired results:

(47)
$$
\begin{array}{ccccc}
k & r & e & \theta & o \\
& & & | & \\
& & (48) & (47) & \\
& & \downarrow & \downarrow & \\
k & r & e & s \quad k & o
\end{array}
$$

We have already examined in detail the types of analyses allowed using counter-bleeding order; all of these analyses will also be allowed under the KSN proposal. Thus KSN allow feeding order and counter-bleeding order. They also allow mutual bleeding orders by a principle called Proper Inclusion Precedence.

Proper Inclusion Precedence states that if the SD of a rule A properly includes the SD of a rule B, then rule A applies first. "Properly includes" means roughly that an SD A properly includes SD B, if A contains all the information contained in B plus more, that is, that A is less general than B. One of the examples they cite is again from Saporta (1965:222). Saporta claims that Latin American Spanish has the following two rules:

(48)                                        ł ⟶ l/____#

(49)                                        ł ⟶ y

That is, palatal laterals become nonpalatal at the end of a word, and they become nonlateral elsewhere. For instance, the form *aquel* 'that' is [akel] and its plural *aquellos* 'those' is [akeyos]. These forms would be derived from underlying /akeł/:

(50)                          akeł    akeł + os
                              ake1     ⎯⎯⎯       (48)
                              ⎯⎯⎯      akeyos     (49)
                             [akel]   [akeyos]

These rules are applied in the correct order by the Proper Inclusion Precedence because the SD of depalatalization ł# properly includes the SD of delateralization ł. Thus we see that the KSN proposal allows feeding order, counter-bleeding order, and certain types of mutual bleeding order.

The KSN proposal excludes counter-feeding order and bleeding orders that do not meet the conditions of proper inclusion. Counter-feeding is excluded from this theory in the same way it is excluded from NGP. Since rules apply to EVERY structure that meets their SD's, there can be no structure exempt from the application of a rule simply because the structure arose after the rule had already applied once. Thus in the Spanish case of counter-feeding discussed earlier, surface [k] and [g] before front V's that do not "soften" can be accounted for by making them /kʷ/ and /gʷ/ at the point at which the velar softening rule applies. But if every rule applies to every structure to which it is applicable, then newly derived [k] and [g] must also be softened. Thus, for KSN, all examples using counter-feeding order will have to be reanalyzed.

The same conclusion follows for bleeding orders. Typically in bleeding orders both rules are applicable (simultaneously) to underlying forms, but if they are allowed to apply in this way, the wrong results will be obtained. As an example of a bleeding order, let us take the Schaffhausen dialect of Swiss German that Kiparsky (1968:178–179) discusses. In this dialect the umlaut rule and a rule that lowers back vowels before dentals, palatals, and /r/ both apply.

(51) $\qquad$ V $\longrightarrow$ [−back] / $\begin{bmatrix} \text{morphological} \\ \text{information} \end{bmatrix}$

(52) $\qquad$ o $\longrightarrow$ ɔ / ___ $\begin{bmatrix} +\text{cons} \\ +\text{coronal} \\ -\text{lateral} \end{bmatrix}$

As we have shown, these rules apply in this order to give the forms [bɔdə] and [bödə] from underlying /bodə/.

(53)

| | Singular | Plural | |
|---|---|---|---|
| | bodə | bodə | |
| | ___ | bödə | umlaut |
| | bɔdə | ___ | lowering |
| | [bɔdə] | [bödə] | |

A simultaneous application will give plural *[bɔ̈də] since both rules could apply to this form. According to KSN, such orderings are not allowed, and cases such as this one should be reanalyzed. The particular reanalysis they suggest involves having another rule or condition in the language stating that front rounded vowels are non-low.

(54) $\qquad$ $\begin{bmatrix} \text{V} \\ -\text{back} \\ +\text{round} \end{bmatrix}$ $\longrightarrow$ [−low]

This will take *[bɔ̈də[ to [bödə], and the correct result will be obtained.

However, as we have seen, this bleeding order is unmarked in the sense that its results are transparent. KSN allow opaque orders, such as counter-bleeding, but exclude this transparent bleeding order. Furthermore, their reanalysis of this case produces a rather strange result. Lowering, which is a phonetic rule motivated only for BACK vowels, applies to a vowel that will be pronounced as a front vowel. This same vowel must then be raised again by rule (54). It appears that their exclusion of bleeding orders will be difficult to support: On the one hand they will have to justify excluding an ordering that is clearly "unmarked"; on the other hand they will have to find well-motivated reanalyses of all cases of unmarked bleeding order.

The KSN proposal, then, allows feeding order, counter-bleeding order, and order determined by the Proper Inclusion Precedence, but disallows counter-feeding order and bleeding orders not determined by the Proper Inclusion Precedence. The problem with this proposal is that no justification is given for allowing some extrinsic orderings and not allowing others. Why, for example, should counter-feeding order and bleeding order be excluded but counter-bleeding order allowed? We have seen in Sections 5.3 and 5.4 of this chapter that counter-feeding and counter-bleeding order have a similar effect on a grammar: They allow extreme degrees of abstractness in rules and underlying forms. KSN cite no evidence in favor of counter-bleeding order or against counter-feeding. They merely state that all examples of counter-feeding order can be reanalyzed. While this is true, they do not show why cases of counter-bleeding order should not also be reanalyzed. (We have seen in Section 5.4 some good reasons to reanalyze counter-bleeding order.) In the absence of any evidence or arguments in favor of their rule-ordering principles, we must conclude that the KSN proposal is empirically unmotivated.

A final word about the Proper Inclusion Precedence. In Section 5.2 we discussed the ordering of the subparts of rules by the Proper Inclusion Precedence (or the elsewhere condition), and we have adopted it for use in NGP. This does not mean, however, as KSN would claim, that all pairs of rules in a proper inclusion relation are valid rules of the grammar. The other constraints on NGP would exclude the rules given above as depalatalization and delateralization. These rules are not valid because they depend upon an abstract underlying segment /ł/ that never occurs in any surface forms in Latin American Spanish. It is simply not reasonable to assume that Latin American speakers would construct such a form to account for the alternation between *aquel* and *aquellos*. How, then, would this alternation be accounted for? In NGP it would be accounted for by a rule that applies to only a few forms. It happens that the only other forms that participate in this alternation are the subject pronouns *el* [el] 'he', *ella* [eya] 'she', *ellos* [eyos] 'they(masc.)', *ellas* [eyas] 'they (fem.)'. These forms will have lexical representations that make them subject to a rule that governs an alternation between /l/ and /y/. No underlying patalized lateral is necessary.

Anderson's (1974) approach to predicting extrinsic rule order is somewhat different. Anderson argues that there is not one continuous sequence of rules, A, B, C, . . . N, in which each rule applies at a fixed point in the sequence, but rather that rules are ordered in pairs, and the order of the two rules is determined with respect to a given form. Thus for form *a*, the rules could apply in the order A, B, while for form *b* the rules could apply in the order B, A. The term LOCAL ORDERING refers to the order being specified individually for a given form, rather than for the whole grammar.

Given a pair of rules, there are two orders in which they could apply. If one of these orders is feeding while the other is nonfeeding (or neutral), the natural or preferred order is feeding order. If one of the orders of the two rules is bleeding while the other is nonbleeding (or neutral), then the natural or preferred order is the neutral order. These notions of "natural" and "unnatural" orders are based on Kiparsky (1968). Feeding order and nonbleeding orders are considered natural because they allow the maximal utilization of the rules. (We return later to a discussion of "natural" order.) In cases where the rules apply to a given form in a natural order, no ordering relation needs to be specified in the grammar. Only unnatural orders need language-specific ordering statements. If two rules do not interact with each other at all, no ordering statement is needed.

Let us consider one of Anderson's examples. In Icelandic there is an alternation between /a/ and /ö/ that Anderson expresses as an umlauting process conditioned by a following /u/:

(55)  U-umlaut: a $\longrightarrow$ ö/____$C_0$u

Some examples:

(56)  
|  |  |  |
|---|---|---|
| *barn* | 'child' | *börnum* (dat. pl.) |
| *svangt* | 'hungry' | *svöngu* (neut. dat. sg.) |
| *(ēg) kalla* | 'I call' | *(við) köllum* 'we call' |

In addition there is a syncope rule, exemplified by these forms:

(57)  
|  |  |  |  |
|---|---|---|---|
| *hamar* | 'hammer' | *hamri* | (dat. sg.) |
| *fifill* | 'dandelion' | *fifli* | (dat. sg.) |
| *morgunn* | 'morning' | *morgni* | (dat. sg.) |

The syncope rule has certain syllable structure constraints that are not relevant here and, in addition, some exceptions. A general formulation given by Anderson is:

(58)  Syncope: $\begin{bmatrix} +\text{syll} \\ -\text{stress} \end{bmatrix} \longrightarrow \emptyset / C\text{____}C + V$

For a certain set of forms the syncope rule precedes the U-umlaut rule. For instance *ketill* 'kettle' has an underlying form (katil/ (the /a/ shows up in dative singular *katli*.) The dative plural form *kötlum* comes from /katil + um/, with syncope deleting the /i/ and creating input to (feeding) the U-umlaut rule. Other forms of this type are *rögnum* (dative plural) 'gods', from /ragin + um/ [cf. *regin* 'the gods' and *ragna* (dative plural)]; *ölnum* (dative plural) 'ell of cloth' from /alen + um/ [cf. *alin* (nominative)]. Since this is the natural order for these forms, no ordering statement is required.

For another set of forms, U-umlaut must apply before syncope because syncope deletes the /u/ that conditions the umlaut:

(59) Nominative Singular    Dative Singular
     *bögull* 'parcel'      *böggli* /bagg + ul + e/ cf. *baggi* 'pack'
     *jökull* 'glacier'      *jökli* /jak + ul + e/ cf. *jaki* 'piece of ice'
     *jötunn* 'giant'      *jötni* /jat + un + e/
     *þögull* 'taciturn'      *þöglan* (masc. acc. sg.) /þag + ul + an/
                       cf. *þagga* 'to silence'

To derive the forms in the second column from stems with underlying /a/, U-umlaut must apply first. The opposite order would be a bleeding order (syncope removes the input to U-umlaut). Thus the order in which the rules apply is the natural order. These examples show that rules need not always apply in the same order for all forms.[5]

The theory of local ordering has a clear advantage over the standard theory of rule order: It does not treat all ordering relations as though they were equivalent. It attempts to distinguish between natural, universally predictable orders and ad hoc, language-specific orders. The problem lies, however, in determining what the natural orders are. Recall now the preceding discussions of various types of order. It seems clear that Kiparsky and Anderson are correct in taking feeding order to be more natural than counter-feeding (see Section 5.2). But what about bleeding versus counter-bleeding? In Section 5.3 we saw that counter-bleeding order is used in cases of absolute neutralization; in Section 5.4 we saw many cases in which bleeding order was the expected order, and nonbleeding order would be impossible. Consider now the second set of forms from Icelandic, the ones in which the rules apply in counter-bleeding order. Are these forms, e.g., *böggli, jökli, jötni*, and *þöglan*, really so natural? There is something unnatural about them: They exhibit an umlauted vowel [ö], the product of U-umlaut, where no [u] is present to condition the umlaut. Notice that the opposite order of these two rules, which is a bleeding order, gives more natural results. The /u/ is deleted before umlaut can apply. The resulting surface forms

---

[5] The example is given here merely to illustrate Anderson's hypothesis and not to argue for one theory over another. However, I will briefly outline the treatment of these forms in NGP. First, U-umlaut cannot be a P-rule because there are surface violations of it, i.e., forms that do not undergo the rule, even though they meet its SD. Examples are *hattur* 'hat' (nominative singular), cf. *höttum* 'hat' (dative plural); *dalar* 'valley' (nominative singular), *dölum* (dative plural). It appears that U-umlaut is an MP-rule, applying only in certain morphological categories, as dative plural, and certain verb categories. U-umlaut does not apply at all to the forms in (59), *bögull, böggli*, etc. These forms have underlying /ö/. Their relations to certain nouns, e.g., *baggi* 'pack', is expressed in a via-rule. Syncope is also an MP-rule, since it has exceptions and apparently requires some morphological information such as a morpheme boundary.

would be *baggli, etc. Such forms are more natural in the sense that where there is no [u], there is no U-umlaut.

Considerations of this sort, which will be discussed further in Chapter 6, led Kiparsky to revise his notions of marked and unmarked orders so that they would be sensitive to the surface forms being generated, rather than sensitive only to the abstract relations between rules. To account for the naturalness of certain bleeding orders, Kiparsky (1971:621–622) formulated a concept of "opacity," which he defines as follows:

(60)  Definition:   A rule A ⟶ B/ C____D is opaque to the extent that there are surface representations of the form:
( i)   A in the environment C____D
(ii)   B in environments other than C____D.

With this definition, it can be said that opaque orders are unnatural or marked while transparent orders are natural or unmarked. Case (i) refers to counter-feeding orders and states that they are opaque. Recall the Spanish velar softening example discussed in Section 5.2. The rule of velar softening in the abstract analysis discussed there is opaque by case (i) because that rule states that a velar before a front vowel will become /s/ or /x/. Yet there are cases where a velar in exactly that environment is not softened, i.e., [ke] 'what', [gera] 'war'. The velar softening rule is opaque with respect to these forms.

Case (ii) of the definition states that forms such as böggli, jökli, jötni, and ɔöglan in Icelandic are opaque with regard to U-umlaut because the umlauted V occurs on the surface in forms where the conditioning environment, the [u], is not present.

It appears, then, that the opacity principle, in the way it separates natural orders from unnatural orders, is more in line with the principles of NGP than the feeding–bleeding principle.

While Anderson discusses opacity, he does not give up the feeding–bleeding principle. Instead he claims that several principles may be at work in determining the order of rules: the feeding–bleeding principle, the opacity principle, and one other principle that we will not discuss here, the self-preservation principle (see Anderson, 1974:Chapter 12). We will return to our critique of local ordering after discussing another suggestion for universal ordering principles.

Kisseberth (1973) makes a suggestion based on Kiparsky's notion of opacity. Kisseberth proposes as a universal principle that all rules apply in the order that makes them maximally transparent. This does not mean that opacity is not allowed in the grammar; as with the authors of the other proposals, Kisseberth does not intend a major revision of the theory. Opacity is allowed, but at the expense of overriding the universal principles with language-specific derivational constraints. The advantage of Kisseberth's approach is that it represents opaque orders as language-specific and ad hoc. The difficulty with his proposal and Anderson's is that opaque orders are allowed at all. The difficulty is both empirical and theory-internal: As I have argued throughout this and preceding chapters, it is precisely these opaque, extrinsic orders that have no empirical support; in fact, the evidence argues strongly against such ordering relations. Beyond this, however, there is a fundamental difficulty in the standard theory that prevents any such universal ordering principles from producing the desired results.

The fundamental problem is that the theory is unconstrained (and neither Anderson nor Kisseberth argue in favor of constraining it to exclude certain analyses). Since there are few constraints on what may be a rule or an underlying form, it will always be possible to find a counter-example to any principle of "natural" ordering. That is, it will be possible to construct a set of rules that apply in the most wildly unnatural fashion, but produce quite natural surface forms from some point of view. Consider a counter-example to Anderson's theory raised by Harris (1973b).

The example concerns a verb paradigm that is perfectly regular and uniform. Some forms of the present tense of *marcar* 'to mark' are given here:

(61)

|  | Indicative | Subjunctive |
|---|---|---|
| 3rd sg.: | *marka* | *marke* |
| 1st pl.: | *markamos* | *markemos* |
| 3rd pl.: | *markan* | *marken* |

We have already discussed, in Section 5.3, the rule of velar softening that Harris posits for Spanish as a very general phonological rule. Notice in the paradigm above that velar softening does not apply in the subjunctive, although a velar consonant appears preceding a front vowel (i.e., the SD of velar softening is met). Harris claims that this rule does not apply to the subjunctive forms because the back theme vowel /a/ occurs immediately after the stem (e.g., /mark + a + e/) and is deleted by truncation (V $\longrightarrow$ $\emptyset$ /____ + V) only AFTER velar softening has tried to apply, as shown in the derivation in (62). This order of rules is unnatural in every way imaginable: It is a counter-feeding order and its output is opaque with respect to velar softening since an unaffected velar occurs in the environment of a front V.

(62)     mark + a + e     (Underlying)
         ―――             Velar softening
         markØe   Truncation
         [marke]  (Phonetic)

But, as Harris argues, the forms generated in this way are not at all unnatural: The paradigm is considered regular, and it is absolutely uniform—there is no alternation in the entire paradigm. A feeding order, where truncation precedes velar softening, would produce an alternation in the paradigm: [marka] but *[marse], and a less natural state of affairs. So a very unnatural order of rules has created a very natural set of forms, and a problem for Anderson and Kisseberth. Of course, there is a solution here: Formulate another principle. The one Harris suggests is that paradigms tend to be uniform.

Now paradigm uniformity is certainly a valid linguistic principle, fully supported by the direction of historical change. (In this regard, paradigm uniformity will be discussed in the next chapter.) But it is very difficult to get such a principle to govern the order of application of rules in a synchronic grammar. At best it would take some sort of transderivational constraint, where the derivation of one form knows what the derivation of another form is like. Such an enormous increase in the power of the theory is certainly unmotivated. There is a much simpler solution.

The obvious conclusion is that Harris's analysis is wrong. There is simply no reason to expect velar softening to apply to [marke] because velar softening is not a generative rule of Spanish, and there is no derivation such as that in (62). But if we exclude such rules on any principled basis, then we would have to exclude all rules that require ad hoc ordering "restrictions," whether they are described by derivational constraints or some other means, and the result would be that we would not need extrinsic rule order at all.

The problem, then, with these proposals for universal ordering principles is that they have not gone far enough. As long as any ad hoc ordering statements are allowed, these can be used to construct ad hoc derivations producing surface forms that appear natural in some way or another. And as long as there are no strong constraints on what may be a rule, there can be no strong statements about the relations among rules. Thus any such proposals attempted in an unconstrained theory will fail.

# 6

# Historical Change in the Morphophonological System

As we have seen, NGP divides up the group of processes that TGP calls phonological rules into three types: phonological rules (a subset of which are syllable structure conditions), morphophonemic rules, and via-rules. NGP claims that these three types of rules represent three different kinds of natural language phenomena. Empirical evidence has already been presented to support this view. Just as each of these rule types has specific characteristics in the synchronic grammar, so each of them behaves distinctly with regard to diachronic change. Because each of these rule types is well-defined, it is possible to constrain the theory of linguistic change to predict only certain types of developments.

## 6.1  Rule Addition

New alternations in a language arise in phonetic environments: this process is often thought of as rule addition—the addition of a new P-rule to the grammar. Most people would agree that the large majority of rule additions are P-rules—rules with a strictly phonetic conditioning—but I would like to suggest that ALL new rules creating new alternations are of this type. In the last section of this chapter we will return to the examination of some apparent counter-examples to this claim, but for now I only want to suggest the plausibility of such a claim and show how it relates to a general theory of historical change.

We have discussed several types of alternations: alternations that have phonetic conditioning and alternations that have morphosyntactic or lexical conditioning. The latter type may either help to signal meaning through a correlation with a particular category, e.g., Andalusian vowel harmony, or it may be an arbitrary suppletive alternation. Which of these alternation types are likely to be added as NEW alternations? Certainly not the arbitrary suppletive type, for these impose a burden on the speaker; there is no reason to expect speakers, either children or adults, to invent new alternations of this type. Rather, alternations of this type tend to be leveled. Alternations that are strongly associated with meaning are not functionless, and they tend to be extended rather than leveled. But these still cannot enter the language abruptly with their correlation to meaning already fixed; rather the alternation must exist prior to its being assigned meaning. Thus, in Andalusian, a distinction between close and open vowels existed before it was assigned meaning. The sound–meaning correspondence is fixed and arbitrary—it is determined by the language and is subject to only minor modifications by speakers.

It appears that the only plausible source for new alternations is in phonetics, where meaning is not concerned, but where the concern is the optimalization of the phonetic string. If P-rules are the only source for new alternations in a language, then it is possible to restrict in a very strong way the set of possible "new rules"; for these would be limited to innovations that have a purely phonetic function, i.e., the class of natural rules. On the articulatory side these innovations reduce to the retiming of a muscular gesture or the increase or decrease in muscular activity (Mowrey, 1975).

While I will continue to speak in terms of "rule addition," it is important to note that "rule addition" is a very misleading label for phonetic innovations. It implies that something has been added to the grammar making it longer, more complicated. As Vennemann (1972a) and Stampe (1973a) point out, when the addition is a natural rule with a phonetic function, as I believe it always is, its addition should be viewed as a simplifying process. Under this view, phonetic innovation is the failure to suppress an innate, universally natural process. But even this view is misleading, because, after the failure to suppress, the grammar contains one more rule.

In reality, phonetic innovation is only rule modification, not rule addition.[1] It has been viewed as rule addition only because phonologists have seldom bothered to write the "low-level" phonetic rules that do not produce salient alternations. Consider as an example the idea of adding a rule of vowel nasalization before a tautosyllabic nasal consonant. We state this as the addition of a rule to the grammar.

(1)    $V \longrightarrow [+ \text{nasal}] / \underline{\quad} [+ \text{nasal}] \$$

This creates an alternation between nasal and oral vowels. Now consider what has really changed in the grammar: A rule has not been added; rather a rule has been modified. The rule that has been modified is the original rule that interprets the distinctive feature [ + nasal]. This interpretation rule is the command to open the velum. There are two quantities that must be specified in the rule: (i) how much to open the velum, and (ii) when to open the velum. The timing might be specified relative to the consonantal obstruction of the vocal tract: Before the assimilation takes place the rule will specify that the velum opening is simultaneous with the vocal closure. What the assimilation represents is a retiming of the velum-opening in relation to the vocal closure— velum-opening precedes vocal closure. No rule has been added: An existing rule has been modified. This modification creates a new alternation, which makes us think that there is a new rule in the grammar. But instead of rule addition we have mere rule modification.

## 6.2   Morphologization and Restructuring

After a phonetic alternation appears in the language, the tendency is for this alternation to work its way up toward the meaning end of the grammar, moving from a purely phonetic function to a semantic function. Schematically:

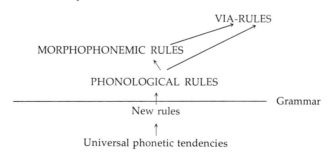

---

[1] The theory that suggests the idea of rule modification is presented in Mowrey (1975). I am very grateful to Richard Mowrey for many stimulating discussions of phonetic change.

Such a progression is suggested in Vennemann (1972e) and Hyman (1973b). The reason for this seems to be a desire on the part of the speaker to interpret alternations as meaningful, where possible. Let us consider the possibilities in more detail.

First, consider the undoing of a phonetic alternation or the loss of phonetic conditioning for a P-rule. There can be two results: restructuring and/or morphologization. Standard accounts of morphologization (the change in a rule from a phonetic conditioning to a morphosyntactic conditioning) usually cite the loss of phonetic conditioning as the motivation for morphologization. A standard example is umlaut in German, which was originally a phonetically conditioned assimilation. A vowel or diphthong became fronted when followed in the same phonological word by a high front vowel or glide. Later the conditioning vowel or glide was reduced in some cases, but the umlauted vowel did not change back. After the reduction or loss of the conditioning vowel, the alternation of umlauted and nonumlauted vowels must be predicted in morphological terms (e.g., umlaut occurs in some noun plurals and certain verb categories). The assumption has always been that morphologization occurs BECAUSE the phonetic environment has been obscured or lost (see Kiparsky, 1971:634).

Examination of actual cases less ancient (and therefore more accessible) than German umlaut suggest that the loss of the phonetic environment is not a condition on morphologization, but rather that morphologization may occur even where the phonetic conditioning is still present and transparent. In this context recall the forms cited from the Granada dialect of Spanish, where a vowel harmony system has developed to mark the singular and plural. In those forms the phonetic conditioning for lax vowels, the final [h], is optionally present in the same forms that exhibit the harmony that is the evidence for morphologization. In this case we cannot tell if the morphologization took place BECAUSE the phonetic environment was being lost, or if the phonetic environment could be lost BECAUSE the alternation has been morphologized. Other examples suggest that the latter is a possibility.

Skousen (1972) discusses a case of morphologization that takes place even where there is no danger of losing the phonetic conditioning. The case involves Finnish consonant gradation, which was a general weakening process affecting consonants at the beginning of closed syllables:

(2)

| | | |
|---|---|---|
| tapa | tavan | 'custom' |
| pato | padon | 'dam' |
| sika | sian | 'pig' |
| piippu | piipun | 'pipe' |
| lantti | lantin | 'corn' |
| kirkko | kirkon | 'church' |

The graduation process created alternations in the noun paradigms. Here are a few examples from *käsi* 'hand': *kätena* (essive), *käden* (genitive), *kädessä* (incessive), etc. For many forms in the language the gradation rule appears to be phonetically conditioned. However, as Skousen points out, there is ample evidence of morphologization. First there is evidence that gradation is nonproductive; borrowings do not necessarily undergo it, e.g., *auto, auton* 'automobile', nor do internally created words such as *sitten* 'then'. Not only does gradation fail to apply where the phonetic environment is met, but it appears to apply even where its phonetic environment is NOT met. For instance, in standard Finnish the possessive suffixes in some persons create a closed syllable, but gradation fails to apply:

(3)      *käteni*      'my hand'
         *kätesi*      'your (singular) hand'
         *kätensä*     'his/their hand'
         *kätemme*     'our hand'
         *kätenne*     'your (plural) hand'

In other dialects, the weak form of the stem is used with possessive suffixes whether a closed syllable is created or not. The forms corresponding to those in (3) are *kädeni, kädesi, kädensa, kädemme, kädenne*. These forms indicate that the alternation of /t/ and /d/ is no longer viewed as related to closed syllables. Forms from the western dialects also indicate morphologization. In these dialects the inessive suffix *-ssa* has been simplified to *sa*, a suffix that creates an open syllable, and gradation still takes place (the reflex of the gradation of /t/ in these dialects is [r]): *käresa* 'hand (inessive)'. Skousen claims, then, that the form of the stem is associated with certain suffixes, which is to say that gradation is a morphologized rule.[2] But observe that in the standard dialect it has become nonproductive and morphologized even though there is no indication of its phonetic conditioning being lost: The language still has closed syllables.

Another similar example is from Maori (Hale, 1971). The verbal forms shown in (4) arose historically because of a rule deleting word-final consonants. Synchronically, the forms with a consonant in the passive could be derived from underlying stems with final consonants by adding /-ia/ for the passive and by deleting the final consonant for the active form. Other evidence, however, suggests that the stems are under-

---

[2] Kiparsky (1973) argues against the position that these alternations are not rule governed. I would agree with Kiparsky that there are some rules involved here. The issue is what sort of conditioning environment for these rules is correct.

(4)

| verb | passive | |
|------|---------|---|
| *awhi* | *awhitia* | 'to embrace' |
| *hopu* | *hopukia* | 'to catch' |
| *aru* | *arumia* | 'to follow' |
| *tohu* | *tohugia* | 'to point out' |
| *mau* | *mauria* | 'to carry' |
| *wero* | *werohia* | 'to stab' |
| *patu* | *patua* | 'to strike, kill' |
| *kite* | *kitea* | 'to see, find' |

lyingly the same as the active forms, and the passive suffix includes an initial consonant. This evidence suggests that the basic form of the passive suffix is /-tia/, and the other forms, /-kia/, /-ria/, etc., are allomorphs. The suffix /-tia/ is used productively in the following cases: when nominals are used verbally in the passive; in derived causatives, even if the verb stem normally takes a different allomorph; in English borrowings; when adverbials are made to agree in voice with the verbs they modify; in compounds; and any time the traditional passive allomorph for a stem is not remembered.

In this case a perfectly straightforward rule of final-consonant deletion is overridden by a morphological analysis, even though the latter is more complicated. This example shows that the tendency to take the unmarked category as the base form is quite strong. Notice further that this morphologization could take place without necessarily disturbing the original consonant deletion rule; such a rule could still exist in Maori.

These examples indicate that even where a phonetic conditioning for an alternation is transparent, speakers may prefer to make a morphological analysis, as I pointed out in Chapter 3. This morphologization tendency (and other types of change as well) seems to be guided by a strong desire to establish a one-to-one correspondence between sound and meaning. Speakers will attempt to assign a meaning to a phonological alternation. This usually occurs where, for some accidental reasons, there is a rather close correspondence between the alternation and some meaning category. Such a correspondence usually does not exist. Still P-rules lose their phonetic conditioning and become nonproductive, causing restructuring and suppletive paradigms.[3] Why should

---

[3] Restructuring is used here in its usual sense of "change in an underlying form." However, in the theory assumed, any restructuring would be accompanied by a change in the rule in question.

this occur? Why and how does restructuring occur? There may be several different types of restructuring and several different causes. I will look into some of these and suggest an explanation for restructuring that occurs without morphologization.

Consider the development of phonemic nasalized vowels. This comes about through the gradual retiming of nasalization so that it occurs during the articulation of the vowel, together with the gradual weakening of the articulation of the nasal consonant. When a sequence of nasalized vowel plus nasal consonant is present on the surface, the nasalization on the vowel is redundant and merely a consequence of the TIMING of the opening of the velum in anticipation of the contrastive feature of nasalization on the consonant. But as the consonant weakens, there will come a time when a generation of language learners will be confronted with a nasalized vowel followed by a consonant so weakened that the nasality will not be considered redundant, i.e., a part of the consonant, but rather will be considered a nonpredictable feature of the vowel. Restructuring will have taken place.

This would be a case of restructuring concomitant with loss of phonetic environment. Restructuring may also occur where the conditioning environment remains, but in these cases it is much less clear what the conditions for restructuring are. Let me briefly suggest a possibility. Often phonetic change takes place through a series of stages, which can be "telescoped" into a single rule that makes a rather radical phonetic change. Consider a typical palatalization progression for velars. Before front vowels and glides a velar will be fronted: (stage I) k——→k$^y$/___i, y. Then [k$^y$] may affricate to [č], producing a rule (stage II) k ——→ č/—i, y. The rule in the first stage is clearly a natural phonetic modification: The relation between [k] and [k$^y$] is quite obvious. In the second stage the situation might be entirely different. The distance between [k] and [č] is much greater than the distance between [k] and [k$^y$]. Can the stage II rule be interpreted as a mere phonetic modification that optimalizes production? There is a possibility that the difference between [k] and [č] is too great phonetically for them to be considered mere variants of one another, and that they will be interpreted as separate entities. Restructuring would occur. Of course, such a process at its inception would be covert; the output of the grammar would not be changed, but it would be subject to change. Occurrences of [k] before [i] and [y] could arise, as well as occurrences of [č] before back vowels, through borrowing or in some other way. I am suggesting that there may be substantive constraints on what may be a phonetically natural alternation and that alternations that progress beyond the natural limit may lead to restructuring. Such a suggestion could be verified with a better understanding of what is a natural process (see Chapter 7). It is clear that the notions of restructuring and morphologization need to be studied in greater detail.

Whatever the causes, the loss of a phonetically conditioned rule leads to restructuring and the development of an MP-rule where productive morphological paradigms are involved, or the development of a via-rule where only lexical correspondences are involved (or, of course, to both).

Changes in MP-rules bring about changes traditionally described as analogy. The expansion of the domain of an MP-rule is analogical extension. This occurs in rules that are strongly associated with meaning. The restriction of the domain of an MP-rule, and its eventual loss, is analogical leveling. Rules that apply to arbitrary classes and do not function in signaling meaning are subject to loss. (Examples are presented in the next section.) This includes via-rules, which are also subject to loss.

In summary, except for cases where borrowing is involved, the typical progression of rules through the grammar is as follows: P-rules are modified to produce new alternations; these may lead to restructuring or the development of MP-rules and via-rules; these in turn may be modified or lost. Other theoretically possible types of changes never occur: MP-rules do not become P-rules; via-rules do not become MP-rules or P-rules. MP-rules and via-rules never spring into the grammar fully formulated (except where they come into the grammar with borrowed forms); they have an evolutionary development that can be traced through the history of the language. These claims for historical change are stronger than any claims that have been made in TGP theory. The rest of this chapter is devoted to justifying the exclusion of two types of changes allowed in other models; rule reordering (Section 6.3) and the addition of new rules with nonphonetic environments (Section 6.4).

## 6.3 Rule Reordering

Kiparsky (1965; 1968; 1971) has argued that rule reordering—the change in the order of application of two phonological rules—is a mechanism of linguistic change. There are two reasons why this claim must be discussed here. One is that rule reordering cannot be a type of change in the theory being presented here because rules are not extrinsically ordered. The other reason is that the existence of rule reordering as a type of change would constitute strong support for the claim that rules ARE extrinsically ordered. Therefore, it is necessary to demonstrate that a theory without extrinsic rule order is able to adequately (or in a superior fashion) account for all historical changes heretofore accounted for by rule reordering, and it is desirable to demonstrate that such accounts are superior to the accounts using extrinsic rule order. Actually, it will not be possible to examine ALL putative cases of rule reordering, but I will try to discuss enough representative cases in such a way that the conclusions arrived at for these cases can be extended to other cases. First, it is necessary to examine in detail the developments in the theory of rule reordering.

Rule reordering is a DESCRIPTION of a particular linguistic change but, in itself, not an explanation. In order for rule reordering to be explanatory, the theory must include principles that predict the direction of reordering and give the motivation for the direction of reordering. Kiparsky (1968; 1971) has proposed to supply the theory with the requisite principle(s).

In his first attempt to formulate the principles predicting the direction of rule reordering, Kiparsky (1968) considered the abstract relations among pairs of rules. He proposed that rule reordering would lead to the maximization of feeding orders and the minimization of bleeding orders. These two predictions may be abbreviated into one general statement: Rules are reordered to allow their fullest utilization in the grammar. The principle predicts that rules in a counterfeeding order may reorder into feeding order and that rules in a bleeding order may reorder into counter-bleeding order, but that the inverse changes may not occur.

As an example of reordering into feeding order, Kiparsky cites an example from standard Finnish and some innovative eastern dialects of Finnish. Both, according to Kiparsky, have a rule deleting medial [γ] (a part of the gradation process) and a diphthongization rule that applies to long mid vowels. In standard Finnish diphthongization does not apply to the results of gradation, suggesting a counter-feeding order:

(5)

|  | /teγe/ | 'make!' | /vee/ | 'take' |
|---|---|---|---|---|
| diphthongization | ____ |  | vie |  |
| gradation | teØe |  | ____ |  |
|  | [tee] |  | [vie] |  |

In the eastern dialects, the long mid vowel resulting from gradation diphthongizes, suggesting a feeding order:

(6)

|  | (teγe/ | /vee/ |
|---|---|---|
| gradation | teØe | ____ |
| diphthongization | tie | vie |
|  | [tie] | [vie] |

Thus, Kiparsky claims, the two sets of dialects have the same rules, but they are applied in different orders, and further that the innovative order is a feeding order.

As an example of reordering out of bleeding order, Kiparsky cites two Swiss German dialects. The relevant rules are umlaut, which applies in certain morphological environments, e.g., the plural in the examples he uses, and a rule lowering mid back vowels before dentals, palatals, and /r/:

(7)     umlaut: V $\longrightarrow$ [−back]/[morphological information]

$$\text{lowering:} \begin{bmatrix} V \\ +\text{back} \\ -\text{high} \end{bmatrix} [+\text{low}]/\underline{\quad} \begin{bmatrix} +\text{coronal} \\ -\text{lateral} \end{bmatrix}$$

In Chapter 5 we discussed the dialects in which these rules allegedly apply in a bleeding order. The derivation Kiparsky gives is as follows:

(8)        Schaffhausen:

|          | bodə (singular) | bodə (plural) |
|----------|-----------------|----------------|
| umlaut   | _____           | ö              |
| lowering | ɔ               | _____          |
|          | [bɔdə]          | [bödə]         |

A related dialect, according to Kiparsky, has the same underlying forms and the same rules, but the rules apply in different order:

(9)        Kesswil:

|          | bodə (singular) | bodə (plural) |
|----------|-----------------|----------------|
| lowering | ɔ               | ɔ              |
| umlaut   | _____           | ɔ̈             |
|          | [bɔdə]          | [bɔ̈də]        |

In this case umlaut does not bleed lowering. The Schaffhausen dialect has the rules applying in the order in which they were added to the grammar; Kesswil is the innovative dialect. Reordering has occurred from a bleeding order into a nonbleeding order.

There are a number of counter-examples to Kiparsky's original attempt to predict the direction of rule reordering. In his 1971 paper, Kiparsky discusses some of these counter-examples and suggests other principles for determining the direction of reordering. These principles do not refer to the abstract relations among rules, but rather refer to the surface forms generated by the rules. This second set of principles produces better results than the first, precisely because they are principles referring to such forms. This is exactly what NGP would claim; since it is a theory that is tied very closely to surface forms, it would predict that all historical changes are motivated by surface forms, not by abstract (ordering) relations among rules. In the discussion that follows we will see that the principles Kiparsky formulates are largely correct, but that his method of representing the changes in the grammar (i.e., rule reordering) can be dispensed with in favor of more straightforward, simpler methods.

Let us begin with the problems encountered by the principle that bleeding orders tend to reorder. We have already discussed in Chapter 5 the problems with the claim that bleeding orders are marked. In a large number of cases, the only imaginable way for two rules to apply is in a bleeding order. The other problem with the principle that bleeding orders tend to be minimized is that there are some cases in which no matter what order two rules apply in, they are in a bleeding order. For these cases the principle is simply not applicable. We will return to such examples below; first let us examine reordering out of bleeding order.

Consider the Swiss German dialects just discussed, where the conservative dialect has umlaut preceding lowering, giving the singular/plural pair [bɔdə], [bödə]. This is a bleeding order, and an unmarked one, as I argued in Chapter 5, since there is no reason to expect a P-rule motivated for back vowels to apply to a front vowel.[4] The innovative dialect has the forms [bɔdə], [bödə], suggesting to Kiparsky a rule reordering. This order produces forms in which the stem vowel has the same height: The only difference between the forms is vowel backness, and this is the marker of plural. Kiparsky (1971) suggests that the principle governing such a change is PARADIGM UNIFORMITY, which he states as follows: "Allomorphy tends to be minimized in a paradigm" (p. 598–599). This, of course, is merely a restatement of the long-observed and time-tested principle of analogical leveling. Nonmeaningful alternations tend to be eliminated. We must certainly accept leveling as a powerful tendency in linguistic change; we must question, however, the formal expression of the principle of paradigm uniformity as rule reordering. Kiparsky (1974) has expressed dissatisfaction with the relation of paradigm uniformity to formal simplification. The problem he recognizes is that there is no direct relation between surface simplification and grammatical simplification in a theory that allows abstract rules. We will see that in NGP this problem is solved, for leveling of surface allomorphy always corresponds to simplifications in the grammar.

In NGP the innovative dialect with the forms [bɔdə], [bödə] would

---

[4] The phonetic motivation for lowering, as explained in Chapter 5, is the lowness of the BACK of the tongue during the articulation of coronal consonants (Vennemann, 1972b).

have an underlying form identical to the singular /bɔdəl/.[5] To derive the plural we only need apply the general umlaut rule. The change that has taken place is merely a restructuring on the basis of the singular form. (And since this is the unmarked category, it is a quite common type of change; see Vennemann, 1972e.) We need not make the strange claim that a phonetic rule motivated only for back vowels applies to a vowel that surfaces as a front vowel. Nor do we need to make the unsupportable claim that speakers register an underlying form with a mid vowel, /o/, for a stem that in all of its occurrences has a low vowel.

Furthermore, if we examine other cases of change by the paradigm uniformity principle, we find that many of them cannot be accounted for by rule reordering; but they can all be accounted for, quite plausibly, by positing a restructured underlying form coupled with a morphologization and eventual rule loss. For example, consider another case discussed in Kiparsky (1971). A rule that was originally a P-rule introduced an alternation into certain Latin paradigms. This rule is stated by Kiparsky as follows (p. 597):

(10)                    rhotacism:   s $\longrightarrow$ r/ V—V

The rule produced an alternation in the paradigm (11a) that was subsequently leveled as in (11b):

(11)  (a)  *honos*    (nominative)   (b)  *honor*    (nominative)
           *honoris*  (genitive)          *honoris*  (genitive)
           *honorem*  (accusative)        *honorem*  (accusative)

To describe the forms in (11a), we can posit an underlying form /honos/ and apply the rhotacism rule. To describe (11b) we need only posit underlying /honor/, to which no rules apply, and paradigm uniformity is described in the same way as in other cases.

Note, however, that an intermediate stage must be postulated (as in the case just discussed). In this intermediate stage, rhotacism has lost its phonetic motivation (perhaps for reasons discussed in Section 6.2), but the alternation of (11a) still exists. This alternation must be accounted for by an MP-rule. Since MP-rules are by their very nature arbitrary, the rule could be stated as s $\longrightarrow$ r or as r $\longrightarrow$ s, depending upon which C is taken to be basic. The direction of the leveling suggests /honor/ as the base form. This is not too surprising, since leveling usually favors the forms of the basic or unmarked category. Evidence in Latin and Early Romance suggest that the accusative is considered the basic category for nouns, since this is the case that came to replace all others when case

[5] This analysis originated with Theo Vennemann (class lectures, 1971).

distinctions were being lost. Thus at this intermediate stage, there is already a restructured underlying form, /honor/, and an inverse rule r ⟶ s, in the nominative of certain nouns. In stage (11b) this arbitrary MP-rule has been lost.

In his 1971 paper, Kiparsky expresses concern about positing underlying /honor/ for stage (11b) because of the existence of the related form *honestus*, which retains the stem-final /s/. But this is a problem only if we assume that all related forms must be derived from the same underlying morpheme. With the concept of the via-rule, *honestus* presents no problem; both /honor-/ and /honest-/ are listed in the lexicon and they are related by via-rules. The fact that *honestus* was unaffected by the restructuring of *honor* supports the idea of separate lexical entries for such forms.

To summarize the discussion up to this point, all cases of changes motivated by paradigm uniformity are formally expressible as restructuring of underlying forms (with rule morphologization and loss). This includes cases formerly expressed as reorderings out of bleeding order, and it includes cases not describable as rule reorderings. Now let us consider reordering in cases of mutual bleeding order, which Kiparsky also claims is motivated by paradigm uniformity.

In cases where two rules have forms such that either order in which they are applied is a bleeding order, the principle of the minimization of bleeding order is simply not applicable. However, the paradigm uniformity principle is. Consider the interaction of final devoicing and g-deletion in German dialects:

(12)      final devoicing:   [-sonorant] ⟶ [-voice] / ___$
             g-deletion:       g ⟶ Ø / [+nasal] ___

In the conservative dialects, devoicing precedes g-deletion giving the following derivation (Kiparsky, 1971:600):

(13)        Conservative   (North German)   'thing'

| | singular | plural | |
|---|---|---|---|
| | /diŋ/ | /diŋ + ə/ | underlying form |
| | diŋg | diŋg + ə | nasal assimilation |
| | diŋk | ———— | devoicing |
| | ———— | diŋOə | g-deletion |
| | [diŋk] | [diŋə] | (phonetic) |

This order produces an alternation of /k/ with Ø. The innovative order, g-deletion before devoicing, gives a uniform output:

(14)         Innovative   (standard German)

| /ding/ | /ding + ə/ | underlying form |
|--------|-----------|-----------------|
| diŋg | diŋg + ə | nasal assimilation |
| diŋØ | diŋØ + ə | g-deletion |
| ____ | ____ | devoicing |
| [diŋ] | [diŋə] | (phonetic) |

Kiparsky claims that the reordering from one bleeding order to another is motivated by paradigm uniformity.

It is certainly true that paradigmatic pressures are at work here. Added evidence of this is the fact that final /k/ after a nasal in paradigms where there is no alternation did not delete: [baŋk], [baŋkən] 'bank (singular and plural)'. But this case can be handled in exactly the same way as the other cases of analogical leveling (Vennemann, 1974a). For standard German we posit an underlying form /diŋ/ to which no MP-rules apply. Notice that in this case the leveling favored the stem in the plural form, /diŋ/, rather than /diŋk/. But the [baŋk], [baŋkən] paradigm is the reason for this. If the *ding* paradigm had leveled in favor of the [diŋk] form, a distinction between paradigms would have been lost.

Let us examine the case in further detail following Vennemann's (1974a) discussion. First consider the NGP analysis of the original state of affairs, the paradigm [diŋK], [diŋə]. This paradigm is the result of the addition of two P-rules to the grammar, the rules mentioned above. But as soon as g-deletion becomes obligatory and [g] no longer appears in the paradigm, the underlying form cannot be /ding/. It must be either /diŋk-/ or diŋ-/. Apparently /diŋ-/ is the choice made (because /diŋk-/ would be confusable with forms such as /baŋk-/). An MP-rule is then needed to insert /k/ in the singular form. The analogical leveling is the loss of the MP-rule.

Now compare the NGP treatment of the [diŋk], [diŋə] stage with Kiparsky's treatment (13). The NGP analysis already shows restructuring with an arbitrary MP-rule and thus predicts the further changes. The ordered rule analysis by itself, however, predicts no change. The situation is depicted as completely stable. Only by looking at the surface forms could one discern that a change might occur; the grammar itself gives no indication of this. In Kiparsky's analysis the surface simplification cannot be expressed as a formal simplification of the grammar, but in Vennemann's analysis (the only one available in NGP) there is a direct reflection of surface simplification in the grammar. This is, of course, because NGP is strongly associated with the surface forms of the language. What the study of rule reordering shows in general is that to find the explanation for changes described as reordering, we must look to the surface. The explanation is not in deep underlying forms nor in abstract relations between rules.

Examples of alleged reordering involving bleeding order give absolutely no evidence for the existence of extrinsic rule order, because the direction of the changes and the explanation of the changes cannot be found in the grammar (that is, the type of grammar that allows reordering) but must be sought outside the grammar. In fact, the example just discussed argues AGAINST the notion of reordering and FOR the restructuring analysis, since only the latter analysis predicts the change. We will see below that the other type of reordering has even less empirical support.

A further note on the motivation for this type of change is on order here. Kiparsky (1968; 1971) is very much concerned to find universal principles that will allow us to describe the change from one stage to another as a change from a marked to an unmarked state. Thus he formulates the principle of paradigm uniformity, and he and others discuss formal simplification in the grammar. In my opinion it is a mistake to try to reduce all types of linguistic change to a single principle of simplification or unmarking. Instead, it is better to view change as being governed by several substantive principles, each of which have as their motivation the optimalization of the grammar, but which cannot all be expressed as formal simplification.

In the examples we have just discussed we find a series of processes operating, all of which were discussed in the first two sections of this chapter. First, a phonetic change takes place, expressed as rule addition. Such changes are motivated by an attempt to optimalize the phonetic string. The phonetic alternation is later reanalyzed as being NOT phonetically predictable. This leads to restructuring of underlying forms and/or rule morphologization (see Andersen, 1973). As I pointed out above, the conditions under which restructuring and morphologization take place are not entirely clear, but the motivation seems to be a desire to associate phonetic alternations with meaning, or the phonetic alternation may simply progress beyond the point of optimalizing the phonetic string and leave an arbitrary alternation. If the residual alternation is not functional in signaling meaning, it is subject to loss, a process that could be considered simplification. The result is a regular paradigm once more. Only in the last stage can we say that the grammar has been simplified, yet each step described above is extremely common and perfectly natural as a change in the grammar.

An auxillary principle formulated by Kiparsky (1971) is the transparency principle: "rules tend to be ordered so as to become maximally transparent" (p. 623). As explained in Chapter 5, transparency is the converse of opacity, which is defined in the following manner:

A rule A ⟶ B/C ____ D is opaque to the extent that there exist surface representations of the form
  (i)   A in the environment C ____ D, or
  (ii)  B in environments other than C ____ D.

The first case of this definition merely characterizes counter-feeding orders and constitutes a restatement of the principle that feeding orders tend to be maximized, i.e., the direction of reordering is from counterfeeding to feeding order. Let us now consider this claim in detail before discussing case (ii) of the definition.

Note first that there is a remarkable scarcity of examples of reordering out of counter-feeding order: As far as I know only two have ever been proposed, the Finnish case previously discussed and a Slavic case to be discussed. This is certainly curious, but we can readily understand why it is so if we consider the plausibility of this type of reordering. One case of counter-feeding order discussed in Chapter 5 involved a rule of velar softening in Spanish (abbreviated as k ⟶ s, g ⟶ x/ ____ front vowels). Forms exempt from velar softening, e.g., *que* [ke], *quien* [kyen[, *guía* [gía], *guerra* [géra], are given underlying forms with labiovelars in Harris's analysis. The delabialization rule counter-feeds velar softening by applying after it. Would we really expect a reordering here, as the transparency principle predicts? Such a reordering would give the forms [se] for *que*, [syen] for *quien*, [xia] for *guía*, [xéra] for *guerra*. I do not have to argue at great length that the sudden emergence of [s] and [x] in these forms (and it would be sudden since rule reordering is by necessity abrupt) would be a strange development indeed. The rule of velar softening (or what is left of it) is simply buried too deeply in the grammar to reemerge in the same form. (This is not to say that a new palatalization rule might not develop, but it would undoubtedly have a different reflex, at least at first.) Observe that the reason that velar softening cannot reorder is precisely because it is opaque. Therefore the claim that rules reorder to eliminate opacity is extremely implausible.

What can be said, then, about the two cases of counter-feeding reordering that have been proposed? Both of these cases have been attacked more than once in the literature. Consider first the Finnish case. Here, in the western dialect, consonant gradation (manifested in this example as the deletion of a voiced velar spirant) fails to feed a diphthongization process. Thus underlying /vee/ gives [vie], but underlying /tege/ gives [tee], with an undipthongized long vowel. In the eastern dialect underlying /tege/ gives [tie]; i.e., in Kiparsky's terms gradation feeds diphthongization.

What has not been demonstrated adequately in this case is that reordering has in fact taken place. There is an additional bit of data that casts doubt on the reordering solution. In the innovative dialect diphthongization is more general than in the conservative dialect: It affects long low vowels ā (——→ oa) and ā̈ (——→ eä) as well as the mid vowels. There are two explanations for the data, neither of which involves reordering. One explanation, discussed in Campbell (1973), suggests that the diphthong in [tie] is the result of a new and different diphthongization process, and the evidence for this is that it affects a different set of vowels. The other explanation is presented in King (1973:554) on the basis of Rapola (1966) and Kettunen (1940). The history of the development and spread of these rules appears to account for the dialect difference. The diphthongization of mid vowels began in the western dialects and spread to the eastern dialects where it was generalized to low vowels. Consonant gradation moved in the opposite direction: It began in the eastern dialects and spread west. Thus by the time gradation reached the western dialects, diphthongization was nonproductive and did not affect the results of gradation. On the other hand, when diphthongization reached the eastern dialects, gradation was well-established so that diphthongization could affect forms produced by gradation. I have no idea which of these suggestions is correct, but the fact that diphthongization is different in the two dialects clearly points to one of these explanations over rule reordering.

The other putative case of counter-feeding reordering is equally weak. This involves the two Slavic palatalization processes (Kiparsky, 1968:363). By the first palatalization /k/ and /g/ became [č] and [j], respectively, before front vowels and glides. Then [j] is deaffricated to [ž]: e.g., *kı̆to > čı̆to 'what', *givŭ > živŭ 'alive'. Later, new instances of front vowels develop by monophthongization of /ai/ to /e/. A second palatalization later affects velars before the new front vowel. The reflexes of this palatalization are [c] and [ʒ]: *k'ena > cena 'price', *g'ĕlo > ʒelo 'very'. The voiced affricate deaffricates in all dialects except Old Church Slavic and modern Polish, giving ʒĕlo > zĕlo. To account for this difference among dialects with regard to deaffrication, Kiparsky suggests that the second palatalization (k ——→ tc,g ——→ ʒ) could have reordered to apply before, and feed, deaffrication, which would be stated as follows:

(15) $\begin{bmatrix} +\text{voice} \\ +\text{coronal} \\ +\text{strident} \end{bmatrix} \longrightarrow [+\text{continuant}]$

(The feature [+coronal] replaces [−grave] in Kiparsky's formulation.) In Old Church Slavic and Polish, where deaffrication does not apply to [ʒ], the second palatalization is said to apply AFTER deaffrication, in the historical order, which is a counter-feeding order. Thus the deaffrication of [ʒ] in the other dialects is described as a reordering out of counter-feeding order.

Koutsoudas, Sanders, and Noll (1974) have proposed another account of this example that is very straightforward and plausible. They suggest that the difference between dialects is simply a matter of the generality of the constraint against affricates (deaffrication). Old Church Slavic and Polish had /ʒ/ but not */ǰ/; the deaffrication rule was more specific, e.g.,

$$(16) \qquad \begin{bmatrix} +\text{voice} \\ +\text{coronal} \\ +\text{strident} \\ -\text{anterior} \end{bmatrix} \longrightarrow [+\text{continuant}]$$

In the other dialects, the affricates underwent a more general rule that disallowed all [+coronal] affricates. Koutsoudas, Sanders, and Noll claim that this is a case of rule generalization [from older (16) to (15)], a well attested type of change, rather than a rule reordering. Another, equally plausible, explanation (suggested by Vennemann, personal communication) is that Old Church Slavic and Polish underwent a new round of deaffrication after the second palatalization. These suggestions show that rule reordering is by no means a NECESSARY description of these developments.

Thus in the two cases of counter-feeding reordering, no case can be made for the necessity of a reordering description. When we couple this with the fact that the principle governing this type of reordering is extremely implausible, we can conclude that it simply does not take place. We saw in the cases of reordering for paradigm uniformity that descriptions involving restructuring are always available (and in fact necessitated by NGP) and further that these descriptions are more explanatory. Thus there appears to be no motivation for positing rule reordering as a type of linguistic change.

## 6.4 Sound Change and Nonphonetic Information

In an attempt to constrain the theory to predict that only certain changes can occur in a morphophonological system, I suggested above

that new alternations always arise as phonetically motivated alternations, i.e., that new alternations are never motivated by the morphosyntactic system. Morphosyntactic alternations are rather the residue of
old phonetic alternations or adaptations of phonetic alternations. I have
already mentioned that any other view is quite implausible, because
speakers do not simply invent new alternations based on meaning or
grammar. In this section we will examine some apparent counter-
examples to this claim.

The position I will defend here is similar to the Regularity Hypothesis, discussed recently by King (1969) and Postal (1968). This hypothesis is stated by King (1969:120) as: "Phonological change is
regular, and its environment can be stated in strictly phonetic terms."
Notice that the regularity clause of the hypothesis seems to follow from
the phonetic environment clause. That is, if a change can be stated in
strictly phonetic terms, then the change would affect every lexical item
or morpheme of the language that provides the correct phonetic environment. However, when the implementation of a sound change in
progress is studied (as in studies done by Labov (1972) and Chen and
Wang (1975), we find that it does not necessarily follow that a change
initiated in phonetic environments will be regular. My position is that
sound changes are always initiated for phonetic reasons and, therefore,
in phonetic environments. They try to apply regularly throughout the
language, but, between the initiation of a sound change and its comple-
tion, many things may happen that prevent the result of a sound change
from being completely regular. Thus exceptions to sound changes and
alleged morphosyntactic conditioning can be explained as developments that arise during the implementation of a sound change.

There are two types of putative counter-examples to the claim that innovations are always phonetically conditioned. One type involves cases
in which an otherwise regular phonetic change has systematic exceptions, determined by grammatical categories. The other, less common
type involves changes that appear to occur only in a certain grammatical
category, but which are not attributable to analogy. The counter-
examples presented by King and Postal are of the first type. King's
(1969:123) example is a case of deletion of final e, phonetically [ə], in the
development of Yiddish from a protolanguage similar to Middle High
German. Unstressed e is deleted in word-final position:

(17)          *tage*    *teg*    'days'
              *erde*    *erd*    'earth'
              *gibe*    *gib*    'I give'

The final e is retained, however, in adjectival inflectional endings:

(18)     *di groyse shtot*     'the big city'
         *dos alte land*      'the old country'
         *a sheyne froy*      'a pretty woman'

Certain other suffixes also retain the *e*. King explains that there is no phonetic reason for the retention of *e* in these forms, nor is there any chance of appealing to analogy. He concludes that the environment for the change is not purely phonetic, that a new rule such as (21) was added to the grammar of Yiddish:

(19)     $\begin{bmatrix} V \\ -stress \end{bmatrix} \longrightarrow \begin{cases} [-\text{next rule}]/ + \underline{\quad} \#]_{\text{adjective}} \\ \emptyset \qquad\quad /\underline{\quad}\ \# \end{cases}$

The feature [−next rule] is merely a formal means of specifying that adjectives are exceptions to the deletion rule.[6]

Postal (1968:245–260) presents counter-examples of the same sort. He claims that a vowel epenthesis rule in Mohawk has exceptions that are conditioned by particular morphemes. Examples of this type are not rare. We often find that certain grammatical categories are exceptions to otherwise general, phonetically motivated rules. The point at issue, however, is whether a rule such as (19) is a possible NEW rule in a morphophonological system. It is my position that King and Postal, in claiming that a rule such as (19) is a possible new rule, have overlooked the important details concerning how a phonological change is initiated and how it develops in the initial stages. Such details are usually ignored when we study linguistic changes as past history, i.e., when we study the result of linguistic changes. But when we observe on-going phonological change, it is possible to understand better the nature of phonological change in general and the development of grammatical exceptions in particular. In the following paragraphs I will outline briefly some of the recent findings of Labov and Chen and Wang concerning linguistic changes. Then I will examine one well-documented phonological change that is exactly analogous to King's example in that grammatical exceptions develop. This example bears out the observations of Labov and confirms the validity of the constraint I am proposing.

Labov's (1972) study of on-going changes in morphophonological

---

[6] The notation could be changed here so that adjectives do not appear to be exceptions:

$$\begin{bmatrix} V \\ -stress \\ -adjective \end{bmatrix} \longrightarrow \emptyset / \underline{\quad}\#$$

In my opinion this notational change does not alter the fact that adjectives are exceptions to the deletion rule.

systems suggests that a description, for instance, of the Yiddish *e*-deletion phenomenon as the mere addition of a rule such as (19) is over-simplified to the extent that the real process of change is obscured. Labov has found that the development of a new rule is a process affected by a number of variables. At first a new rule is always variable; the rule may or may not apply in any given situation. Furthermore, the amount of phonetic variation produced by the rule differs from utterance to utterance. In this variable stage certain definite tendencies develop; that is, the frequency of application in a particular situation tends to be systematic. For instance, in a certain grammatical category the rule may be applied more frequently than in another category. As successive generations attempt to learn the system that governs the application of rules, the new rule stabilizes and becomes obligatory in certain environments and inapplicable in others.

Wang (1969) and Chen and Wang (1975) have studied the lexical diffusion of sound changes. They argue against the position that a sound change affects all lexical items simultaneously. It seems, rather, that a phonological change works its way through the lexicon, moving from item to item. All the factors that influence lexical diffusion are not known, but it is clear that phonological factors and grammatical factors are relevant. Recent work (Fidelholtz, 1975; Hooper, 1976b) supports an older claim (Schuchardt, 1885 [1972]) that the frequency of use of a lexical item plays a part; i.e., more frequent items undergo change before less frequent items.

The observations of Labov, Wang, and Chen contribute significant details to our understanding of sound change, which make it possible to investigate the claim that all "new rules" come from a finite set of phonetically motivated processes. The sound change has a strictly phonetic motivation when it enters the language as an optional or variable rule (although, according to Labov, even the phonetic motivation may vary a bit at first). Very soon, the new rule runs headlong into the established morphophonological processes in the language and a conflict sometimes results, particularly if the output of the new rule obscures some morphological distinctions or violates some other phonological constraints active in the grammar. When the new rule stabilizes as an obligatory process, the conflict must be resolved. If the established processes of the language win out over the new rule, then the stabilized rule will have exceptions. To see how this process works, we will examine a well-documented case of rule addition in the recent history of Spanish. The case to be discussed here is parallel to the example cited by King.

Between the twelfth and fifteenth centuries the predecessor of Modern Spanish underwent a deletion of word-final *e* (phonetically [e]), after a consonant. In a TGP analysis of Modern Spanish, there is a rule that deletes word-final *e* after certain consonants.

$$(20) \qquad e \longrightarrow \emptyset\,/\,V \begin{Bmatrix} r \\ l \\ n \\ d \\ s \\ y \end{Bmatrix} \underline{\quad}\#$$

In Modern Spanish this rule has grammatical exception because conjugated verb forms with final *e* retain it. The following forms are in standard orthography:

(21)

| Infinitive | Gloss | Conjugated form |
|------------|-------|-----------------|
| *poder*   | 'to be able to' | *puede*  3 sg. pres. ind. |
| *salir*   | 'to leave'      | *sale*  3 sg. pres. ind. |
| *poner*   | 'to put'        | *pone*  3 sg. pres. ind. |
| *ganar*   | 'to win'        | *gane*  1 and 3 sg. pres. subj. |
| *quedar*  | 'to stay'       | *quede*  1 and 3 sg. pres. subj. |
| *casarse* | 'to marry'      | *se case*  1 and 3 sg. pres. subj. |
| *poder*   | 'to be able to' | *pude*  1 sg. pret. ind. |
| *venir*   | 'to come'       | *vine*  1 sg. pret. ind. |

Thus *e*-deletion in a TGP would be rendered as (22).[7]

$$(22) \qquad e \longrightarrow \begin{Bmatrix} [-\text{next rule}]\,/+\underline{\quad}\#\,]_{\text{verb}\,[-\text{finite}]} \\ \emptyset\,/\,V \begin{Bmatrix} r \\ l \\ d \\ n \\ s \\ y \end{Bmatrix} \underline{\quad} \end{Bmatrix}$$

The feature [−finite] is necessary in this analysis because the infinitive is said to have a final /e/ that is deleted, e.g., /amare/ [amar] 'to love' (cf. Section 3.1 and Harris, 1969).

Rule (22) is exactly analogous to King's rule (19), and it might also constitute a counter-example to the position advocated here. However, the history of (22) is known, and this history shows that rule (22) was

[7] There are also a few other exceptions that need to be accounted for, e.g., *doce* 'twelve', *trece* 'thirteen', which no doubt retained the final /e/ on analogy with *once* 'eleven', *catorce* 'fourteen', and *quince* 'fifteen'.

not added to the grammar in this form. In fact, at the time that *e*-deletion began to affect Spanish words, it did not have any grammatical exceptions. The history of *e*-deletion shows exactly what Labov's observations would predict. According to Menéndez Pidal (1968:167–70), *e*-deletion was optional at its inception and optionally affected every word-final *e* in the language (syllable structure permitting) throughout the twelfth and thirteenth centuries. Some possible variants during this period were:

(23)   a. *pane*        *pan*        'bread'
          *mare*        *mar*        'sea'
          *amare*       *amar*       'to love'
          *mercede*     *merced*     'mercy'
          *fi(d)ele*    *fiel*       'faithful'
          *me(n)se*     *mes*        'month'
          *paze*        *paz*        'peace'

       b. *monte*       *mont*       'mountain'
          *puente*      *puent*      'bridge'
          *arte*        *art*        'art'
          *hueste*      *huest*      'host'
          *humilde*     *humilt*[8]  'humble'
          *dulce*       *dulz*       'sweet'

       c. *noche*       *noch*       'night'
          *leche*       *lech*       'milk'
          *principe*    *princep*    'prince'
          *nueve*       *nuef*[8]    'nine'
          *nieve*       *nief*[8]    'snow'
          *calle*       *cal*        'street'

       d. *pude*        *pud*        1 sg. pret. of *poder* 'to be able'
          *vine*        *vin*        1 sg. pret. of *venir* 'to come'
          *di[š]e*      *di[š]*      1 sg. pret. of *decir* 'to say'
          *faze*        *faz*        3 sg. pres. ind. of *hacer* 'to make'
          *sale*        *sal*        3 sg. pres. ind. of *salir* 'to leave'
          *quiere*      *quier*      3 sg. pres. ind. of *querer* 'to want'
          *peche*       *pech*       1 and 3 sg. pres subj. of *pechar* 'to pay'
          *pese*        *pes*        1 and 3 sg. pres. subj. of *pesar* 'to weigh'

The forms in (23) are divided according to the situation produced by the application of *e*-deletion. The forms in (23d) are verb forms; the forms in (23b,c) after deletion have final C's or C clusters that violate the modern syllable structure conditions (SSC) for Spanish. The forms in

---

[8] These forms were apparently affected by final devoicing, a process that does not survive in Modern Spanish.

(23a) have final C's that are allowed by the modern SSC. There is only one type of word that was not ever affected by the apocation rule; these are forms that would have highly marked syllable structure if a final V were deleted.

(24)

| | | |
|---|---|---|
| pobre | *pobr | 'poor' |
| padre | *padr | 'father' |
| roble | *robl | 'oak' |

In the forms with an asterisk, a relatively strong C is followed by a very weak C, and the cluster is far less acceptable as a syllable-final cluster (see Chapters 8–12). Compare the forms in (23b): The resultant syllable-final cluster has a weaker C followed by a stronger one. These clusters are not allowed in Modern Spanish, but they do not violate the universal constraints on syllable structure (see Chapter 12). We must assume, then, that the SSC of twelfth and thirteenth century Spanish was somewhat more flexible than it is today.

It is clear, then, that the original $e$-deletion rule was sensitive to consonantal strength. The rule may be stated as (25):

(25)
$$V \longrightarrow \emptyset / \left\{ \begin{bmatrix} V \\ C \\ m \text{ strength} \end{bmatrix} \right\} \begin{bmatrix} C \\ n \text{ strength} \end{bmatrix} \underline{\quad}, \quad \text{if } m < n$$

The quality of the vowel need not be specified because, according to the universal constraints proposed in Hooper (1972b) (see Chapter 13), only the minimal V may be deleted. The strength conditions require that if there are two C's, the first must be weaker than the second.

The SD of the rule deserves some further comment. Above I have described this deletion as taking place in word-final position. If this were correct, $e$-deletion would not have a purely phonetic motivation; it would have a # (word-boundary) in its SD, and it would be a sandhi rule. I believe, however, that $e$-deletion is not a sandhi rule; the reason is that this apocope is related to the process of syncope that occurred in the language. One round of syncope occurred less than a century before the appearance of apocope (Otero, 1971:310,313). This syncope affected weak V's in pretonic and posttonic position, provided that clusters of three C's did not result, which is to say, provided that the SSC was not grossly violated. For example, [kaled$^z$e] > [kald$^z$e] 'wedge', L. *pectine* [peitene] > [peitne] (Modern Spanish *peine*) 'comb'. Apocope is only the final stage of this quite general deletion of weak V's and, for this reason, should be considered a phonetically motivated process.

The easiest way to state a rule that will generate the correct results is to add the # to the SD. But this statement would be incorrect, because it would in effect claim that the # conditioned the deletion. It is more difficult to check, but to my knowledge rule (25) generates the correct results, without claiming that the deletion was motivated by a syntactic boundary. Rule (25) does not delete word-internal V's, because these have already been deleted. It does not delete /e/ in the first syllable of the word, because a V or a C weaker than the second C must precede the obligatory C.

At the beginning rule (25) was variable. The lexical representations of affected forms retained the word-final /e/. We have already noted that the result of e-deletion in forms such as (23b) was to produce a syllable-final sequence not previously allowed (and not allowed in Modern Spanish). In forms such as (23c) the existing SSC is violated; C's such as /č/ /p/, /f/, /ł/ are too strong to occur in syllable-final position (and in the case of /ł/ the C itself was altered to be acceptable as syllable-final). Nevertheless, the apocope rule applied to these forms. Similarly, apocope in verb forms such as (23d) disrupts the pattern of the verb paradigm. It does not, however, cause any morphological distinction to merge. In the present tense it merely violates the general pattern in which a V follows the root of the verb.

As mentioned above, Labov has found that variable rules are applied with greater frequency in some environments than in others. In this case, the apocope rule was applied with greater frequency in environments in which it did not conflict with the SSC or the verb pattern. The forms in (23a) were affected by apocope more regularly than any other forms, and apocope in these forms stabilized very early; only the forms without [e] were used. In NGP these forms would now be entered in the lexicon without final /e/, and at this point the noun and adjective pluralization rule must provide the final V to produce pairs such as [pan] (singular), [panes] (plural) 'bread'. The e-deletion rule remained variable for a century or more after this development, and the pairs in (23b,c,d) coexisted, governed by variables that are not reconstructable now.

The outcome was that the forms in (23b,c,d) retained the final /e/.[9] The verb paradigm and the SSC won out over the deletion rule. In an NGP, the result is represented as the loss of the deletion rule (which no doubt was preceded by a stage in which the application of the rule to forms (23b,c,d) became less and less frequent). Notice that, under this account, there was no point at which the rule had exceptions of any sort. Rather the phonetically motivated rule was optional at first and

---

[9] The only conjugated verb form that lost the /e/ is the familiar imperative of a few verbs: *pon* (*poner* 'to put'), *ten* (*tener* 'to have') etc.

could apply in all environments. As time went on, the frequency of application was governed by phonotactic, grammatical, and (no doubt) social factors, but the rule did not enter the language with any but a phonetic motivation. I would suggest, then, that all exceptions to phonological rules develop in just this way; all phonological rules have their source in universal phonetic constraints, and new rules never arrive at the door of the grammar with their grammatical exceptions in tow.

A less common type of apparent counter-example to the claim that all sound changes are phonetically conditioned are cases in which a sound change appears to operate ONLY in a certain morphosyntactic environment. Bear in mind that we are not concerned with changes due to analogy, i.e., the extension or restriction of an MP-rule, but rather with true innovation in a particular morphosyntactic category. The cases of this type that I am aware of lend themselves to the same sort of interpretation as the preceding example. In these cases the phonetic innovation is natural (phonetically explanatory) and can be shown to be a part of a more general change that has gone through for a certain morpheme while remaining variable in the rest of the language. I will present only one example here merely to suggest, as with the previous example, that the phonological, grammatical, and social factors influencing the implementation of a sound change are very complex, but the original impetus for a sound change is always phonetic.

The second person plural morpheme in Spanish derived from Latin *-tis*, and in Old Spanish was *-des* (*amádes* (present indicative), *amábades* (imperfect indicative) 'to love'). The intervocalic /d/ or [ð] in this morpheme was deleted in penultimately stressed forms in the thirteenth century, as in *amádes* > *amáis*, and in antepenultimately stressed forms in the fifteenth century, as in *amábades* > *amábais* (Menéndez Pidal, 1968:278). Other verbal morphemes, such as the past participle *-do* from Latin *-to*, maintained the dental fricative, e.g., *amádo* [amáðo] in standard pronunciation. Forms of other categories maintained the intervocalic dental: *vída* [bíða] from Latin *vita* 'life', *ciudádes* 'cities' (note the identical phonetic environment), *nádes* 'swim' (second person singular present subjunctive).

This development would appear to be the result of the addition of a rule with a positive morphological environment, e.g., delete /d/ in the second plural morpheme, if we did not know that this deletion is a part of an extremely general weakening process affecting intervocalic consonants from the Vulgar Latin period to the present (see Chapter 13). Today the deletion of [ð] is well established in dialects considered substandard and becoming more and more common even among educated speakers. While the general process has a phonetic explanation, the restructuring of the second plural morpheme at this particular period was probably due to a combination of nonphonological factors. One of these factors could have been frequency: The suffix -*des* occurred on second person plural forms in every tense of every verb, which would make it one of the most frequent items containing an intervocalic /d/. Thus it is possible that its frequent use encouraged its reduction. Further, there are the social factors. In Modern Spanish the deletion of /d/ is stigmatized, and it was no doubt stigmatized in Old Spanish. But it is possible for the pronunciation of a particular form to lose its stigma while similar pronunciations of other forms remain stigmatized.

Consider now a hypothetical situation that would have arisen if the general process of weakening of intervocalic consonants had been arrested after the restructuring of the second plural suffix. Then it would appear that an isolated change had occurred in this morpheme only and give the impression that a sound change can be morphologically conditioned. I would like to suggest that the examination of a large number of cases will reveal that the initiation of a sound change always has a very straightforward phonetic explanation but that the implementation of a sound change is subject to diverse influences that create complex situations.

# 7

# Underlying
# Representations

## 7.1 Phonetic Variation

In NGP the phonological forms of underlying representations are closely related to surface phonetic forms. We will be discussing several models of the lexicon in this chapter, all of which require that the surface phonetic forms guide the choice of underlying forms. Therefore it is necessary to discuss a problem that always arises in considerations of phonetic representations, the problem of the huge amount of phonetic variation that is found in all languages. If we formulate a constraint on underlying forms to the effect that underlying forms be identical to surface phonetic forms, or be archisegmental representations of surface phonetic forms, then the problem is of WHICH surface phonetic forms, since any word or morpheme has a number of surface realizations predicted, not morphophonemically, but phonetically and by speech style or tempo. Furthermore, to the extent that the variation is predictable, it should be represented in the grammar.

Several important facts suggest a model for representing variable forms in the grammar. One fact is that variable representations of the same form are relatable to one another by general rules. For instance, the careful form for *security* [səkyɨ́rɨti] is related to the more casual form [ṣkyɨ́rɨ̇ri] by the processes of schwa-deletion and flapping. The second important fact is that the casual form may be derived from the careful form, but not vice versa. This is because the rules that apply in more casual styles are largely reductive rules, e.g., neutralizations such as flapping, vowel reduction rules, and deletion rules. The careful forms contain more information than the more casual forms. These facts, which hold for all languages, suggest that the most careful style of speech should be taken as the basis for the phonological shape of un-derlying forms, and the more casual forms derived from this by variable rules, as proposed in Abaurre (1974) and Rudes (1975). The careful or explicit form of speech we have in mind here should be distinguished from artificially explicit or hypercorrect forms of speech, which may be derived by adaptive rules, as proposed by Anderson (1973). The under-lying representations should be based on the most explicit, naturally occurring spoken forms. Thus the underlying representation of *security* would be based on [səkyɨ́rɨti], and [ṣkyɨ́rɨ̇ri] will be derived by rule.

Most languages exhibit a number of styles or tempos all related to one another by rules. Furthermore, some of the variable rules appear to be interdependent, as Kučera (1973) has observed. That is, the application of one rule to a form necessitates the application of other rules in order to arrive at an acceptable output. For example, in the word *security*, it is possible to have an output to which flapping has been applied, but not schwa-deletion, [səkyɨ́rɨ̇ri]; but an unacceptable output results from applying schwa-deletion without applying flapping,*[ṣkyɨ́rɨti]. This fact could be accounted for by setting up at least three styles or tempos in English, each of which REQUIRES certain rules to apply, as in Rudes (1975). The rules, then, are not optional but OBLIGATORY, given the proper combination of factors, both phonological and social. Three forms for *security* could be generated as follows:

(1)     Andante:    [səkyɨ́rɨti]    underlying form with all
                                            redundancies filled in
    Allegretto:   [səkyɨ́rɨ̇ri]   flapping
    Presto:      [skyɨ́rɨ̇ri]    flapping
                                            schwa-deletion

If the rules were truly optional or variable, it would be difficult to account for the dependency of schwa-deletion on flapping, especially since these processes are quite unrelated phonologically. The explanation of their interrelatedness in Rudes's hypothesis is that both flapping and schwa-deletion are characteristic of Presto speech and obligatory within this style. Kučera (1973:514) found that such interdependencies could be identified in Czech even across word boundaries, but the farther removed the two interdependent elements were in the string, the less glaring the inconsistency. This is because it is possible to change styles within a sentence but rarely within a word.

Our example also shows a characteristic asymmetry in the relations among styles. Schwa-deletion is dependent upon flapping, but flapping is completely independent of schwa-deletion. If we think of the styles in a hierarchy, the most explicit style being the highest and the most casual being the lowest, we find that the reflexes of rules that apply in higher styles persevere into the lower styles; the result of a rule in a higher style is never undone in a lower style. Put another way, each lower style produces a further reduction of the phonetic string. This characteristic of the relations among styles suggested to Abaurre (1974) that the various styles be generated by a block or cycle of rules for each style. Each cycle of rules applies to the output of the higher cycle.

Let us consider Abaurre's examples from Brazilian Portuguese. In Largo, the relevant rules are palatalization, which palatalizes coronal stops (/t/ and /d/) before the high front vowel, and nasalization, which nasalizes a vowel before a nasal consonant. In Andante, final unstressed mid vowels become high (vowel raising). These vowels condition a reapplication of palatalization. In Allegretto, high front vowels after palatal consonants are deleted (vowel deletion). The variants of *teatrinho* 'little theater' and *morte* 'death' exemplify the process:

(2)

| | *teatrinho* | *morte* | rules |
|---|---|---|---|
| Largo: | [čiatrĩɲo] | [mɔhte] | palatalization nasalization |
| Andante: | [čiatrĩɲu] | [mɔhči] | vowel raising palatalization |
| Allegretto: | [čatrĩɲu] | [mɔhč] | vowel deletion |

Observe that the palatal consonant derived by the fully productive rule in Largo for *teatrinho* and in Andante for *morte* persists in Allegretto despite the deletion of the vowel that conditions it. Similarly, in the Presto version of *teatrinho*, final vowel and nasal are deleted, but the nasalization remains on the vowel: [čatrĩ:]. The reflexes of rules applied in a higher style remain constant in the lower styles.

Furthermore, there is a certain coherence among the styles that I believe is characteristic of the relations among styles. Each style does not derive from the underlying forms using totally different processes, but rather each style continues a progression in the same direction as the preceding style. Thus the vowel raising process in Andante, which is a reductive process, is carried further in Allegretto and Presto as the unstressed high vowels are deleted. This coherence among the styles may be expressed by having the rules of each style operate on the output of the rules of the immediately preceding style.

An apparent paradox in this model is the representation of more casual and faster forms of speech as being affected by more rules than the slower, more careful forms. One would expect careful speech to require more rules than sloppy speech. Of course, since these rules are all natural processes, one could speak of the SUPPRESSION of natural processes in careful speech (as in Stampe, 1973). The effort in careful speech would be in the suppression; in casual speech the speaker merely lets the natural processes take over. However, I am not totally satisfied with this characterization either. The difficulty lies, it seems to me, not in the particular model of stylistic variation, but rather in the conception of the phonological process or rule on which this model is based.

As I pointed out in the last chapter, the prevailing notion that if there is no assimilation (for example), there is no rule, and if there is an assimilation, there is a rule, draws a distinction between having a rule and not having one that is simply erroneous. Consider a sequence of segments, /ti/, that is classified as a sequence of a segment that is [+ stop, + coronal] followed by a segment [+ vocalic, + palatal]. In a language where this sequence is phonetically [ti], we posit no rule. Yet technically there has to be some rule to implement the phonetic realization of this string: The classificatory representation contains the information that the coronal closure precedes the palatal vowel; the exact timing of the two articulations must be governed by a rule. In particular, the palatal positioning of the tongue must not follow the articulation of [t] too closely or the result is likely to be a palatalization of [t]. On the other hand, in a language in which the phonetic realization of /ti/ is [či], the rule that specifies the relative timing times the palatal articulation to begin during the stop closure. Whether the phonetic realization is [ti] or [či], some rule is needed. We tend to represent the output with phonetic [ti] as the unmarked situation—the situation that would exist if no language-specific rules applied. But it is not clear that this is an accurate representation; a number of unrelated languages realize /ti/ as [či] (e.g., Brazilian Portuguese and Japanese). As Stampe has argued, it is the NONAPPLICATION of a natural process that is a language-specific phenomenon. But again Stampe is assuming that it takes a process to derive [či] and no process to derive [ti]. It is important to remember, however, that in reality it takes the same number of rules to derive [ti] from /ti/ as to derive [či] or [č] from /ti/. More casual styles of speech do not derive from the application of more rules but merely from the modification of rules. Even the progression of [či] to [č] in (2) does not really represent the addition of a deletion rule; it represents the ultimate stage in the regressive retiming of the palatal vowel: The palatal articulation of the vowel occurs simultaneously with the articulation of the consonant and is no longer a separate gesture.

The remarkable coherence we find in the processes applying in the various styles is due to the fact—not that the rules of each style apply to the output of a previous style in a synchronic sense—but rather that processes of each style are further modifications of rules existing in higher styles, and these modifications advance in a predetermined direction. However, the model that Abaurre and Rudes develop for deriving speech styles is a useful descriptive device, as long as we bear in mind what our rules represent and what they do not represent.

Let us now refer back to the variation found in Brazilian Portuguese to make another point. Because of the reductions and deletions characteristic of fast, casual speech, certain feature values appear to be contrastive in these forms that are not contrastive in the more careful styles. For example, the [č] in Brazilian Portuguese occurs in Allegretto in environments where it is not entirely predictable from the forms in that style; that is, it occurs before vowels other than [i] and at the ends of words, e.g., [čatrĩɲu] and [mɔhč]. Although in the model I have been discussing, all surface contrasts are represented as lexical contrasts, the existence of these Allegretto forms does not mean that [č] must be entered in the lexicon as a contrastive segment. Rather the contrastive units are established on the basis of the most careful (but not hypercorrect) form of speech. Since a single speaker may use forms such as [mɔhte], [mɔhči], and [mɔhč], we surmise that the relationship between the forms is part of his grammar. The speaker knows, in effect, that [mɔhč] is derived from [mɔhči] and [mɔhte], and since these forms actually exist in spontaneous speech, the derivation is considered real. The palatal consonant [č] is not phonemic in Brazilian Portuguese as long as stylistic forms (of the same words) exist in which the conditioning environment is present. If, in the future, the forms [mɔhte] and [mɔhči] are no longer used, and [mɔhč] is the Largo form, the palatal consonant will have to be entered in the lexicon.

Abaurre discusses another point in connection with speech styles that is characteristic of stylistic variation and illustrates the complexities in the notion of phonetic representation. A form such as [mɔhč], common in Allegretto speech, violates a very strong syllable structure condition that applies in Largo and Andante speech. In Largo and Andante, a syllable may not end in a stop (or affricate). Historically, vowel epenthesis applies to correct violations of this condition: In Largo *tecnico* 'technician' is [tékiniko]; *ritmico* 'rhythmic' is [híčimiko]; *etnico* 'ethnic' is [éčiniko] (in the latter two examples the epenthetic [i] conditions palatalization). This vowel epenthesis is productive in more recent borrowings; e.g., *futbol* is [fúčibol]. Yet in Allegretto the vowel that is inserted to avoid syllable-final obstruents in careful speech is deleted after palatals in casual speech, e.g., Allegretto [híčmiku], [éčniku], [fúčbol], producing syllable-final affricates in blatant violation of the syllable structure conditions of Largo and Andante speech. This example illustrates a situation I believe is typical of phonetic structure. There are few absolutes; there is rather considerable variation in styles and tempos produced by a complex interplay of productive rules and conditions.

## 7.2  Underlying Representation of Phonetic Alternations

To this point, I have discussed the constraints on NGP in terms of a condition on rules, the True Generalization Condition, and a condition on their application, the No-Ordering Condition. All writers in the area of natural generative phonology agree that these conditions are correct (Hudson, 1974b; Vennemann, 1974b; Hooper, 1975; Rudes, 1975). While these two conditions have definite implications for underlying representations, they unfortunately have little bearing on certain details of underlying representation. We have already seen that the two conditions, in effect, rule out all phonological abstractness in the form of imaginary or abstract segments, because rules that are true generalizations cannot apply to segments that are abstract. Despite this, a number of questions involving the lexical representation of alternations remain to be answered. These questions will be discussed here in two parts: first, the underlying representations of forms undergoing phonetically conditioned alternations and, second, the representations of forms undergoing morphosyntactically conditioned alternations.

We begin with Vennemann's original proposal for constraining natural generative phonology. His first formulation of the theory called for the No-Ordering Condition and another condition that was stated as a condition on underlying forms, rather than a condition on rules. This condition, the Strong Naturalness Condition (Vennemann, 1971), has two parts, stated as follows:

(3)    (a)    The underlying forms of nonalternating morphemes are identical to their phonetic representations.

(b)  For alternating forms (a morpheme with one or more al-
     lomorphs), one of the allomorphs is listed in the lexicon
     in its phonetic representation, and the others are de-
     rived from it.[1]

This is the strongest possible condition on the abstractness of underlying forms, since it does not allow any abstractness at all. Under this
condition there will be a great deal of redundancy in the lexical representations, but this does not mean that any generalizations that are considered valid are left unexpressed. Rather, the P-rules apply vacuously
to lexical representations as redundancy rules. They also apply generatively, changing feature values, if the rule's structural description arises
in the course of a derivation. MP-rules do not apply redundantly in the
lexicon; rather they apply generatively to derive surface allomorphs
from the basic underlying allomorph.

The Strong Naturalness Condition, along with the No-Ordering Condition, has the same effect as the True Generalization Condition: It requires that surface forms be related to one another in the most direct
fashion possible so that the rules of the grammar represent transparent
surface generalizations rather than abstract generalizations. This is, of
course, the desired result, as we have already seen.

However, the Strong Naturalness Condition as stated above must be
revised. There are two problems with it. The first is that syllable structure conditions and rules motivated by syllable structure cannot apply
to lexical representation since these are in the form of morphemes,
which are not necessarily composed of complete syllables. That is,
while all phonetically motivated rules apply vacuously to lexical representations, syllable structure rules (which are considered to be phonetically motivated) cannot apply without producing incorrect results.
Consider the very familiar process of syllable-final devoicing in
German, which produces alternations such as the following: *Bund*
'league' has the forms [bunt] (nominative singular) and [bundəs] (genitive singular). Suppose we enter in the lexicon a representation /bund/
for 'league' from which we will derive [bunt] and [bundəs]. We do
not want the syllable-final devoicing rule to apply to /bund/ because it
would give us /bunt/ as an underlying representation, and it would be
impossible to derive the surface form [bundəs] without postulating a
totally unmotivated rule of voicing. Of course, the point is that syllable-
final devoicing should not apply to underlying forms such as /bund/ be-

---

[1] The Strong Naturalness Condition has also appeared in Vennemann (1974a,b). It is
quoted here with the permission of Georgetown University Press and the Chicago
Linguistic Society.

cause the final consonant here is not syllable-final; in fact, at this point syllabification is completely irrelevant. Syllabification can be determined only after the inflections are added and words are formed. We could merely state that syllabically motivated rules are barred from the lexicon, but this would be only an ad hoc solution since all other rules would be allowed to apply to lexical representations. (See Vennemann (1974b) and Hooper (1975) for further discussion.) This problem would not seem so serious if another related problem did not exist for the Strong Naturalness Condition as stated above.

The second problem arises when there is a paradigm in which there is no ONE surface allomorph from which the other allomorphs can be derived without devising ad hoc rules. A good example of this sort is a case in Palauan discussed in Schane (1974:300). Consider the following alternations:

(4)

| Present middle verb | Future past (conservative) | Future past (innovative) | |
|---|---|---|---|
| ma-dáŋəb | dəŋób-l | dəŋəb-áll | 'cover opening' |
| ma-té?əb | tə?ib-l | tə?əb-áll | 'pull out' |

Palauan has a productive P-rule that reduces unstressed vowels to schwa. Such a rule is clearly natural and, being a neutralization rule, can only proceed in one direction: from an underlying full vowel to a surface reduced vowel. The problem is that there can never be a surface allomorph of the stem that has both vowels in the full form. Thus there cannot be ONE surface allomorph from which all other allomorphs can be derived unless we devise rules that convert schwas into particular full vowels given certain arbitrary markers on stems. Clearly we want to avoid such a solution as long as the vowel reduction rule is productive.

This problem arises because the requirement that morphemes be listed lexically is not necessarily compatible with the requirement that phonetic detail be present in the lexicon. Morpheme boundaries are determined by meaning and are completely irrelevant to phonetic rules, while phonetic rules are determined universally by physiological constraints and are often unaffected by morphological considerations. Thus a problematic situation for the Strong Naturalness Condition can arise given an accidental combination of morphological and phonetic factors. To see better why this is the case, consider a hypothetical example of a language with the following two P-rules: (a) a neutralization of the distinction between /o/ and /ɔ/ in unstressed syllables: ɔ ⟶ o / [ − stress]; (b) a rule palatalizing /t/ to [č] before /i/. Given these rules, there is no doubt about what the underlying representations should be like, since the directionality of the rules is determined independently. We can derive [o] from /ɔ/, but not vice versa, since there are also contrastive /o/'s in the language; [č] must be derived from /t/ by palatalization, and not the reverse, since we know that palatalization is phonetically natural. Now a problem would arise if, for accidental morphological reasons, this language happened to have paradigms such that a stressed stem happened to be ALWAYS followed by a high front vowel. Allomorphs such as the following would occur:

(5)  (a)  *kɔ́rči*
     (b)  *kortáno*
     (c)  *korčilo*

We cannot take any one of the three allomorphs [kɔ́rč-], [kort-], or [korč-], and derive the other two without devising ad hoc rules. The underlying form must contain /ɔ/, yet the only allomorph with /ɔ/ has a palatal [č] and not [t]. This is a hypothetical example and yet it is a possible example, and we would certainly want the theory to be able to handle such cases.

The Strong Naturalness Condition needs to be revised so that the P-rules can be formulated and apply independently of the morphology. There are two modifications of the theory that have been suggested to rectify this problem. Vennemann (1974b) advocates listing ALL the words of the language in the lexicon in fully specified phonetic form. Thus all three words in (5) would be listed in phonetic form, and the P-rules would serve merely as redundancy rules that relate these forms. On the other hand, the approach advocated in Hudson (1974b; 1975b) and Hooper (1975) allows morphemes to be listed in the lexicon but does not require fully specified matrices; partially specified archisegmental representations are allowed for features predictable by P-rule. Thus, for the paradigm in (5), an archisegmental underlying stem could be posited: /kɔrt-/.

The difference between these approaches revolves around two basic issues: (i) whether or not all the words of the language should be listed in the lexicon, and (ii) whether phonological representations should be fully specified in phonetic form or partially specified in archisegmental form. We turn now to a discussion of some of the arguments on both sides of these two controversies, but two points must be made clear from the outset. One is that these issues regarding underlying forms are important, but they have no consequences for the issues discussed in the preceding chapters. The different models of the lexicon do not have distinct empirical consequences with regard to the issues of abstractness or extrinsic rule order.[2] Second, our evidence concerning lexical representations is quite indirect, and, in general, the hypotheses we will be discussing are not subject to direct empirical disconfirmation because, as I pointed out before, we have access to the lexicon only through the rules of the grammar. Given our state of ignorance about "mental representations" and the fact that the particular issues to be discussed here do not bear on the general issues of concern in this book, I will attempt to summarize the arguments concerning lexical representations without belaboring the points unduly.

Let us begin by discussing the arguments for and against listing ALL the words of the language in the grammar. Notice, first, that I am assuming that SOME words have to be listed in the lexicon. As explained in Chapter 4, these are the words formed by nonproductive processes, where the phonological and/or semantic structure of the word is not totally predictable by general rules. The point here concerns whether or not to list in the lexicon all words formed by productive morphological processes, e.g., inflectional processes, and productive derivational processes such as Spanish diminutive (-ito) and superlative (-ísimo) or English -un-, -ness, -able. One argument given in Thompson (1974) for listing ALL the existing words of the language somewhere in the grammar is that native speakers know what are and what are not the words of their language. For instance, Thompson argues that the -able suffix in English is productive for transitive verbs. Yet speakers feel a definite difference between words such as *washable, unbelievable, readable,* which speakers recognize as English words, and words such as *bathable, driveable, packable,* which speakers recognize as possible, but nonexistent, words of English. This difference can be accounted for in Thompson's model by listing the occurring words in the grammar and, in addition, by allowing the productive processes to generate words that are not listed in the grammar.[3]

Notice, however, that the distinction Thompson draws between

---

[2] Except, as I mentioned in Chapter 5, in Hudson's model, where all MP alternations are lexicalized, but phonetic alternations are not. The MP-rules are, in effect, applied before the P-rules.

[3.] In Chapter 4 I indicated that it would not be necessary to list in the lexicon words derived by productive derivational processes. Thompson advocates listing these words on the basis of the fact that speakers know they are occurring words. It is not clear to me that this is linguistic knowledge. It may rather be mere familiarity with the derived forms, on a par with the familiarity speakers have with phrases such as "my fellow Americans" or "We'll return after a word from our sponsors." In any case, it is of no great consequence to the model whether these words are listed in the grammar, since the rules that derive them must also be listed; and the argument does not affect inflected forms, as I shall point out.

*washable* and *bathable* does not exist for productive inflectional processes. While a verb may exist in the language without an *-able* form, except in special cases, verbs do not exist without inflected forms. Consider the verb Thompson invents, *to foil*, meaning to wrap something in aluminum foil. This word produces a reaction of unfamiliarity at first, but once we have accepted it, we can, without further strangeness, use it in the forms *foils, foiled,* and *foiling*. However, the adjective *foilable* produces another reaction of unfamiliarity. My point here is that the existence of the verb *to foil* implies the existence of the inflected forms but does not imply the existence of derived forms such as *foilable*. This difference between inflected and derived forms indicates that even if strong arguments are found for listing the forms produced by derivational processes in the grammar, it will not imply that forms produced by inflectional processes must also be listed.

In most languages the vast majority of words that undergo inflectional processes are treated in an absolutely regular and systematic way. For this reason it seems unnecessary to include in the grammar a complete specification of every paradigm, whether regular or suppletive. One argument given for including a list of all paradigms concerns defective paradigms (Shopen, 1971; Halle, 1973). For instance, Halle points out that certain Russian verbs lack first person singular forms of the non-past tense. Halle reports that "Russian grammar books frequently note that such forms . . . 'do not exist', or 'are not used', or 'are avoided'" (p. 7).

(6)     *lazŭ*               'I climb'
        *pobezŭ* (or *podeždu*)   'I conquer'
        *deržu*              'I talk rudely'
        *muču*               'I stir up'
        *erunžu*             'I behave foolishly'

Halle feels the absence of these forms is an "accidental gap" (on a par with the lack of a form *blik* in English) and should be expressed by the fact that these forms do not occur in the all-inclusive list of actual Russian words.[4]

There are two points that can be made about this argument. First, the missing members of defective paradigms do not seem to be accidental

---

[4] It is hardly worth mentioning that the formal apparatus proposed in Halle (1973) to account for "gaps" in the set of actual words is absurd. Halle proposes a "filter," which takes as input the unconstrained output of the word-formation rules and marks the nonoccurring words as [ − lexical insertion]. The filter can accomplish this only if it contains a list of all potential, but nonoccurring words of the language. Thus in Halle's model the grammar contains a list of all occurring words AND a list of all nonoccurring words.

gaps in the sense that *blik is, or even in the sense that forms such as *arrivation (from arrive) and *derival (from derive) are. The latter three nonwords could become words quite easily if a meaning were assigned to them. But the Russian first singular present forms have meaning, yet they are not words. Second, the fact that a list might be used for incomplete paradigms does not imply that all paradigms must appear in list form. That is, a list of all forms derived by regular inflectional processes is simply unnecessary.

A complete list of all the words of a language (including all inflected forms) is necessary in NGP only if lexical forms are given in fully specified phonetic representations, as Vennemann (1974b) proposes. Now we must examine the question of whether lexical forms should be given in fully specified phonetic representation or in archisegmental representation.

Vennemann's proposal is that lexical items be represented as words in the phonetic form that they take on when pronounced in isolation. Thus lexical items would be the minimal pronounced units of the language. One argument for this position concerns the explanation of the development of certain sandhi processes in Sanskrit. Of particular interest here is a process that arose at word boundaries and never applied word internally. First, consider the alternations between obstruents in word-internal position (7a) and in prepausal position (7b):

(7)

|  | (a) | (b) |  |
|---|---|---|---|
|  | vācam | vāk | 'voice' |
|  | bhiṣajam | bhiṣak | 'physician' |
|  | samrājam | samrāṭ | 'universal ruler' |
|  | marutam | marut | 'wind' |
|  | padam | pāt | 'foot' |
|  | -vṛdham | -vṛt | 'increasing' |
|  | -stubham | -stup | 'praising' |

The data show a neutralization of some point of articulation features that will not be of interest to us and a complete neutralization of voicing and aspiration in favor of the voiceless unaspirated stop. Word-final obstruents before words beginning in a voiceless obstruent appear in the same form as in the prepausal position in (7b). Before words with a voiced onset (i.e., a vowel, resonant, or voiced obstruent), the final obstruent becomes voiced (asti means 'is'):

(8)     vāg asti
        pād asti
        -stub asti

Notice that the result is the same whether the word-internal variant is voiced, voiceless, or aspirated (compare (7a)). Let me emphasize again that the voicing observed here is restricted to word boundaries and does not occur internally (see (7a) again). Similarly, nasal consonants condition assimilation across word boundaries but not internally. Before *mām* 'me' an obstruent becomes voiced: *vāg mām, marud mām,-stub mām;* or the obstruent becomes nasalized: *vāŋ mām, marun mām, -stum mām.* Such assimilations do not occur inside of words: *runadhmi* 'I hinder', *ātman* 'soul', *agni-* 'fire'.

The proposed explanation for the development of these assimilations across word boundaries is that the final consonants first weakened to voiceless unaspirated stops before a pause, which is a natural environment for weakening. These weakened variants were taken as basic and used word-finally in all positions. Because the final consonant was weak, it was subject to assimilation to the following segment. In Vennemann's model the weakened prepausal consonants are entered in the lexicon in phonetic form, since all words are listed as they are pronounced in isolation. These lexical forms, the adpausal variants, "may next appear in connected speech and may cause or undergo further changes in their new context" (Vennemann, 1974b:364). Thus Vennemann posits the following sequence:

(i) A rule weakens prepausal consonants to voiceless, unaspirated.

(ii) The voiceless, unaspirated consonants are entered in the lexicon in fully specified phonetic detail.

(iii) As a result, the weakened variant is generalized to all positions.

(iv) Assimilation affects the weakened consonants when they occur internally in an utterance.

Vennemann uses this example to argue that fully specified WORDS should be entered in the lexicon. But even if we accept his proposed explanation for the development of this external sandhi process as correct, this does not commit us to adopt his view of the lexicon. The external sandhi can also be explained in a model that allows archisegmental representations of morphemes. The first stage is as in (i) above, the addition of a rule that weakens prepausal consonants. The second stage is the generalization of this rule to word-final position. Then, as above, the weakened segments are subject to assimilation. The difference here is that the model that allows archisegmental representation does not require the immediate restructuring of lexical representation to be identical with prepausal forms, but rather must explain the generalization of weakening to word-final position as rule generalization based on a TENDENCY to take the adpausal variant or the "pronunciation in isolation" form as basic.

Further examples show that the archisegmental model is correct. Vennemann's requirement that the adpausal form of a word ALWAYS be represented in the lexicon is too strong. With this requirement his model is unable to describe certain situations that exist in natural language. These are situations in which a neutralization or a weakening occurs in the adpausal variant of a word and renders it impossible to predict the internal variants from the form of the adpausal variant. For example, in some dialects of American English, at the end of a syllable, /t/ is always reduced to [ʔ]. Thus the word *hit* will be [hɪʔ] before a consonant (as in *hit Carl*) and before a pause. For Vennemann's model this would mean a lexical form [hɪʔ] for the word *hit*. However, when this word occurs before a vowel, the final segment is a flap [r] rather than a glottal stop: [hir] in *hit Alice, hit 'er*. In Vennemann's model then, there would have to be a rule changing a glottal stop into a flap before a vowel. This is an inverse rule; it would not be phonetically natural. Vennemann's model predicts that there can be no synchronic grammar of a natural language in which a phonetically natural weakening or neutralization takes place in utterance-final or syllable-final position. It is clear, however, that such synchronic grammars do exist and that, therefore, the phonetic representation of a word in isolation cannot always be taken as the basic form.

Consider an example of a neutralization in prepausal position in Tuscarora.[5] Word-final [ʔ] and [h] contrast in internal position with each other and with words ending in vowels. However, in prepausal positions these contrasts are neutralized, and words with internal final [ʔ], [h], or a vowel all end in a weak glottal trill, which we will symbolize as [H]. The following singular and plural pairs illustrate the neutralization:

(9)

| Singular | Plural | |
|---|---|---|
| uhčíhrɜH | uhčihrɜʔkɜháʔnɜH | 'bear' |
| tkɜhwǽ·nuH | tkɜhwæ·nuhkɜháʔnɜH | 'panther' |
| θkwarí·nɜH | θkwarinɜkɜháʔnɜH | 'wolf' |

These singular forms above are the prepausal forms. Inside an utterance, the contrast is maintained. The word for 'bear' ends in [ʔ], while 'panther' ends in [h] and 'wolf' in a vowel.

(10)    Rɜ·kwæh    haʔ    uhčíhrɜʔ    waʔná·tkɜH.
        The man    the    bear    he it saw.
        'The man saw the bear.'

---

[5] I am grateful to Blair Rudes for the information about Tuscarora.

Rə̀·kwæh    ha?    tkəhwæ·nuh    wa?ná·tkə̀H.
The man saw a panther.
Rə̀·kwæh    ha?    θkwarí·nə̃    wa?ná·tkə̀H.
The man saw a wolf.

Under Vennemann's proposal, we must take the "pronunciation in isolation" to be the base form, e.g., /uhčíhrə̀H/ for 'bear.' But from this
form it is impossible to predict the feature values of the final segment in
internal position, since some words that end in [H] will internally end
in [?], some will end in [h] and others in vowels. In Tuscarora this neutralization is completely productive and transparent. There is no evidence that it is anything but a simple prepausal neutralization, and it
should be represented as such.

Vennemann's model cannot account for cases such as these, since it
REQUIRES that the adpausal form always be the underlying form. However, observe that in some cases the direction of historical change indicates that there is a TENDENCY for the adpausal variant to be taken as
basic, causing restructuring and rule inversion. One example of rule inversion discussed in Vennemann (1972e) illustrates this point. Many
dialects of English have lost syllable-final /r/. In some dialects a sandhi
rule has developed that supplies final /r/ after a schwa in final position,
before a vowel, e.g., *water may* [wɔrəmey], *water is* [wɔrərɨz]. That
the /r/ is inserted before a vowel and not present in underlying representation is evident from the fact that the /r/ shows up where it does
not occur etymologically: *idea is* [aydiyərɨz]. This case is typical in that
the prepausal form, the form without the /r/, was taken as basic; restructuring seems to favor the adpausal form. However, Vennemann's
model does not represent the favoring of adpausal variants as a tendency, but rather as an absolute: In his model there can be no stage in
English in which there are underlying words that end in /r/ and an
obligatory rule deleting syllable-final /r/.

The argument just given, however, is not an argument against representing lexical forms in fully specified phonetic matrices, but only an
argument against the choice of phonetic forms. Presumably the
problem of the choice of the surface phonetic form to be entered in the
lexicon could be solved. But since the proposal made in Vennemann
(1974b) does not work, the Sanskrit sandhi example cannot be used to
support a lexicon of fully specified phonetic words.

What, then, is the evidence that bears on the choice of a fully specified or an archisegmental lexicon? As I pointed out before, there really is
no empirical evidence that can decide this issue. Rather the preference
for one model over the other seems to be based on assumptions about

what a grammar is like and how the lexicon and rules function. For instance, Vennemann (1974:358) and Stampe (1973a:35) find it desirable to have a model in which underlying forms are pronounceable (although they present no arguments to the effect that they should be pronounceable). On the other hand, I see no reason whatsoever to suppose that lexical forms are pronounceable independently of the P-rules, because the sole and unique function of P-rules is to make forms pronounceable. While Vennemann views P-rules as redundancy conditions on phonetic structure, I view them as dynamic processes that describe the act of articulation. In this view, lexical forms need only contain enough classificatory information to trigger the correct P-rules. With a dynamic view of P-rules, lexical forms should not be pronounceable in themselves; furthermore, it would make no sense to enter in the lexicon the effects of a P-rule (i.e., phonetic detail) except where the information ceases to be predictable (in which case it is no longer detail). Thus if P-rules are viewed as dynamic processes, lexical representations should be archisegmental.

There are two traditional objections to archisegmental representations. One is that leaving blanks in lexical matrices can lead to spurious simplification or the improper use of blanks. This problem does not arise in NGP, for, as Stanley (1967) has shown, if the rules that fill in blanks are not extrinsically ordered, or if a True Generalization Condition is imposed on the rules, the blank values cannot be used improperly. (See also Hooper, 1975.)

The other objection is that one cannot always tell which feature values to leave blank (Stanley, 1967). For instance, if a language has only voiceless obstruents, one could formulate a redundancy rule of the form [− sonorant]⟶[− voice], or the condition could take the form [− voice]⟶[sonorant]. But both generalizations could not be made, for then both [sonorant] and [voice] would be left blank and neither rule could apply. Or, to take an example cited in Schane (1973:44), an English morpheme structure condition states that the first segment in an initial sequence of nonsonorants must be /s/ and can therefore have the feature value for [strident] left blank. But because all strident segments are necessarily nonsonorant, the value for [sonorant] could also be left blank. Since they cannot both be left blank, a choice must be made; but, it is claimed, such a choice would be arbitrary.

This problem also does not arise in NGP. The only rules that fill in blanks are P-rules, the natural phonological processes. Constraints on sequences of major class features (such as [syllabic] and [sonorant]) are expressed in syllable structure conditions, which are positive conditions that do not fill in blanks. (These are discussed in detail in Part II.)

Thus there are never blanks for major class features. Since in all cases in which there is a problem concerning what feature to leave blank, one of the rules concerned predicts a major class feature from a "manner of articulation feature," this problem cannot arise if major class features do not have blanks.[6]

In general, then, the model I am adopting characterizes productive processes, such as regular word-formation processes and regular phonetically conditioned processes, as generative and dynamic rather than static. Output predicted by these processes, both words and phonological features, will not be listed in the grammar. Only phonological and morphological sequences NOT predicted by productive rules will be listed in the lexicon.

## 7.3 The Lexical Representations of Morphophonemic Alternations

The remaining problem relevant to lexical representation is the problem of alternations that take place under morphological conditions in inflectional paradigms. Such alternations may be totally suppletive and involve only one form, as the English alternation between *go* and *went*, or they may apply in small classes, as, for example, the alternation in English *sing, sang, sung*, etc. Or, they may involve larger classes, such as the verbs that have a monophthong/diphthong alternation in Spanish. The question to be discussed here concerns what sort of underlying representation to give to a stem that undergoes alternations in morphological environments.

The model that I have been assuming to this point is the one normally used in generative grammars. In this model totally suppletive forms have to be listed in some component of the grammar (either in the lexicon or in the morphological spell-out rules). Alternations that affect classes of forms (either small or large) are represented in rules that change the feature values of the underlying morpheme into the feature values occurring in the surface allomorphs. (We have already discussed the constraints on the choice of segments occurring in the underlying form—these must be archisegmental representations of segments oc-

---

[6] Furthermore, the type of "rule" that causes the problem, i.e., the type that predicts a major class feature from a lower-order feature, is a rather suspicious type of rule. As we shall see in Section 7.4, the rules that fill in blanks, the P-rules belong to a universal set of phonetically natural processes that describe the possible modifications a phonetic string may undergo in articulation. Rules of the type [−voice] ⟶ [−sonorant], [+strident] ⟶[−syllabic], do not appear to belong to this set.

curring in the surface allomorphs.) The members of an alternation class are identified by an arbitrary diacritic marking in the lexical entry, which matches the diacritic in the rule that governs that alternation. For example, verbs in Spanish that have the *e/ie, o/ue* alternation have to be marked with a diacritic, because there are both verbs with mid vowels and verbs with diphthongs that do not alternate:

(11) | | *montar* | *contar* | *amueblar* |
|---|---|---|---|---|
| | | 'to mount' | 'to tell, count' | 'to furnish' |
| sg. | 1 | *mónto* | *cuénto* | *amuéblo* |
| | 3 | *mónta* | *cuénta* | *amuébla* |
| pl. | 1 | *montámos* | *contámos* | *amueblámos* |

Whether the underlying form of *contar* is /kont-/ or /kwent-/, a diacritic must be used. Similarly, the rule, whether it is a diphthongization rule or a monophthongization rule, must contain a diacritic feature.

This model gives a good representation of several important facts about morphologically conditioned alternations. Such alternations add complexity to the grammar. This complexity is represented by a rule that is necessarily language-specific and contains nonphonetic information. It is also represented by the added complexity of the lexical representations that must include a diacritic marker. The fact that the class of items that undergo the rule are arbitrary and must be learned one by one is represented by the arbitrariness of the diacritic and by the fact that each item must be separately marked. The final fact that is represented is that paradigms with such alternations are subject to leveling in favor of some basic form. The basic form is the underlying form, and leveling is represented as the loss of the language-specific rule. The leveling in Chicano of *contar* and similar forms to *cuentár, cuénto, cuénta, cuentámos*, etc., is viewed as the loss of the diacritic for these forms, with the emergence of the underlying morpheme /kwent-/ in all surface forms. Leveling takes place one paradigm at a time. When all paradigms have been leveled, the rule is lost.

A different model of lexical representation is proposed in Hudson (1974a, and 1975b). Hudson proposes that all nonproductive alternations be represented in the lexicon as suppletive. Instead of using diacritic features to identify lexical items that undergo morphophonemic alternations, these items are identified by the existence of variant forms, or parts of forms, in the lexicon. For example, instead of listing standard Spanish *contar* as in (12a), with the diacritic [ + M] (for monophthongization), Hudson would list *contar* as in (12b):

(12)      a.   /kwent/     b.   /k $\left\{ \begin{matrix} o \\ we \end{matrix} \right\}$ nt/
              +M

The diacritic analysis, (12a) requires a rule that changes /we/ into /o/ when unstressed, and this rule contains the feature [+M]. The suppletive analysis, on the other hand, requires a rule that distributes the allomorphs. The rule would be as follows (but see Chapter 8 for a reformulation):

(13)
$$\left\{ \begin{array}{c} o \\ we \end{array} \right\} \longrightarrow \left\{ \begin{array}{ll} o\,/\,[-\overline{\text{stress}}] \\ we & \text{elsewhere} \end{array} \right\}$$

(The "elsewhere" case can be dispensed with for greater simplicity since it is understood that an alternate not specifically mentioned occurs elsewhere.) No diacritic is needed since the suppletive representation itself serves as a trigger for the distribution rule. The rule obviously does not apply to lexical items such as *montar*, whose underlying form is /mont/, nor to *amueblar*, whose underlying form is /amwebl/, since no suppletion is represented in these forms. One obvious advantage of this type of lexical representation is that lexical forms and the rules that distribute them are related directly, rather than through the intermediate stage represented by the diacritic.

But there are a number of more important arguments for Hudson's model. One is that it does not require any distinction be made between totally irregular alternations such as *go, went* and minor alternations such as *contar, cuento*. All alternations are represented lexically by listing the alternate forms. There are two advantages of this model over the model that uses diacritics for minor alternations. First, no clear-cut distinction can be drawn between "irregular" forms and minor alternations. We simply do not know how many lexical items undergoing the same alternation suffice to form a clause and justify a diacritic, or how few justify separate listings. Furthermore, there does not seem to be any way to find out. Hudson therefore argues on the basis of a general principle of science (which he calls Anaximander's Principle) that if we can find no boundary between totally suppletive and minor alternations, then we had better assign no boundary. Instead, all alternations should receive the same sort of treatment. Another reason for not positing different representations for irregular versus minor alternations is that historical change makes no distinction between the types: ALL morphophonemic alternations are subject to leveling (unless they have a clear association with meaning). In Hudson's model the leveling of alternations is represented as the simplification of lexical entries (with the eventual loss of the distribution rule). Hudson proposes that the direction of leveling is always toward the form designated by the elsewhere case of the distribution rule, since this form is considered to be the basic, or more usual, form. (Note that these advantages apply also to Vennemann's (1974b) model, which we have rejected for other reasons.)

The representation of alternations in lexical entries eliminates a number of formal oddities from the derivation of allomorphs. Starting in the lexicon, it eliminates the notion of one underlying form for two or more allomorphs. Thus we do not have to claim that the lexical representation of the *contar* paradigm is of the phonological form /kwent-/ or /kont-/. Instead we can claim that underlying the *contar* paradigm is a stem with a syllabic nucleus of variable interpretation, depending upon the morphological context. Also, in Hudson's model MP-rules do not CHANGE feature values; they merely state the distribution of alternates. The grammar does not have to include in the derivation of *contamos* a step in which /we/ IS CHANGED INTO /o/. Rather, in the grammar, just as on the surface, /we/ and /o/ exist side by side, and their particular occurrence is determined by the environment.

A related formal oddity that is eliminated in Hudson's model is the existence of an intermediate stage where impossible sequences or strings occur. Consider, as an example, Hudson's analysis of regular plural formation in English. The phonological shape of the lexical entry for plural is as follows:

(14)
$$
\left\{ \begin{bmatrix} +\text{vocalic} \\ +\text{front} \\ +\text{high} \\ +\text{mid} \end{bmatrix} \right\}
\begin{bmatrix} +\text{obstruent} \\ +\text{continuant} \\ +\text{alveolar} \\ +\text{strident} \\ \{+\text{voice}\} \\ z\,/\,s \end{bmatrix}
$$

The braces represent an alternation with Ø: /I/ alternates with Ø, and the feature [+voice] alternates with Ø; which is to say, in some occurrences voicing is neutralized and can be represented by an archisegment, while in other instances the segment is obligatorily voiced.

Now compare this analysis to the one in which the plural morpheme is represented lexically as /+ z +/. As we saw in Section 5.4, when this morpheme is added to a word such as *kiss*, the string /kɪs + z/ is produced. This is an unacceptable string, and two rules are applicable to it: an epenthesis rule that inserts /ɨ/ and the devoicing rule. Recall that with the No-Ordering Condition the devoicing rule is technically applicable to this string, but the rule should not apply, since in the phonetic output the /z/ will not directly follow the /s/; instead a vowel will intervene. The problem in this example and the other bleeding order examples discussed in Section 5.4 is the formal problem of having a stage at which the BASE forms of allomorphs are strung together. As we pointed out earlier, in Hudson's model the problem simply does not arise.

Another aspect of Hudson's model can be illustrated with the example of English plural formation. Phonetically determined variants are also represented in the lexicon. These usually take the form of archisegments, whose values are determined by P-rules. In the case of the alternation in the plural of /ɪ/ with Ø, the alternates are distributed in Hudson's analysis by a surface phonetic constraint that bars sequences of sibilants from occurring in phonetic forms. A distinction is maintained between phonetically conditioned allomorphs, which are distributed by independently necessary P-rules, and morphologically conditioned allomorphs, which are distributed by rules whose only function is just this, to distribute allomorphs. Further intricacies of morphophonemic description will be discussed in Chapter 8.

## 7.4  Naturalness

In this section I will describe the treatment of markedness and rule naturalness in NGP. There are two major ways that this theory of naturalness differs from the theory of marking and linking proposed in Chapter Nine of the "Sound Pattern of English": (i) There is no difference posited between underlying naturalness of phonemic inventories and the naturalness of rules; i.e., there is no difference between static and dynamic naturalness (Stampe, 1973a,b; Chen 1973). (ii) There is no evaluation measure for computing degrees of naturalness among rules; rather, ALL P-rules are natural. The purpose here will be merely to outline this theory, to show how a theory incorporating (i) works, and to present the advantages of (ii). I will not undertake a full-scale presentation of the merits of this theory over the Markedness Theory of Chomsky and Halle. For arguments that bear on this issue, see Chen (1973) and Stampe (1973b).

The treatment of naturalness in NGP is a modification of the notion of naturalness developed by Stampe (1969; 1973a,b) and based on Jakobson (1941 [1968]). Stampe draws a distinction between "natural processes" and "acquired rules." Natural processes are the obligatory, inviolable phonological rules of the language. They do not have exceptions, although they may be restricted to casual speech (i.e., they may be variable). They make minimal phonetic substitutions, and they have a phonetic function; i.e., they are natural. There is a universal inventory of such natural processes, which are, according to Stampe's theory, innate. Acquired rules, on the other hand, have many exceptions and are easily suppressed (for example, they do not "interfere" in second language acquisition). They make more radical substitutions. They are not natural; rather, they are arbitrary, language-specific, and must be learned.[7]

The distinction Stampe draws is quite similar to the distinction in NGP between P-rules, on the one hand, and MP-rules and via-rules, on the other. An example that Stampe gives of an acquired rule is the K ⟶ S rule of English, exemplified by pairs such as *electri* [k], *electri* [s] *ity*. This rule would be a via-rule in our framework. Stampe's natural processes include the rule of flapping in English, e.g., *write* and *wri*[ɾ]*er*, and the rule of syllable-final devoicing in German. These are P-rules in NGP. The major difference between the two frameworks is that Stampe allows his natural processes to be extrinsically ordered and therefore allows more abstractness in underlying representation than is allowed in NGP.

The more concrete approach of NGP has two advantages over Stampe's approach. One advantage is that the rules postulated in NGP are always subject to empirical confirmation or disconfirmation. In Stampe's theory, however, because he allows rule order and some abstractness, the existence of a postulated natural process in a particular language cannot always be proven or disproven. For instance, Stampe (1973:32) posits for English a context-free, paradigmatic process, ŋ ⟶ n. This process bars all velar nasals from lexical representation. This paradigmatic process is overridden in derivation by two syntagmatic processes, nasal assimilation and g-deletion, which convert a phonemic representation /sɪŋg/ into a phonetic representation [sɪŋ]. The evidence for the paradigmatic process, ŋ ⟶ n, is the English adaptation of the Vietnamese name *Nguyen*, with initial [ŋ] in Vietnamese, which is modified to [nuyen] in English. But this adaptation can be accommodated by the more restricted rule, which is surface-true in English.

(15)              [ + nasal] ⟶ [ + anterior] / #＿＿＿

The existence of a more general rule cannot be confirmed or disconfirmed, and, therefore, such a rule should not be allowed. Indeed the more general rule would not be allowed by the True Generalization Condition.

The second advantage of NGP is also a consequence of the True Generalization Condition. The natural rules of NGP are FORMALLY distinct

---

[7] Although I am using some basic concepts of Stampe's theory, I do not agree that natural rules are innate in the sense that he claims they are. His hypothesis predicts that all rules of phonetic detail are innate; however, it is clear that even these rules must be acquired. That is, English speaking children must LEARN to aspirate voiceless stops, even though this aspiration becomes automatic and nonsuppressable.

from all other rules because they are the ONLY rules with purely phonetic conditioning. Thus we can make the strongest possible claim about rule naturalness, i.e., that ALL phonetically motivated rules are natural.

Compare this claim to TGP accounts of rule naturalness in which some rules are thought to be natural while others are considered less natural and even "crazy." Under this weaker hypothesis it is necessary to develop an evaluation measure that can characterize degrees of rule naturalness. A moment's reflection will reveal that this would be an infinite task in a theory with no constraints on what may be a rule, since the theory must be able to evaluate the naturalness of every logically possible rule constructable within the formalism provided by the theory. Furthermore, in a theory that allows abstract rules, it is not clear how a notion of "naturalness" could be developed and characterized. Naturalness in this theory could not have a phonetic base, since the abstract rules it allows apply at a deep level far from the realities of surface phonetics.

The task of a theory of rule naturalness in NGP is much more manageable. The theory must specify the set of possible phonetically conditioned rules for any language. This set may be large but it is certainly finite, for it is well known that many of the same processes apply in language after language. Just as there is a finite set of phonetic features that can characterize the phonetic possibilities of the languages of the world, so there is a finite number of possible assimilations, deletions, insertions, metatheses, etc., that occur as P-rules in the languages of the world. The hypothesis is that all of these processes are phonetically explainable or natural. And the theory of rule naturalness can be more than a list of processes, since a general phonetic explanation can be associated with each rule, and, furthermore, certain implicational relations will hold between rules of related types (Chen, 1973, 1974; and Part II of this book).

Even if this very strong hypothesis turns out to be wrong, it is an extremely useful hypothesis. Theories of rule naturalness have all suffered so far from the same basic inadequacy—the lack of coherent characterization of what is meant by "natural." The practice has been to make subjective judgments about what is natural (Schane, 1972). Faced with a particular process, a phonologist will call it natural if it has a rather obvious phonetic explanation, as, for instance, the assimilation of point of articulation in contiguous consonants; or the process will be called natural if it has been observed to occur in several distinct languages, even if the phonetic cause is unknown. Neither of these criteria is reliable, however. The first is deficient because in many cases pho-

netic explanation has not been developed; the second is unreliable because it is usually based on an individual's experience, which is typically haphazard. The usual approach to the problem of naturalness
turns out to be circular. We cannot determine what the natural rules are
until we have some well-developed concept of naturalness, but we
cannot develop a concept of naturalness until we have the empirical
input, i.e., the corpus of natural rules.

As a working hypothesis, our strong hypothesis cuts the circularity
out of the methodology. If we predict that all surface-true, phonetically
conditioned rules are "natural," then we have a body of data on which
to base a substantive concept of naturalness. Of course, the hypothesis
would not be worth much if it did not have some a priori plausibility,
but it does. First, the great majority of P-rules in any language DO have
obvious and well-known phonetic explanations, so it is not a great leap
to claim that they all do if such explanations could be developed. Second, we assume that all linguistic phenomena have some raison d'être
and that there is no reason to have a P-rule if it does not optimize the
phonetic string in some way.

Let me illustrate some of the dangers of approaching naturalness with
only subjective criteria. In "How Do Languages Get 'Crazy' Rules?"
Bach and Harmes (1972) assume that languages may have unnatural or
"crazy" rules even among the phonetically statable, productive rules. A
rule that they claim is "crazy" is the Japanese rule affricating /t/ to [ts]
before /ɯ/. Another facet of the same general process, the palatalization
of /t/ to [č] before /i/, is considered natural.[8] On what basis do Bach and
Harms consider t ⟶ ts/____ɯ unnatural? There are two bases: One is
that such a process is quite unfamiliar to them; and the other is that the
rule, collapsed with the t ⟶ č/____i rule, looks quite unnatural in
Chomsky–Halle features because it requires an agreement of the features [back] and [anterior] (Bach and Harmes, 1972:14).

(16) $\begin{bmatrix} -\text{sonorant} \\ +\text{coronal} \end{bmatrix} \longrightarrow \begin{bmatrix} +\text{delayed release} \\ +\text{strident} \\ \alpha\,\text{anterior} \end{bmatrix} / \underline{\hspace{1em}} \begin{bmatrix} V \\ +\text{high} \\ \alpha\,\text{back} \end{bmatrix}$

Since [anterior] and [back] express almost opposite notions, their agreement cannot be an assimilation. So this rule must be considered unnatural.

---

[8] There is another complication in the general process, because among the voiced consonants [dz] from /d/ before /ɯ/ is variably [z], and the palatalized version of /z/ before /i/ is
[j]. I will not deal with these details here, although they obviously demand an explanation.

Their judgment on the naturalness of this rule was premature. But such a judgment is allowed by a theory that allows unnatural rules. Consider now how this rule would be evaluated under the hypothesis that all P-rules are natural. First, we must establish that this rule is a P-rule, but it is quite clear that it is. It is a very regular, very strong, and virtually unsuppressable process in Japanese. The next step, then, is to see if there is any way this rule can be interpreted as natural. Actually, there is a rather straightforward phonetic explanation for the affrication of /t/ in the transition to the high back vowel. In anticipation of the high vowel, the tongue is high; when the coronal consonant is released, the tip of the tongue is pulled straight back for [ɯ], creating friction at the alveolar ridge, and thus affrication. Viewed articulatorily, the process does not seem unnatural. I would argue, then, that the strong hypothesis is more useful than the weaker one, because it forces us to look more carefully for substantive explanations. Under the strong hypothesis we can base our concept of naturalness on the linguistic data, rather than on a priori assumptions and haphazard experience.

Notice further that a theory of natural rules calls for the development of a feature system that can adequately capture the motivation for natural processes. The feature systems developed by Jakobson, Chomsky and Halle, and Ladefoged are all directed toward the expression of phonemic and phonetic contrasts and are only partially adaptable to the expression of processes. The Japanese process discussed here is not well described in classificatory features. In fact there is no reason to expect classificatory features to be useful in describing or explaining phonological processes (see Mowrey, 1975).

To this point we have established that natural generative theory will specify the universal set of P-rules occurring in the languages of the world. In this way the notion "possible P-rule" will be strictly defined. The "markedness" of individual segments will be defined by the same universal set of rules. In this theory markedness and naturalness are not two separate concepts, but rather result from a single concept and a single set of rules.

In contemporary theories phonological markedness describes the naturalness of phonemic inventories. Markedness theory attempts to account for certain universals of language, such as the fact that all languages have voiceless obstruents, or, stated differently, if a language does not have a voicing contrast in obstruents, its obstruent phonemes are all voiceless (Jakobson, 1941 [1972]). This fact leads Chomsky and Halle to formulate a marking convention of the following form:

(17) $\qquad$ [u voice] $\longrightarrow$ [ $-$ voice] / [ $-$ $\overline{\text{son}}$ ]

This convention states that voiceless obstruents are unmarked (natural) and voiced obstruents are marked (less natural).

In the theory I am proposing, based on Stampe's theory, the fact that a language may have ONLY voiceless obstruents and no voiced obstruents is represented by the following rule, which is a member of the universal set of natural rules:

(18)                 $[-\text{son}] \longrightarrow [-\text{voice}]$

Few languages have this rule in its unrestricted form, but it exists as a possibility. The opposite possibility, $[-\text{son}] \longrightarrow [+\text{voice}]$, does not exist; there are no languages in which all obstruents are voiced.

Context-free rules of this sort account for naturalness in phonemic systems. However, we need not separate the notion of naturalness in phonemic systems from the naturalness of rules; phonemic systems are natural because they result from the application of natural rules. This context-free rule is only a part of a larger rule schema that specifies the natural values of the feature [voice] in several contexts. The following is a part of a universal rule for specifying [voice] for obstruents:[9]

(19)   $\begin{bmatrix} -\text{sonorant} \\ <+\text{continuant}> \end{bmatrix} \longrightarrow \begin{cases} [+\text{voice}]/V\underline{\phantom{xx}}V & \text{(a)} \\ [-\text{voice}] & \text{(b)} \end{cases}$

A language may utilize any one of the subparts of this rule; however, if both (a) and (b) apply, they must be disjunctively ordered with (a) preceding (b). The angled brackets around [+continuant] mean that the rule may affect only fricatives, or it may affect all obstruents, but it may not affect ONLY stops (except trivially where a language has only stops). This reflects the claim that if there is a voicing contrast for fricatives, there will also be one for stops (because there is no rule [−continuant] $\longrightarrow$[−voice]), and that if stops undergo a context-sensitive process involving voicing, fricatives do as well (Foley, 1972). That is, intervocalic voicing affects fricatives before stops (as in Latin and Old English). The following language situations are predicted, given rule (19).

1. All obstruents are phonetically voiceless ((b) without [+continuant]).
2. All fricatives are phonetically voiceless ((b) with [+continuant]).
3. Voicing is not contrastive, and obstruents are voiced in vocalic environments (part (a)), voiceless elsewhere (part (b)).

---

[9] I am not in a position to argue for the details of the CONTENT of this rule; the point here is to illustrate the form of such rules. The rule for voicing will have a number of other subparts, e.g., a rule of syllable-final devoicing and various assimilation rules.

4. The same as (3) but for fricatives only ((a) and (b) with [+continuant]).

5. Voicing is contrastive, but the contrast is neutralized in favor of [+voice] intervocalically (part (a) only).

6. The same as (5) but for fricatives only (part (a) with [+continuant]).

At the same time, a number of situations are considered impossible. Here are some examples. The theory predicts there will be no language in which the following occur:

1. All obstruents are phonetically voiced.

2. A voicing contrast exists for fricatives only.

3. Intervocalic obstruents are DEVOICED by rule (or voicing is neutralized intervocalically in favor of the voiceless value).

These are strong claims, subject to empirical disconfirmation. However, they represent the TYPE of statements that a theory of naturalness should contain.

Notice further that the claims made in this theory are consistent with Jakobson's implicational universals in a way that the Marking Conventions are not. The Marking Convention given by Chomsky and Halle regarding [voice] in obstruents states merely that voiceless obstruents are unmarked and voiced obstruents are marked. A system in which all obstruents are voiced is considered possible; it is merely deemed to be a complex system. Such systems, however, do not exist, and the theory should reflect this fact.

Another positive aspect of the treatment of naturalness described here is a consequence of the fact that there is no fully specified phonemic level in NGP. A fully specified phonemic level leads to counterfactual representations and statements. For example, in the model of Chomsky and Halle if the point of articulation of a nasal consonant is completely neutralized before another consonant, as it is in Spanish, then in each of its occurrences the nasal consonant would be represented as /n/, the unmarked nasal. That is, *bomba, donde, ganga* would be /bonba/, /donde/, /ganga/. But it has been pointed out (by Vennemann, 1972f; Schane, 1973) that /n/ is not natural or unmarked before a labial or a velar consonant; rather, the natural situation is the one in which the nasal is assimilated. However, the difficulty in the Chomsky and Halle theory cannot be remedied merely by adding a marking convention to that affect, because Marking Conventions apply at the phonemic level of representation. Phonemically, Spanish *ganga* is /ganga/, since there is no /ŋ/ phoneme in Spanish. Thus the phonemic representation itself is unnatural, although the phonetic representation is natural. This contradiction results entirely from the decision to posit a fully specified phonemic level, which leads to the counterfactual representation of [gaŋga] as /ganga/. Such representations lead in turn to erroneous statements about naturalness. (See also Hooper, 1975.)

This example nicely illustrates the inseparability of underlying naturalness and rule naturalness. As I mentioned before, underlying representations are natural if they feed into a system of natural rules. In Spanish, where a natural rule supplies the values for the point of articulation features for nasals before consonants, these feature values are unspecified lexically. The fact that it is natural for these feature values to agree with the feature values of the following consonant is represented by the existence of the nasal assimilation rule in the grammar and by the attendant reduction of lexical complexity resulting from the occurrence of blanks rather than plus or minus values.

# 8

# Morphophonemics in Spanish Verbs

When introducing a new theory, it is customary to demonstrate how the theory handles linguistic data by analyzing in some detail a substantial portion of some language. Such an analysis serves as a model for further analyses and demonstrates the ability of the theory to handle a wide range of data. Since the present theory is developed from a well-known theory (transformational generative phonology), certain aspects of the model do not need to be further illustrated here. In particular, the representation of surface-true, phonetically conditioned rules will be the same in this theory as in previous theories. Certainly a great deal remains to be learned about these rules, i.e., what is their phonetic motivation, what is the universal set of such rules, how naturalness can be defined, and what is an appropriate feature system for stating such rules. But these questions go beyond the scope of what I set out to demonstrate in this book. For our purposes the representation of phonetically conditioned alternations is noncontroversial. The controversy instead centers around the representation of morphophonemic alternations.

In previous chapters I have discussed the consequences of limiting the use of phonological abstractions in describing morphophonemic phenomena, and I have indicated that the alternative usually involves including more nonphonological information in the rules of the grammar. But this is not the end of the problem: There is still a wide range of solutions to many morphophonological problems. To give the theory better predictive powers, some important questions about morphology and the interaction of morphology and phonology need to be answered. Some of these questions will be discussed in this chapter, but none of them will be given a final answer. I can only attempt to identify the problems and some potential solutions.

The data to be analyzed include the regular verb conjugations plus certain classes of verb stems that have vocalic alternations. These forms have been analyzed many times before (Saporta, 1959; Foley, 1965; Harris, 1969; Brame and Bordelois, 1973; Harris, 1974b, 1975; just to name a few) and part of the analysis is noncontroversial; however, it is necessary to present an NGP analysis of both problematic and nonproblematic data to demonstrate that the theory works for a fairly substantial body of data.

In Section 3.1 we have discussed the important role that stress plays as an indicator of tense. We will assume that the stress rules as developed there are incorporated into the grammar and concentrate here on the segmental representations of morphemes. We will illustrate below the role of the stress rules in the derivations.

The discussion will be organized as follows: In Sections 8.2, 8.3, and 8.4 we examine the morphological composition of the Spanish verb, dealing primarily with the generation of the correct allomorphs. In Sections 8.5 and 8.6 the alternations in the stem vowels of certain verbs are analyzed. In Section 8.7 some additional problems regarding these analyses are discussed.

## 8.1 Person/Number Markers

Again let me emphasize that the analysis presented here is tentative. There are many places where a choice between two or more alternative analyses must be made arbitrarily. I would like to emphasize the arbitrariness of certain decisions because these are precisely the cases that need to be studied in order to develop a theory of morphology that has psychological validity. In (1) I have given a complete list of the forms of regular verbs in Spanish (omitting compound tenses), and I have assigned morpheme boundaries to the forms. Following Harris (1974b), will assume that a verb form consists of a stem and at most three suffixes: [stem + theme vowel (ThV) + tense/mood (TM) + person/number (PN)]; e.g., imperfect indicative, third person plural: [cant + a + ba + n]. Not all forms contain all three suffixes: e.g., present indicative lacks an explicit marker of TM; first singular present indicative also lacks a ThV.

I will begin the discussion of morphological spell-out rules with the PN markers and progress leftward towards the stem giving the underlying representation of the various formatives. To refer to the morphological categories, I will use the traditional names (e.g., present subjunctive, future, etc.) rather than designating these by binary features, since in most cases the latter results in more cumbersome formalism. I will use binary morphological features that designate conjugation classes. Second and third conjugations function identically for many forms; thus they will be referred to as [− 1st conjugation]. Then second and third will be further distinguished by the feature [± 3rd conjugation]. Further I will refer to the future and conditional tenses together as the subsequent tenses and distinguish between them with the feature [past]. Future is [− past], that is, the future is "subsequent" to the present, and conditional is [+ past], i.e., subsequent to some time in the past.

In the following table, orthography is used except where othographic *i* represents [y]. Regular verb conjugations are given.

| (1) | *cantar* 'to sing'<br>First Conjugation | *comer* 'to eat'<br>Second Conjugation | *vivir* 'to live'<br>Third Conjugation |
|---|---|---|---|
| **Present Indicative** | | | |
| sg.1 | cánt +    + o | cóm +    + o | vív +    + o |
| 2 | cánt + a + s | cóm + e + s | vív + e + s |
| 3 | cánt + a | cóm + e | vív + e |
| pl.1 | cant + á + mos | com + é + mos | viv + í + mos |
| 2 | cant + á + ys | com + é + ys | viv + í + s |
| 3 | cánt + a + n | cóm + e + n | vív + e + n |
| **Present Subjunctive** | | | |
| | cánt + e | cóm + a | |
| | cánt + e + s | cóm + a + s | |
| | cánt + e | cóm + a | |
| | cant + é + mos | com + á + mos | |
| | cant + é + ys | com + á + ys | |
| | cánt + e + n | cóm + a + n | |

| *cantar* 'to sing'<br>First Conjugation | *comer* 'to eat'<br>Second Conjugation | *vivir* 'to live'<br>Third Conjugation |
|---|---|---|

**Preterite (Indicative)**

| | |
|---|---|
| cant +   + é | com +   + í |
| cant + á + ste | com + í + ste |
| cant +   + ó | com +   + yó |
| cant + á + mos | com + í + mos |
| cant + á + steys | com + í + steys |
| cant + á + ron | com + yé + ron |

**Imperfect Indicative**

| | |
|---|---|
| cant + á + ba | com + í + a |
| cant + á + ba + s | com + í + a + s |
| cant + á + ba | com + í + a |
| cant + á + ba + mos | com + í + a + mos |
| cant + á + ba + ys | com + í + a + ys |
| cant + á + ba + n | com + í + a + n |

**Imperfect Subjunctive**

| | |
|---|---|
| cant + á + ra | com + yé + ra |
| cant + á + ra + s | com + yé + ra + s |
| cant + á + ra | com + yé + ra |
| cant + á + ra + mos | com + yé + ra + mos |
| cant + á + ra + ys | com + yé + ra + ys |
| cant + á + ra + n | com + yé + ra + n |

**Imperfect Subjunctive**

| | |
|---|---|
| cant + á + se | com + yé + se |
| cant + á + se + s | com + yé + ses |
| cant + á + se | com + yé + se |
| cant + á + se + mos | com + yé + se + mos |
| cant + á + se + ys | com + yé + se + ys |
| cant + á + se + n | com + yé + se + n |

**Future**

| | | |
|---|---|---|
| cant + a + ré | com + e + ré | viv + i + ré |
| cant + a + rá + s | com + e + rá + s | viv + i + rás |
| cant + a + rá | com + e + rá | viv + i + rá |
| cant + a + ré + mos | com + e + ré + mos | viv + i + ré + mos |
| cant + a + ré + ys | com + e + ré + ys | viv + i + ré + ys |
| cant + a + rá + n | com + e + rá + n | viv + i + rá + n |

**Conditional**

| | |
|---|---|
| cant + a + ría | com + e + ría |
| cant + a + ría + s | com + e + ría + s |

| *cantar* 'to sing'<br>First Conjugation | *comer* 'to eat'<br>Second Conjugation | *vivir* 'to live'<br>Third Conjugation |
|---|---|---|
| cant + a + ría<br>cant + a + ría + mos<br>cant + a + ría + ys<br>cant + a + ría + n | com + e + ría<br>com + e + ría + mos<br>com + e + ría + ys<br>com + e + ría + n | |

Infinitive

| cant + á + r | com + é + r | viv + í + r |
|---|---|---|

Present Participle

| cant + á + ndo | com + yé + ndo | viv + yé + ndo |
|---|---|---|

Past Participle

| cant + á + do | com + í + do | viv + í + do |
|---|---|---|

Imperative

| cant + á + d | com + é + d | viv + í + d |
|---|---|---|

The first person singular has a discrete marker only in the present indicative and the preterite. In the present indicative the /o/ of first singular is clearly a PN marker, since it is constant in the three conjugation classes. No ThV appears before the /o/, but a rule will be presented later to take care of the ThV's. In the preterite the matter is not so clear. The first singular suffixes /e/ and /i/ carry information about both the person/number of the verb and about its conjugation class. In fact the [− 1st conjugation] form is identical to the ThV for past tense forms. Thus we must ask whether /e/ and /i/ are ThV's or PN markers. Since the /i/ of *comí* is identical to the ThV, it could be considered the ThV. However, the same tack cannot be followed for the /e/ of *canté*, since it differs in quality from the ThV. Therefore I will generate both V's as PN markers. But note that /i/ and /e/ are restricted to first and non-first conjugation by the rule, in effect, signaling the conjugation class of the verb. The morphological spell-out rule for first singular is tentatively given as:

$$(2) \quad [\text{1st sing.}] \longrightarrow \left\{ \begin{array}{l} \varnothing / [\text{pres ind}] + \underline{\quad} \\[4pt] \left[ \begin{array}{l} +\text{syll} \\ -\text{low} \\ -\text{back} \\ \alpha\text{high} \end{array} \right] / [-\alpha \text{1st conj.}] + [\text{pret.}] + \underline{\quad} \\[4pt] \varnothing \end{array} \right\}$$

Rule (2) rewrites the first singular morpheme as /o/ in the present indicative, as /i/ or /e/ for the preterite. For all other categories first singular has no segmental realization, signified by ∅ as the elsewhere case. A simplification of the notation, following Hudson (1975b), allows for the omission of ∅ with the understanding that if no elsewhere case is stated, the morpheme rewrites as ∅ for all categories not mentioned in the rule. Bear in mind also that these rules produce archisegmental representations, which are subject to all the P-rules of the language.

Let us turn now to the third singular marker, which has a nonempty realization only in the preterite. Again, the conjugation classes differ: /o/ appears in first conjugation (e.g., *cantó*) and /yo/ occurs in second and third conjugations (e.g., *comió, vivió*). For first conjugation, /o/ will be a PN marker, as /e/ is. The problem with /yo/ is in deciding whether it is bimorphemic, consisting of a ThV plus PN marker /i + o/, which can be converted to [yo] by a general P-rule of Spanish, or monomorphemic, a PN morpheme consisting of two segments. I have chosen the second alternative. My only reason is this: If the /y/ of *comió* were a ThV, then we would expect it to be stressed, as are the other ThVs: *comí, comiste, comimos*, etc. Since it is not stressed, I suspect that it is underlyingly a glide. Thus the rule for third singular is (3).

(3)     [3rd sing.] ⟶ ⟨y⟩ o /⟨– 1st conj.⟩ +[pret.] + ____

(This rule reads: Third singular rewrites as /yo/ in the second and third conjugation of the preterite, as /o/ elsewhere in the preterite, and as ∅ in all other categories.) Historically, these preterite forms (from the Latin perfect tense) contained both a transparent theme vowel and a person/number marker, as in Vulgar Latin (Menéndez Pidal, 1968:310).

(4)          1st   *canta + i*      *comi + i*
             3rd   *canta + ut*    * *comi + ut*

In these forms the PN markers are /-i/ for first singular and /-ut/ for third singular. When /ai/, /au/, and /ii/ monophthongized, the ThV and PN markers fused. In an abstract grammar one could reconstruct ThV's and the PN markers /-i/ and /-u/ for these forms, as Harris (1969) does. The rules that derive the surface forms are restricted for the most part to just these derivations (see Harris, 1969:81–86; 1974b). The abstract analysis is motivated by a desire to set up just one underlying phonological representation for each morpheme. It results in simpler morphological spell-out rules and more complex phonological rules. By contrast, in the analysis I am proposing, the morphological rules are slightly complicated but no other rules are needed at all. This is a typical difference between TGP and NGP. To my knowledge the TGP assumption that all allomorphs should be traced to a common source in a synchronic grammar has never been justified. On the other hand, the more direct representation of allomorphy is easy to justify, since it assumes that the speaker–hearer associates the sound directly with the meaning. The burden of proof is clearly on those who propose that speakers make the sound–meaning correspondence in a less direct manner.

Second person singular is /-s/ in all tenses except preterite, where it is /-ste/ in standard Spanish. Second person plural is /-ys/ everywhere except after /i/ in present indicative, where the /y/ is deleted because of the preceding /i/, and in the preterite, where the form is /steys/. There are two ways of analyzing the /-ste-/ that is characteristic of second person preterite: It could be generated as a preterite marker occurring only in second person or a second person marker occurring only in the preterite. The difference between these approaches is minimal; I will arbitrarily opt for the second.

Let us consider the singular forms first. They may be generated by the following rule:[1]

(5)
$$\begin{bmatrix} \text{2nd person} \\ \text{singular} \end{bmatrix} \longrightarrow \begin{cases} \text{ste} / [\text{preterite}] + \underline{\quad} \\ \text{s} \end{cases}$$

The rule for plural is similar:

(6)
$$\begin{bmatrix} \text{2nd person} \\ \text{plural} \end{bmatrix} \longrightarrow \langle \text{ste} \rangle \, \text{ys} / \langle \text{preterite} \rangle + \underline{\quad}$$

The angled brackets relate /ste/ to the preterite only; /ys/ occurs for all other tenses. The /y/ does not appear phonetically in third conjugation, present indicative, *vivís*. The reason is that sequences of vowels and glides agreeing in backness and height do not occur in Spanish. Let us suppose that this is a phonetic constraint in Spanish. There are two ways to handle the alternation of /y/ with ∅. We can adopt the model proposed in Hudson (1975b) and represent the second plural morpheme as /(y)s/. This represents two allomorphs, /ys/ and /s/. To choose the correct allomorph we invoke the phonetic constraint, which, given a structure such as (7a), will reject the ill-formed string, leaving (7b).

---

[1] I have made no attempt to relate the /s/ in /ste/ to the /s/ of the elsewhere allomorph, because this would make it impossible to relate the rules for singular and plural. Furthermore, in many dialects of Latin America an /s/ is added to /ste/, e.g., *cantastes* or *cantates* (Rosenblat, 1946:222–278), indicating that /ste/ is not analyzed as containing the second person morpheme. In these dialects it might be more accurate to generate /ste/ as a preterite marker.

(7)  (a) $viv + i + \left\{\begin{matrix} y \\ \varnothing \end{matrix}\right\}$ s

(b) $viv + i + \varnothing$s

Alternatively, we could generate second person plural as /ys/ and apply a rule to delete the /y/ after /i/. There are no clear empirical differences between the alternatives. I have adopted the latter because, for phonetically conditioned alternations, there is no motivation for representing all alternants lexically.

The rules for the second person morphemes may be abbreviated as one rule, since there are many similarities between the singular and plural forms:

(8)  $\left[\begin{matrix} \text{2nd person} \\ \langle \text{plural} \rangle \end{matrix}\right] \longrightarrow \left\{\begin{matrix} \text{ste } \langle \text{y s} \rangle / [\text{preterite}] + \underline{\quad} \\ \text{y} \quad \text{s} \end{matrix}\right\}$

The first person plural morpheme is the most constant in standard Spanish, always appearing as /-mos/:

$\left[\begin{matrix} \text{1st person} \\ \text{plural} \end{matrix}\right] \longrightarrow \text{mos}$

The third person singular has no explicit marker except in the preterite, which was treated in rule (3). The third person plural is always marked by /-n/ and marked additionally by /ro/ (giving /ron/) in the preterite. Parallel to the second person /ste/, I will take /ro/ to be a third plural marker occurring in the preterite. The rule for third plural is quite simple:

(9)  $\left[\begin{matrix} \text{3rd person} \\ \text{plural} \end{matrix}\right] \longrightarrow \langle \text{ro} \rangle \text{ n} / \langle \text{preterite} \rangle + \underline{\quad}$

## 8.2 Tense/Aspect Markers

TM morphemes show up in the present subjunctive, the imperfect indicative and subjunctive, and the future and conditional. In the present subjunctive the /e/ of first conjugation and the /a/ of second and third conjugation could be considered as altered forms of the ThV. But it is more direct to generate these vowels as TM markers and not generate a ThV, since there are, as I mentioned above, other cases where the ThV does not appear. Thus the rule for the present subjunctive marker is (10).

(10)  [present subjunctive] $\longrightarrow \left\{\begin{matrix} \text{a} / [-\text{1st conj.}] + \underline{\quad} \\ \text{e} \end{matrix}\right\}$

The imperfect indicative forms consist of a stem, the ThV (which is stressed), and a TM marker, which is /ba/ for first conjugation, /a/ for second and third conjugation, as in *cantába, comía,* and *vivía* (first or third singular). Harris (1969) sets up one underlying form /ba/ for all conjugations and deletes the /b/ in the environment following /i/ and a morpheme boundary. On the other hand, we will generate /ba/ and /a/ directly as two allomorphs by the following rule:[2]

(11)      imperfect indicative $\longrightarrow$ $\left\{ \begin{array}{l} \text{a/}[-\text{1st conj.}] + \underline{\phantom{xx}} \\ \text{ba} \end{array} \right\}$

I have chosen to use a completely morphological environment to predict the nonoccurrence of /b/ rather than a partial phonological environment referring to the quality of the theme vowel, because there is no indication that the properties of /i/ influence the nonoccurrence of /b/. There is, for example, one irregular verb, *ir* 'to go', which has the /b/ in the imperfect, *iba* (first or third singular), despite a preceding /i/.

The past subjunctive has two alternate markers, /ra/ and /se/. The choice of one or the other alternate is partially grammatical, partially stylistic, and varies a great deal according to regional dialects. I will not go into the problem here but will merely state an informal rule that generates both allomorphs:

(12)                [past subjunctive] $\longrightarrow$ $\left\{ \begin{array}{l} \text{se} \\ \text{ra} \end{array} \right\}$

The future and conditional tenses raise a number of questions, largely because of their historical source. They were derived historically from a compound construction consisting of the infinitive followed by an auxiliary, a finite form of *haber*, e.g., *cantar* + *he* $\longrightarrow$ *cantaré, can-*

---

[2] A shorter statement of rule (11) would be the following:

(i) imperfect indicative $\longrightarrow$ $\langle$ b $\rangle$ a/$\langle$+ 1st conj.$\rangle$

This rule, however, implies that /ba/ is the special case and /a/ is the elsewhere case. This implication is incorrect, for first conjugation is the unmarked conjugation class. Since only conjugation class is involved in this allomorphic distribution, it is best to represent the first conjugation form as the elsewhere form. Dialectal evidence points in this direction as well, since there have been reported forms such as *traíba* and *tráiba* for standard *traía* (Rosenblat, 1946:238), but there are no cases of the allomorph /a/ being used in first conjugation.

The situation with these allomorphs is slightly unusual. Ordinarily, the shorter form segmentally is the elsewhere form, i.e., the unmarked form. This is the case for second person, where /s/ is unmarked singular, /ys/ unmarked plural, and /ste/ and /steys/ are the preterite forms. Similarly, third plural /ron/ occurs in the preterite and /n/ elsewhere. In these cases the simpler rule formulation allowed by the use of angled brackets is appropriate.

*tar* + *había* ⟶ *cantaría*. In a synchronic grammar, we could take the stem for the future and conditional to be the infinitive, but this would involve making some claims about meaning that are untenable. In particular, we would have to claim that the /r/ marker of the future and conditional means the same thing as the /r/ of the infinitive. If we take the parts of the future and conditional forms that occur after the /r/ (e.g., *e*, *as*, *a*, *emos*, *eyes*, *an*, and *ia*, *ias*, *iamos*, *iays*, *ian*) and try to trace them to the forms of *haber* (similar in function to the English auxiliary *have*), we run into semantic and phonological trouble. Harris (1969) gives syntactic and semantic arguments for this analysis, but he has more recently (Harris, 1974b) stated that these arguments are rather weak. The phonological difficulties arise primarily in the conditional: The imperfect forms of *haber* are *había*, *habías*, etc., but the conditional suffix has no *hab* /ab/. Since the /ab/ does not occur in the conditional, there is no evidence for its being there underlyingly.

I will propose, therefore, that the future and conditional forms are not synchronically derived from the infinitive and *haber* and will proceed as though they are simple inflected forms analogous to the other forms we have been discussing. Still some questions arise. One question involves the number of morphemes in these forms and the composition of these morphemes. Consider the following two analyses:

(13)  (a) *cant* + *a* + *r* + *e* + *mos*
          *cant* + *a* + *r* + *ia* + *mos*
      (b) *cant* + *a* + *re* + *mos*
          *cant* + *a* + *ria* + *mos*

In both (13a) and (13b) the vowel following the stem is taken to be the theme vowel; as we mentioned above, it is identical to the vowel of the infinitive in all three conjugations. In (13a) /r/ is considered a morpheme that occurs in both future and conditional forms. We could call this a subsequence marker. The only reason for not adopting (13a) is that it requires four suffixes to follow the stem, rather than three, which is the maximum found in other tenses. That is, the subsequent forms would be the only ones with separate markers for tense and aspect. In the interest of keeping the word-formation rule for verbs simple, I will not separate morphological spell-out rules for /r/, /e/, and /ia/; however, the solution I propose incorporates basically the same information, since the choice of /re/, /ra/, or /ria/ depends on morphological information. The choice of /ria/ versus the other two forms depends on the tense, and the choice between /re/ and /ra/ depends on the person.

(14)

$$[\text{subsequent}] \longrightarrow r \left\{ \begin{matrix} \begin{Bmatrix} e/\underline{\quad} \\ a \\ ia \end{Bmatrix} + \begin{Bmatrix} [\text{1st person}] \\ [\text{2nd person plural}] \end{Bmatrix} / [-\text{past}] \end{matrix} \right\}$$

Another alternative would be to generate /e/ and /a/ of the future more directly as person/number morphemes. This would mean modifying (and complicating) all of the rules given above for PN markers to generate an extra vowel for the future. The choice seems to be between two claims: (a) that /e/ and /a/ are person/number markers occurring only in the future, or (b) that /e/ and /a/ are TM markers for future, determined by person and number. The difference is small. I have chosen the latter interpretation because /e/ and /a/ identify person only in the first and third singular, but they are a necessary part of all the future forms. It would be preferable to make decisions of this sort on empirical bases, but our understanding of morphology as a psychological phenomenon has not been sufficiently developed.

Imperative forms will be dealt with under the heading of tense/mood. For formal imperatives in the singular and plural, subjunctive forms are used, e.g., *cante usted, coma usted, canten ustedes, coman ustedes.* No additional morphological rules are needed for these forms. The familiar imperative singular is *canta tú, come tú, vive tú,* that is, verb stem plus ThV, with no other markers. Since there are no TM or PN markers, no rules are needed. The plural familiar, however, has a marker /d/, e.g., *cantad, comed, vivid,* added after the ThV. For this marker a rule is needed:

(15)

$$\begin{bmatrix} \text{imperative} \\ \text{plural} \end{bmatrix} \longrightarrow d$$

## 8.3   Theme Vowels

Finally, we must deal with the theme vowels. As we mentioned before, there are three conjugation classes; but the second and third are nondistinct in all forms except present indicative, first plural (*comemos, vivimos*), the infinitive (*comer, vivir*), and the subsequent forms. Conjugation class membership is a property of the stems, determined arbitrarily, and not correlated with any phonological properties of the stem. Thus there is first conjugation *crear* 'to create' and second conjugation *creer* 'to believe', first conjugation *sentar* 'to seat' and third conjugation *sentir* 'to feel, regret'. In first conjugation the ThV is uniformly /a/, where it occurs, and in second and third conjugation it is /i/, /e/, /ye/, or absent. In the analysis I will propose, there are two steps in the derivation of the ThVs. The first rule merely generates a ThV in the positions where a ThV occurs on the surface. This rule applies to all conjugation classes, since the occurrence or nonoccurrence of a ThV is the same for all classes. In the second stage, the quality of the ThV is determined by rule.

In general the ThV (which is sometimes a diphthong /ye/) occurs before inflections that begin in consonants and does not occur before inflections that begin in vowels. The only exception is found in the imperfect indicative, which, in second and third conjugations, has the ThV /i/ occurring before the TM marker /a/, e.g., *comía, comíamos.* Harris (1969:72, 76) generates a ThV in all verbs and deletes that vowel if it occurs before a formative beginning in a vowel. For Harris the imperfect indicative morpheme is /ba/ for all conjugations, so that /kom + i + ba/ underlies *comía.* The ThV does not delete because the /b/ is present; the /b/ is deleted only after the vowel deletion rule has attempted to apply but failed. (This is a counter-feeding order.) Harris's analysis gives the diachronic explanation for the exceptionality of imperfect forms; that is, the ThV occurs in *comía* because a consonant used to intervene between the ThV and TM vowel. But synchronically the explanation is somewhat different: The ThV in the imperfect does not delete because it is stressed, and the stress that occurs on it is a signal of past tense. Thus we will view the appearance of a ThV in the imperfect, despite a following vowel, as a property of the tense.

There is no motivation for generating a ThV in all verbs and then deleting it in some cases. Rather, we will generate the ThV's only in the forms in which they occur on the surface. There are several ways of stating the environment of such a rule. For instance, we could list environments in which the ThV occurs in morphological terms or we could give the environment in partially phonological terms, stating that the occurrence of the ThV depends in part on the following segment. I will adopt the latter approach to the environment, since one of the functions of the ThV is to fill out the syllable between the stem and the TM marker, in case the TM marker begins in a consonant. Thus the ThV has a partially phonological function, and the imperfect indicative must be viewed as exceptional in a way. Given the phonological function, there are two ways to predict the occurrence of the ThV. One generalization is that the ThV does NOT occur before vowels, except in the imperfect, but does occur elsewhere; the other generalization is that the ThV occurs before consonants, before the end of the word, and before the imperfect markers, and does NOT occur elsewhere. I choose the former statement only because it is shorter.

Thus every verb will be generated with a marker "ThV" following the stem, but this "ThV" will not always get a phonological interpretation. It is subject to the following rule:

(16)　[theme vowel] $\longrightarrow$ $\begin{cases} \emptyset / \underline{\hspace{1cm}} \text{ ([−cons])[+syll] except in} \\ \phantom{\emptyset / \underline{\hspace{1cm}}} \text{the imperfect} \\ \text{V} \qquad \text{elsewhere} \end{cases}$

The [ − consonantal] in parentheses in the first line of (16) is a complication that results from the analysis of *comió* [komyó] that I adopted above. I chose not to analyze the /y/ as derived from the ThV because it is not stressed; I chose rather to analyze the third singular preterite PN marker as an underlying diphthong and not generate a ThV. Thus the ThV should not be generated before a glide followed by a V; the ThV does, however, appear before a glide followed by a C, as in *cantays, comeys.*

Rule (16) generates either $\emptyset$ or an unspecified V. Another rule will specify the features of this vowel, according to conjugation class. The first conjugation theme vowel is invariably /a/:

(17)　$\begin{bmatrix} \text{V} \\ \text{ThV} \\ +\text{1st conj.} \end{bmatrix} \longrightarrow [+\text{low}]$

(Since /a/ is the only [ + low] vowel in Spanish, the features [ + back, − high, − round] may be added by existing rules.)

In both the second and third conjugations the ThV may be /i/, /e/, or /ye/, but in a few cases the conditions vary in the two conjugations. The following table summarizes the distribution of the three realizations of the theme vowel:

(18)　Second and Third Conjugation Theme Vowels:

*e*

Second conjugation
Infinitive (*comér*)
Present indicative (*cómes, cóme, cómemos,* etc.)
Subsequent (*comeré, comería,* etc.)

Third conjugation
Present indicative, unstressed (*víves, víve,* etc.)

*ye*

Both conjugations
Preterite, third plural (*comiéron, viviéron*)

Past subjunctive (*comiéra, comiése, viviéra, viviése*)
Present participle (*comiéndo, viviéndo*)

*i*

BOTH CONJUGATIONS
Preterite (except third plural) (*comíste, comímos, vivíste, vivímos*)
Imperfect indicative (*comía, vivía*)
Past participle (*comído, vivído*)

THIRD CONJUGATION
Present indicative, stressed (*vivímos, vivís*)
Infinitive (*vivír*)
Subsequent (*viviré, viviría*)

The usual approach to second and third conjugation in the generative framework (Harris, 1969; Brame and Bordelois, 1973) is to posit an underlying /e/ for the ThV in second conjugation and an underlying /i/ for third conjugation.[3] This is because the ThV's in second and third conjugation are distinct in the first and second plural of the present indicative, in the infinitive, in the subsequent forms, and in the plural imperative, and where they are distinct, the second conjugation has /e/ and the third conjugation has /i/. In other cases, the underlying vowel is changed into /e/, /i/, or /ye/ by rules.

Hudson's model for generating allomorphs, which we have adopted at least in part, suggests a different approach. Rather than generating one underlying vowel for each conjugation class and changing it to derive surface forms, we will generate the alternates directly. The fact that the vowels that participate in the alternation are the same in both conjugations, /i/, /e/, and /ye/, suggests that they can be generated by the same rule; i.e., we do not need a separate rule for second and third conjugations.

The conditioning environments in this rule are almost entirely morphological. Except for present indicative and preterite, each tense has a uniform ThV for all persons and numbers. There are no phonological factors that could determine what this uniform vowel is; therefore, the vowel will be predicted on the basis of tense and mood. In the present indicative, however, where the third conjugation ThV is /e/ or /i/, there is a correlation with stress: /i/ occurs stressed, /e/ occurs unstressed. We will use stress to predict this alternation. The ThV for third plural of the

---

[3] More recently, Harris (1975) adopts an approach similar to ours: He generates /e/ for second conjugation only in the non-past, and /i/ elsewhere.

preterite differs from the other preterite ThV's in that it is /ye/ and the usual ThV for preterite is /i/. Harris (1969) and Brame and Bordelois (1973) give a partially phonological environment for the derivation of the diphthong. They claim that the /ye/ occurs before /rV/ and before /nd/. There are several reasons for rejecting this as conditioning environment. First, as argued in Harris (1975), there is no reason why /rV/ and /nd/ should function together to condition a diphthongization, and second, this is not a true generalization, even about verb forms. The future and conditional forms have the ThV occurring before /rV/ (*comeré*, *comería, viviré, viviría*), yet the ThV does not become /ye/. Furthermore, if we take into account the alternate forms of the past subjunctive, *comiese, viviese*, etc., we see that the morphological generalization is more appropriate. The diphthong occurs here before /s/, in violation of the putative phonological environment, but consistent with the morphological environment.

The rule for generating the theme vowels for second and third conjugation is as follows:

$$(19) \quad \begin{bmatrix} ThV \\ -1st \ conj. \end{bmatrix} \longrightarrow \left\{ \begin{array}{l} e \ / \ [-3rd \ conj.] + \underline{\quad} + \left\{ \begin{array}{l} present \\ subsequent \\ infinitive \end{array} \right\} \\ \qquad\qquad [-\overline{stress}] + present \\ ye \ / \underline{\quad} + \left\{ \begin{array}{l} past \ subjunctive \\ preterite + 3rd \ plural \\ present \ participle \end{array} \right\} \\ i \end{array} \right\}$$

Rule (19) claims, then, that second and third conjugation theme vowels are identical except in a few special cases. A similar approach is adopted in Harris (1975). However, in earlier analyses (Harris, 1969; Brame and Bordelois, 1973) second and third conjugation ThV's are differentiated in underlying form, and this contrast is neutralized in certain contexts. The validity of the former approach over the latter is supported by widespread dialectal developments that level most of the remaining contrasts between second and third conjugation ThV's. In many dialects of Latin America (Rosenblat, 1946:216–218), especially in New Mexico (Espinosa, 1946:65) and Guanajuato, Mexico (Boyd–Bowman, 1960:164), the ThV distinction in the present indicative has been leveled in favor of the second conjugation. That is, third conjugation *vivimos* is now *vivemos*, analogous to *comemos*. These dialects do not use the second plural form, so the result is /e/ throughout the present indicative in non-first conjugation forms. In some other dialects the analogy runs in the opposite direction: The second conjugation present form *comemos* becomes *comimos*. These developments support the general approach taken here, for if all second and third conjugation forms contrasted in underlying form, it would be extremely unlikely for either form to change. On the other hand, if second and third conjugation forms are viewed as basically the same, with a distinction being made only in special cases, the loss of these special cases is to be expected.

To summarize this analysis of Spanish verbal forms, I give below the word formation rule for verbs and a list of the rules proposed to spell-out the morphemes (and allomorphs). Below that is a sample derivation. In this derivation the place of the verb stress rule is illustrated. The only rule I have given in (22) that refers to stress is rule L, the rule for spelling out second and third conjugation theme vowels. Since [− stress ] is mentioned in this rule (I assume that prior to the application of the stress rules all segments are unspecified for stress; the stress rule assigns the value[+ stress] to some vowels, [− stress] to all others), it is necessary for the stress rules to apply before L applies. On the other hand, the stress rules are stated in terms of phonological segments, C and V, and therefore cannot apply until the morphemes of the verb are given a phonological shape. The stress rules, then, are intrinsically ordered between rules K and L. The stress rules for verbs are repeated here for convenience. For present tense, since we are dealing with the standard dialect, I have chosen to use the penultimate rule (20c), but bear in mind the discussion in Section 3.1.

(20)     $V \longrightarrow [+\text{stress}] /$
$$\left\{ \begin{array}{l} \left] \begin{bmatrix} \text{stem} \\ \text{verb} \\ \left\{ \begin{array}{l} +\text{past} \\ -\text{finite} \end{array} \right\} \end{bmatrix} + \underline{\quad} \right. \quad \text{(a)} \\ \text{r[subsequent]} \quad \text{(b)} \\ \underline{\quad} C_0VC_0\#]_{\text{verb}} \quad \text{(c)} \end{array} \right.$$

Subrule (20a) assumes that morphological information is carried on the stem, even after word formation. I also assume that all morphemes retain their morphological categorization even after the application of the morphological spell-out rules. Thus, the word formation rule functions as follows. All the relevant morphological information appears as a bundle of features on a verb:

verb
[conjugation]
[TM]
[PN]

This information is copied in the correct order, to the right of the stem, and a ThV is added, by the following rule:

(21)
$$\begin{bmatrix} \text{verb} \\ \text{[conjugation]} \\ \text{[TM]} \\ \text{[PN]} \end{bmatrix} \longrightarrow \text{[verb]} \begin{bmatrix} \text{stem} \\ \text{[conjugation]} \\ \text{[TM]} \\ \text{[PN]} \end{bmatrix} + \text{ThV} + \text{TM} + \text{PN}$$

For example, consider the derivation of the first plural present indicative form *comemos*, which follows the restatement of the rules in (22).

(22)
PERSON/NUMBER

A. [1st singular] $\longrightarrow$ $\left\{ \begin{array}{l} \text{o/[pres. ind.]} + \underline{\quad} \\ \begin{bmatrix} +\text{syll} \\ -\text{low} \\ -\text{back} \\ \alpha\text{high} \end{bmatrix} /[-\alpha\text{1st conj.}] + \text{[preterite]} + \underline{\quad} \end{array} \right\}$

B. [3rd singular] $\longrightarrow$ $\langle y \rangle$ o/$\langle -1\text{st conj.}\rangle$ + [preterite] + $\underline{\quad}$

C. $\begin{bmatrix} \text{2nd person} \\ \text{plural} \end{bmatrix} \longrightarrow \left\{ \begin{array}{l} \langle \text{ste} \rangle \text{ ys/[preterite]} + \underline{\quad} \\ \text{y} \quad \text{s} \end{array} \right\}$

D. [1st plural] $\longrightarrow$ mos

E. [3rd plural] $\longrightarrow \langle \text{ro} \rangle$ n/$\langle \text{preterite} \rangle$ + $\underline{\quad}$

TENSE/MOOD

F. [present subjunctive] $\longrightarrow \left\{ \begin{array}{l} \text{a/}[-1\text{st conj.}] + \underline{\quad} \\ \text{e} \end{array} \right\}$

G. [imperfect indicative] $\longrightarrow \left\{ \begin{array}{l} \text{a/}[-1\text{st conj.}] + \underline{\quad} \\ \text{ba} \end{array} \right\}$

H. [past subjunctive] $\longrightarrow \left\{ \begin{array}{l} \text{se} \\ \text{ra} \end{array} \right\}$

I. [subsequent] $\longrightarrow$ r $\left\{ \begin{array}{l} \left\{ \begin{array}{l} \text{e/}\underline{\quad} + \left\{ \begin{array}{l} \text{[1st person]} \\ \text{[2nd person plural]} \end{array} \right\} /[-\text{past]} \\ \text{a} \end{array} \right. \\ \text{ia} \end{array} \right\}$

J. $\begin{bmatrix} \text{imperative} \\ \text{plural} \end{bmatrix} \longrightarrow$ d

THEME VOWEL

K. [ThV] ⟶ $\left\{\begin{array}{l} \emptyset / \underline{\hspace{1em}} \ ([-\text{cons}])[+\text{syll}] \text{ except imperfect} \\ V \end{array}\right\}$

L.
$\begin{bmatrix} \text{ThV} \\ -1\text{st conj.} \end{bmatrix} \longrightarrow \left\{\begin{array}{l} e / [-3\text{rd conj.}] + \underline{\hspace{1em}} + \left\{\begin{array}{l} \text{present} \\ \text{subsequent} \\ \text{infinitive} \end{array}\right\} \\ \qquad\qquad \overline{[-\text{stress}]} + [\text{present}] \\ ye / \underline{\hspace{1em}} + \left\{\begin{array}{l} [\text{past subjunctive}] \\ [\text{preterite}] + [3\text{rd plural}] \end{array}\right\} \\ i \end{array}\right\}$

M. [ThV] ⟶ a / [+1st conj.] + _____

SAMPLE DERIVATION

(23) *Comemos*

$\begin{array}{l} +\text{com}+ \\ \begin{bmatrix} -1\text{st conj.} \\ +2\text{nd conj.} \\ \text{present} \\ \text{indicative} \\ [1\text{st plural}] \end{bmatrix} \end{array} \longrightarrow \begin{array}{l} [\text{com}]_{\text{stem}} + \text{ThV} + \begin{bmatrix} \text{present} \\ \text{indicative} \end{bmatrix} + [1\text{st plural}] \\ \begin{bmatrix} -1\text{st conj.} \\ +2\text{nd conj.} \end{bmatrix} \end{array}$

$\begin{array}{llll} [\text{com}]_{\text{stem}} & + & \text{ThV} & + \text{ pres. ind.} + 1\text{st plural}] \\ \begin{bmatrix} -1\text{st conj.} \\ +2\text{nd conj.} \\ \text{pres. ind.} \\ 1\text{st plural} \end{bmatrix} & & & \end{array}$

|  |  |  |  |
|---|---|---|---|
|  | _____ | _____ | mos | D |
|  | V | ∅ | _____ | K |
|  | V́ | | | (20c) |
|  | é | | | L |

*com é mos*

## 8.4 Stem Vowel Alternations

We turn now to a discussion of the alternations found in the stem vowels (the last vowel of the stem) of certain Spanish verbs. In this section we will discuss three alternations: (i) the alternation in first and second conjugation stem vowels of /ye/ with /e/ and /we/ with /o/; (ii) the alternation in third conjugation of /i/, /e/, and /ye/, and /u/, /o/, and /we/; (iii) the alternation in third conjugation stem vowels of /e/ with /i/. These alternations have been discussed extensively in the generative framework by Harris (1969; 1974a; 1975), and Brame and Bordelois (1973; 1974). My purpose here is merely to present an analysis of these alternations in the framework of natural generative phonology and not to make a detailed comparison with these previous analyses. However, I will make reference to the earlier analyses where important theoretical issues arise, and in particular I will compare the analysis to be developed with the most recent analysis by Harris (1975).

The first alternation, that of /e/ with /ye/ and /o/ with /we/, has been mentioned repeatedly in previous chapters. In the standard language in a certain class of verbs the diphthongs occur in the present, in stressed syllables. Here are some illustrative forms:

(24)

|  | *contar*<br>'to tell, count' | *sentar*<br>'to seat ' |
|---|---|---|
| **Present Indicative** | | |
| sg. 1 | *cuénto* | *siénto* |
| 2 | *cuéntas* | *siéntas* |
| 3 | *cuénta* | *siénta* |
| pl. 1 | *contámos* | *sentámos* |
| 2 | *contáis* | *sentáis* |
| 3 | *cuéntan* | *siéntan* |
| **Present Subjunctive** | | |
| sg. 1 | *cuénte* | *siénte* |
| 2 | *cuéntes* | *siéntes* |
| 3 | *cuénte* | *siénte* |
| pl. 1 | *contémos* | *sentémos* |
| 2 | *contéis* | *sentéis* |
| 3 | *cuénten* | *siénten* |

In all other forms the stem vowel is an unstressed, simple vowel. As I mentioned in Chapter 7, in Hudson's model of lexical representation the verbs that have this alternation are distinguished from those that do not by their complex lexical entries:

(25)

$$contar / k \left\{ \begin{array}{c} o \\ we \end{array} \right\} nt\text{-}/ \qquad sentar / s \left\{ \begin{array}{c} e \\ ye \end{array} \right\} nt\text{-}/$$

To formulate the rule that distributes the alternants, two points must be decided: (i) what conditions the alternation, and (ii) what is the basic or "elsewhere" alternant. In many cases it is not clear whether an alternation of this nature has phonological conditioning, morphological conditioning, or both, but in this case it is fairly clear that stress is conditioning the alternation. Unlike some other phonological conditioners, stress can be used to predict the alternants no matter which one we choose for the basic variant. Therefore, a decision about which is the basic variant must be made independently of the decision regarding conditioning. Either of the following two rules could correctly predict the distribution of the alternants.

(26) $\begin{Bmatrix} o/e \\ we/ye \end{Bmatrix} \longrightarrow \begin{Bmatrix} we/ye/[+\overline{stress}] \\ o/e \end{Bmatrix}$

(27) $\begin{Bmatrix} o/e \\ we/ye \end{Bmatrix} \longrightarrow \begin{Bmatrix} o/e/[-\overline{stress}] \\ we/ye \end{Bmatrix}$

Rule (26) designates the simple vowels as the elsewhere case, while rule (27) designates the diphthongs.

The other alternation type that involves the diphthongs and the mid vowels helps us make a choice between (26) and (27). As seen in (28), some verbs have a three-way alternation between diphthongs, mid vowels, and high vowels.

(28)

| *mentir* 'to lie ' |
| --- |

PRESENT

| | | Indicative | Subjunctive |
| --- | --- | --- | --- |
| sg. | 1 | *miénto* | *miénta* |
| | 2 | *miéntes* | *miéntas* |
| | 3 | *miénte* | *miénta* |
| pl. | 1 | *mentímos* | *mintámos* |
| | 2 | *mentís* | *mintáis* |
| | 3 | *miénten* | *miéntan* |

IMPERFECT

| | | Indicative | Subjunctive |
| --- | --- | --- | --- |
| sg. | 1 | *mentía* | *mintiéra* |
| | 2 | *mentías* | *mintiéras* |
| | 3 | *mentía* | *mintiéra* |
| pl. | 1 | *mentíamos* | *mintiéramos* |
| | 2 | *mentíais* | *mintiérais* |
| | 3 | *mentían* | *mintiéran* |

PRETERITE

| | |
| --- | --- |
| sg. | *mentí* |
| | *mentíste* |
| | *mintió* |

| *mentir* 'to lie ' |
| --- |
| pl. *mentimos*<br>*mentisteis*<br>*mintiéron* |

| Infinitive | Past Participle | Present Past |
| --- | --- | --- |
| *mentir* | *mentido* | *mintiéndo* |

Subsequent: *mentiré, mentiría,* etc.

In these verb forms, the diphthongs occur under stress, as in *contar* and *sentar,* but both the high vowels and the mid vowels may occur in unstressed syllables. This fact suggests that it is [ + stress] that is associated with diphthongs, as in rule (26), rather than [ − stress], which is associated with mid vowels, as in rule (27). Therefore, we will take rule (26) and expand it to account for the three-way alternation in (28).

To predict the distribution of the high and mid vowels, I will adopt the phonological environment suggested in Harris (1969) and, before that, in Saporta (1959). That is, the mid vowel occurs before a high front vowel in the next syllable.[4] The high vowel occurs elsewhere. The rule for distributing the alternants for the *mentir* class and the *contar, sentar* class is as follows:

(29)
$$\begin{Bmatrix} ye\,/\,we \\ e\,/\,o \\ \langle i\,/\,u\rangle \end{Bmatrix} \longrightarrow \begin{Bmatrix} ye\,/\,we\,/\,[+\overline{stress}] \\ e\,/\,o\,\langle\,/\underline{\quad}C_0 i\rangle \\ \langle i\,/\,u\rangle \end{Bmatrix}$$

(Of course, this rule can be stated in terms of distinctive features, but for the purposes of this discussion, alphabetic symbols will be used.) The lexical representation of *mentir* is

$$/m \begin{Bmatrix} ye \\ e \\ i \end{Bmatrix} nt\text{-}/$$

Since all three alternants are present in this stem, the entire rule (29), including all the material in angled brackets, is used for *mentir*. For verbs such as *contar* and *sentar,* which are listed lexically as having a diphthong/mid vowel alternation, only the first two cases of the rule are applicable. The material in angled brackets is not used, so the mid

---

[4] Actually, Saporta (1959) and Harris (1969) restrict the environment to before a STRESSED /i/. But as Harris (personal communication) has pointed out, this restriction is not necessary, and, in fact, it is incorrect for my analysis of subsequent forms.

vowels are not restricted to any phonological environment, but occur elsewhere for these verbs.

No revisions of the rule are necessary to account for the third alternation type, the alternation between /i/ and /e/, exemplified in (30).

(30)

| | | *pedir* 'to ask for' |
|---|---|---|

PRESENT

| | | Indicative | Subjunctive |
|---|---|---|---|
| sg. | 1 | *pído* | *pída* |
| | 2 | *pídes* | *pídas* |
| | 3 | *píde* | *pída* |
| pl. | 1 | *pedímos* | *pidámos* |
| | 2 | *pedís* | *pidáis* |
| | 3 | *píden* | *pídan* |

IMPERFECT

| | | Indicative | Subjunctive |
|---|---|---|---|
| sg. | 1 | *pedía* | *pidiéra* |
| | 2 | *pedías* | *pidiéras* |
| | 3 | *pedía* | *pidiéra* |
| pl. | 1 | *pedíamos* | *pidiéramos* |
| | 2 | *pedíais* | *pidiérais* |
| | 3 | *pedían* | *pidiéran* |

PRETERITE

| | | |
|---|---|---|
| sg. | 1 | *pedí* |
| | 2 | *pedíste* |
| | 3 | *pidió* |
| pl. | 1 | *pedímos* |
| | 2 | *pedísteis* |
| | 3 | *pidiéron* |

| Infinitive | Past Participle | Present Participle |
|---|---|---|
| *pedir* | *pedído* | *pidiéndo* |

Subsequent : *pediré, pediría,* etc.

(There are no verbs that have a parallel alternation of back vowels. This will be regarded as an accidental gap.)

The lexical representation of *pedir* is / p{$\frac{e}{i}$}d-/. The first part of rule (29) is not applicable to *pedir* since no diphthong occurs in the lexical form; the second and third cases of (29) apply to *pedir* and correctly distribute the stem vowel alternants, for the material in angled brackets will be used.

Rule (29) also accounts automatically for three other verbs, *jugar* 'to play', *adquirir* 'to acquire', and *inquirir* 'to inquire'. These verbs have the diphthongs /we/ and /ye/ in stressed forms but the high vowels in all other forms. Their lexical representations are:

$$(31) \qquad /x \left\{ \begin{matrix} we \\ u \end{matrix} \right\} g\text{-}/ \qquad /ink \left\{ \begin{matrix} ye \\ i \end{matrix} \right\} r\text{-}/$$

For these verbs only the first and last cases of rule (29) are used; the second is simply inapplicable because no mid vowel appears in the lexical form. Thus rule (29) accounts for all three alternation types, plus the three verbs mentioned here.

Three further facts need to be represented in the grammar. First, no third conjugation verb has a nonalternating mid stem vowel. Second, no second conjugation verb stem has a high stem vowel (Harris, 1975). These two generalizations are expressed together in rule (32). Third, only third conjugation verbs have the mid/high and the mid/high/diphthong alternations, rule (33). These generalizations are expressed in lexical redundancy rules relating the form of the stem vowel to the conjugation class of the verb.

$$(32) \qquad \begin{bmatrix} +syll \\ -low \end{bmatrix} \ \text{IS ALWAYS}[\alpha high] / \underline{\hspace{1cm}} C_0 \ \underset{\begin{bmatrix} -1st\ conj. \\ \alpha 3rd\ conj. \end{bmatrix}}{verb}$$

$$(33) \qquad \left\{ \begin{matrix} \left( \begin{bmatrix} -syll \\ +high \end{bmatrix} \begin{bmatrix} +syll \\ -back \\ -high \end{bmatrix} \right) \\ \begin{bmatrix} +syll \\ -high \end{bmatrix} \\ \begin{bmatrix} +syll \\ +high \end{bmatrix} \end{matrix} \right\} \ C_0]_{verb} \ \text{IS ALWAYS } [+3rd\ conj.]$$

The analysis of stem vowels just presented attempts no account of stem vowels in non-verb forms, nor were non-verb forms taken into consideration in the analysis. The decision to exclude non-verb forms was made on the basis of the principles established in Chapter 4. The forms of the verb paradigm are considered to be productively related and are thus derived from a common stem by the application of morphological rules, MP-rules and P-rules. There are a few verb–noun and verb–adjective relations that may be productive. For instance, a verb may be formed from a noun or adjective by the suffixing *-ear*, e.g., *telefonear* 'to telephone', *golpear* 'to strike', from *golpe* 'strike, blow'. However, all such verbs are first conjugation and will not have stem vowel alternations. Adjectives and nouns may be formed from the past participle of verbs, but no additional MP-rules are needed. A productive noun-formation process involves the suffixation of *-miento* (meaning "act or effect of X") to forms containing the theme vowel /i/ for second and third conjugations and /a/ for first conjugations (Harris, 1975). For alternating verb stems, the stem vowel is exactly as expected before ____$C_0$i; it is the mid vowel for stems having the mid/high alternation: e.g., *pedír, pedimiénto, rendír, rendimiénto.* The rules already formulated will predict the correct vowel for this and all of the other productive processes involving verbs and non-verbs.

In nonproductive relations between verbs and non-verbs, however, we sometimes find the stem vowel affected. While this chapter is meant to treat verbs primarily, non-verbs deserve some discussion because other generative treatments of stem–vowel alternations (e.g., Harris, 1969, 1975; Brame and Bordelois, 1973) do take non-verbs into account and thus account for a wider range of data. To make the present analysis comparable to these previous analyses, I will briefly discuss stem vowels in non-verbs as they relate to verb forms.

We have already seen in Chapter 4 that words related by nonproductive derivational morphology are listed in the lexicon, and the relations between them are described in via-rules that express the semantic, syntactic, morphological, and phonological generalizations. Let us now consider the three types of relations that may exist between verbs and non-verbs, with regard to alternations in the stem vowel.

The simplest cases are those in which a nonalternating verb stem is identical to the stem found in non-verbs. Consider these examples:

(34)   SECOND CONJUGATION

| | |
|---|---|
| *comer* 'to eat' | *comedor* 'dining room' |
| *vencer* 'to conquer' | *vencible* 'conquerable' |
| *mover* 'to move' | *movil* 'mobile' |
| | *movible* 'moveable' |
| *vender* 'to sell' | *vendija* 'public sale' |
| | *vendible* 'salable' |

THIRD CONJUGATION

| | |
|---|---|
| *escribir* 'to write' | *escritura* 'writing' |
| *transcribir* 'to transcribe' | *transcripción* 'transcription' |
| *distinguir* 'to distinguish' | *distinción* 'distinction' |
| *discutir* 'to discuss' | *discusión* 'discussion' |
| *producir* 'to produce' | *producción* 'production' |

Let us assume that for these pairs of words, the verb is basic and will appear fully specified for semantic information (meaning of the stem), syntactic information (selectional restrictions and subcategorization features), morphological information (conjugation class), and phonological information (the phonological representation of the stem) (Vennemann, 1972c). For example, *discutir* will have all such information specified. However, the related non-verb is, at least in part, described in terms of the verb. Thus *discusión* will have the marking "related to lexical entry *m*," where *m* is *discut-*, the verb. Inasmuch as there is identity between the verb stem and non-verb, no rules are needed. That is, since both *discutir* and *discusión* have the same stem vowel, no rule regarding stem vowels need be referred to. On the other hand, to describe the difference in stem final consonants, a via-rule relating /t/ to /s/ is referred to.

Now consider cases in which the verb stem has alternating vowels. There are verb/non-verb pairs such as the following:

(35)  FIRST CONJUGATION

| | |
|---|---|
| *contar* (o / we) 'to count' | *contaduria* 'accountancy' |
| *nevar* (e / ye) 'to snow' | *nevásca* 'snowfall', 'blizzard' |
| | *nevázo* 'snowfall' |
| *rogar* (o / we) 'to beg' | *rogación* 'petition' |
| | *rogatívo* 'supplicatory' |

SECOND CONJUGATION

| | |
|---|---|
| *doler* (o / we) 'to ache, hurt' | *dolór* 'pain' |
| | *doliénte* 'suffering, sufferer' |
| *perder* (e / ye) 'to lose' | *perdición* 'perdition, loss' |

THIRD CONJUGATION

| | |
|---|---|
| *pedir* (i / e) 'to ask for' | *petición* 'petition' |
| *servir* (i / e) 'to serve' | *servício* 'service' |
| *cenir* (i / e) 'to gird' | *cínto* 'belt' |
| *maldecir* (i / e) 'to curse' | *maldición* 'curse' |
| *mentir* (ye / i / e) 'to lie' | *mentíra* 'lie' |
| *divertir* (ye / i / e) 'to amuse' | *diversión* 'diversion' |
| *morir* (we / u / o) 'to die' | *mortecíno* 'dying' |
| | *mortál* 'mortal' |
| | *muérte* 'death' |
| *dormir* (we / u / o) 'to sleep' | *dormitório* 'dormitory' |
| | *durmiénte* 'sleeping, sleeper' |

In each of these cases, the verb stem will contain a complex entry for the stem vowel, and the non-verb will contain one of the vowels found in the verb stem. For most of the non-verbs, the stem vowel is predictable by the rule presented earlier for stem vowels in verbs, rule (29). The /e/ in *petición* and *mentíra* and the /o/ in *dormitório* occur before an /i/ in the next syllable; the /we/ in *muérte* occurs under stress; the /i/ in *maldición*, *servício*, and *cínto* and the /u/ in *durmiénte* are in the same environments as for verbs. This predictability is accounted for by a via reference to rule (29) contained in the lexical entry for the non-verbs. Here is an example of two related entries:

(36)    Entry *m*                    Entry *n*

$$[m \begin{Bmatrix} ye \\ e \\ i \end{Bmatrix} nt\text{-}]$$    [mentira]
                                     noun

        verb                         related to *m* via
                                     (a)  rule (29)
                                     (b)  morphological rules
                                     (c)  semantic rules

Some of the non-verbs contain vowels present in the verbs but not predictable by rule (29), e.g., *diversión, mortál*. These non-verbs will be related to verbs by some via-rules but not by rule (29). Still the phonological relation is apparent from the identity of the non-verb stem vowel with one of the verb stem vowels.

A third type of relation obtains between nonalternating verb stems and non-verbs that have a different stem vowel (examples from Harris, 1975):

(37)    SECOND CONJUGATION

        *cometir* 'to commit'        *comisión* 'act of committing'
                                     *comiténte* 'committing'
        *corromper* 'to corrupt'     *corrúpto* 'corrupt'
                                     *corruptór* 'corrupter'
                                     *corrumpénte* 'corruptive'


        THIRD CONJUGATION

        *cubrir* 'to cover'          *cobertúra* 'covering'
                                     *cobertór* 'bed cover'
        *dirigir* 'to direct'        *dirección* 'direction'
                                     *dirécto* 'direct'
        *mullir* 'to soften'         *molície* 'softness'
                                     *molitívo* 'softening'

A comparison with the forms in (34) reveals that there is no way to predict whether the verbs and non-verbs will have the same or different stem vowels. Thus the vowel differences in (37) must be viewed as somewhat idiosyncratic. However, a minor generalization is apparent in (37): The difference between the stem vowels is a difference between high and mid vowels. As we mentioned earlier, second conjugation stem vowels may not be high, while third conjugation nonalternating stem vowels may not be mid. The redundancy rule (32) formulated to express this generalization serves as the via-rule relating the verbs and non-verbs in (37).

## 8.5 Suppletive Representation versus Diacritic Features

The preceding section sets the stage for a comparison of the present analysis to the one presented in Harris (1975). In treating non-verbs I have purposely relied heavily on Harris, since my objective was to account for approximately the same body of data with regard to stem vowels as his analysis. The primary difference between Harris's treatment of non-verbs and the NGP treatment is that in his analysis verbs and (nonproductively related) non-verbs derive from a common underlying stem. Thus *cometer* and *comisión* are derived from /comit/; *cometer* undergoes a rule for verbs similar to rule (32). Similarly, *cubrir* and *cobertura* are derived from /cobr/ with the verb undergoing Harris's version of rule (32).

Of greater interest, however, is the comparison of Harris's treatment of vowel alternations in the verb paradigms with the treatment developed here using Hudson's model. Harris's analysis is of particular interest because he uses diacritics to trigger the vowel alternation rules. In the last chapter we compared the diacritic approach to MP alternation with Hudson's approach and found them to be similar in many respects. Both approaches are, in general, consistent with the constraints on NGP. However, in the case under discussion here, the stem vowel alternations in Spanish verbs, we find independent evidence for adopting Hudson's model of representing MP alternations over the diacritic approach. We proceed now to an outline of the diacritic approach, as presented in Harris (1975).

Under the diacritic approach, the verbs with a diphthong/mid vowel alternation are represented with underlying mid vowels marked with the diacritic [ + D] (Harris 1969, 1975). Rule (38) applies to these vowels:

(38)
$$\begin{bmatrix} e \\ o \\ +D \end{bmatrix} \longrightarrow \begin{bmatrix} ye \\ we \end{bmatrix} / [+\overline{stress}]$$

Another logical possibility under the diacritic approach is to have underlying diphthongs with a diacritic [+M] (for monopthongizing) and the following rule:

(39)

$$\begin{bmatrix} ye \\ we \\ +M \end{bmatrix} \longrightarrow \begin{bmatrix} e \\ o \end{bmatrix} / [-\overline{stress}]$$

Harris (1973) argues that the diphthongization analysis should be chosen over the monophthongization analysis because diphthongization also occurs in theme vowels (e.g., *comiéron, comiéndo, viviéron, viviéndo*). This argument will be discussed in the last section, where we examine the relation or lack of relation between stem vowel and theme vowel alternations. It should also be observed that the rule accounting for the diphthong/mid vowel alternation will also be needed in the high/mid/diphthong alternation, a point that we will also return to.

For the alternation between high and mid vowels, as in *pedir*, Harris posits a high vowel in the dictionary representation, which corresponds to the NGP lexical level. (Harris, adopting the model formulated by Halle (1973), also has a deeper, lexical level, at which the stem for *pedir* has a mid vowel. The vowel is raised by a morphological rule corresponding to (32) above.) The high vowel is chosen for two reasons: (i) the mid vowel is easily predictable in environment ____$C_0 i$ and (ii) if /pid-/ underlies *pedir*, the generalization can be made that all third conjugation non-low stem vowels are high. The stem /pid-/ and others like it are marked [+L] (for lowering). The following rule applies:

(40)                  $[+L] \longrightarrow [-high]/\_\_\_C_0 i$

Verbs such as *mentir* with a three-way alternation have underlying high vowels and are marked with the two diacritics, [+L] and [+D]. The diphthongization rule is generalized to apply to high vowels:

(41)

$$\begin{bmatrix} +D \\ +stress \end{bmatrix} \longrightarrow \begin{Bmatrix} ye / [-\overline{back}] \\ we / [+\overline{back}] \end{Bmatrix}$$

The underlying representations are as follows:

(42)

| | *sentar* | *pedir* | *mentir* |
|---|---|---|---|
| | /sent-/ | /pid-/ | /mint-/ |
| | +D | +L | +D |
| | | | +L |

Both Harris's diacritic analysis and my analysis using Hudson's model account for the forms of standard Spanish in practically equivalent ways. However, if we extend the body of data to be accounted for to include evidence concerning analogical leveling, a major difference between the approaches emerges.

I am assuming here as I have throughout that it is desirable for a theory of grammar to go beyond the synchronic analysis and give a natural account of diachronic developments. The alternations discussed here, like all MP alternations, are subject to analogical leveling. In some dialects of Spanish (in particular the Chicano dialects described by Espinosa (1946) and Reyes (1972) and the Mexican dialect of Guanajuato described by Boyd-Bowman (1960)) leveling has already occurred. These dialects are of great interest to us in the construction of a theory, because the leveling gives us evidence of a real native speaker analysis of the data in question. Before leveling occurred, these dialects had the same alternations as the standard language. We assume that, in leveling, the more basic allomorph of a paradigm replaces the other allomorphs. Thus by examining the direction of leveling we learn which allomorphs the speakers considered more basic, and we gain evidence about the way real speakers analyze alternations. Of course, different speakers may arrive at different analyses of the same data, but leveling gives evidence for at least one psychologically real analysis.

The facts are as follows. The diphthong/mid vowel alternation levels out in favor of the diphthong; that is, the diphthong occurs in all forms, stressed and unstressed. Examples are *cuentár, cuentámos, cuentába*. The high/mid vowel alternation levels in favor of the high vowel, as in *pidír, pidémos, pidía, pidíste*. The three-way alternation loses all mid vowels; that is, diphthongs occur under stress, high vowels elsewhere.[5]

(43)

PRESENT

|  | | Indicative | Subjunctive |
|---|---|---|---|
| sg. | 1 | *miénto* | *miénta* |
| | 2 | *miéntes* | *miéntas* |
| | 3 | *miénte* | *miénta* |
| pl. | 1 | *mintémos* | *miéntanos* |
| | 2 | —— | —— |
| | 3 | *miénten* | *miéntan* |

Imperfect Indicative: *mintía, mintías*, etc.
Imperfect Subjunctive: *mintiéra, mintiéras*, etc.

[5] The table reveals three other differences between these dialects and the standard dialect: (i) The stress on the first plural present subjunctive form occurs on the stem vowel (see Section 3.1); (ii) the first person plural marker is *-nos* in the present subjunctive; and (iii) in the first plural present indicative the theme vowel is /e/ rather than /i/ (see Section 8.3).

| PRETERITE | | |
|---|---|---|
| sg. 1 | *mintí* | |
| 2 | *mintíste* | |
| 3 | *mintió* | |
| pl. 1 | *mintímos* | |
| 2 | —— | |
| 3 | *mintiéron* | |

| Infinitive | Past Participle | Present Participle |
|---|---|---|
| *mintír* | *mintído* | *mintiéndo* |

Given rule (29), repeated here for convenience, the leveling is accounted for by the mere loss of the mid vowel case in each alternation.

(29)
$$
\begin{Bmatrix} ye/we \\ e/o \\ \langle i/u \rangle \end{Bmatrix} \longrightarrow \begin{Bmatrix} ye/we/[+\overline{stress}] \\ e/o \langle /\underline{\quad} C_0 i \rangle \\ \langle i/u \rangle \end{Bmatrix}
$$

Subsequent to this loss, verbs such as *contar* are underlying /kwent-/, verbs such as *pedir* are underlying /pid-/, and verbs such as *mentir* are underlying /m{$\frac{ye}{e}$}nt-/. Rule (44) applies to the latter class of verbs.

(44)
$$
\begin{Bmatrix} ye/we \\ i/u \end{Bmatrix} \longrightarrow \begin{Bmatrix} ye/we/[+\overline{stress}] \\ i/u \end{Bmatrix}
$$

Thus the analysis involving rule (29), based on Hudson's model, gives a uniform account of the leveling of all three alternation types.

Under the diacritic proposal, however, it is impossible to account for this leveling. The diacritic representation of MP alternations implies that, through historical simplification, the diacritic will be lost, and the underlying form will replace all other allomorphs. Recall that the underlying forms in Harris's analysis are as in (42), repeated here.

(42)
| | *sentar* | *pedir* | *mentir* |
|---|---|---|---|
| | /sent-/ | /pid-/ | /mint-/ |
| | +D | +L | +D |
| | | | +L |

For *pedir* and *mentir* the leveling described above is represented by the loss of the lowering rule and the diacritic [ + L ]. For *pedir* the underlying form shows up in all positions; for *mentir* the underlying form occurs except where diphthongization applies. For *sentar*, on the other hand, this analysis does not make the correct prediction; it predicts that leveling will eliminate all diphthongs in favor of the simple mid vowel.

In order for a diacritic analysis to make the correct prediction for *sentar*, the diphthong would have to be taken as underlying, with a diacritic [+M] to trigger the rule that derives the mid vowel. There are some considerations, independent of leveling, that would suggest that the diphthong is basic. The strongest of these is that the mid vowel is the neutralized alternate, while the diphthongs are the nonneutralized alternates. Ordinarily, one chooses the nonneutralized variant as the underlying form. Related to this matter is the fact that the diphthongs occur under stress and should be considered the full form, while the mid vowels are obviously the reduced versions. Again, one ordinarily chooses the full form as underlying, even where there is no neutralization. These considerations should lead to the choice of the diphthong as underlying in the diacritic approach. But there is one major obstacle. If the rule is one of monophthongization, the diphthongs in the *mentir* class must either be underlying or be derived by a different rule. If they are derived by a different rule, then we cannot capture the relatedness of the two types of alternations involving diphthongs. If we take the diphthongs as basic for *mentir*, then there will have to be a rule to derive the high vowels from the mid vowels (which would be derived from diphthongs by monophthongization). For such a rule to apply to the *pedir* class (which it must, since the high/mid alternations of this class are clearly related to the alternations of the *mentir* class), the mid vowel must be underlying for *pedir*. But with an underlying mid vowel, we cannot account for the leveling in *pedir*, which favors the high vowel. The problem is this: The diacritic approach calls for the choice of ONE allomorph for the underlying form, but for *mentir* there are TWO allomorphs that can be considered basic. Hudson's model provides the perfect framework for reflecting such facts. Of course, the diacritic approach could be modified to allow for more than one underlying form in some cases, but such cases would be impossible to identify without the extra leveling evidence, which is ordinarily not available.

The case of stem vowel alternations in Spanish, then, provides precisely the evidence that demonstrates the empirical differences between the diacritic model and Hudson's model. Both models account adequately for the synchronic facts of standard Spanish, but only Hudson's model provides a natural account of the analogical changes that have occurred in this system in nonstandard dialects.

## 8.6 Further Problems

In this section I will discuss some problems and pseudoproblems regarding the alternations just analyzed. First, we take up a question that I promised earlier to return to: The environment used to predict the occurrence of the mid vowels. For the purposes of expediting the analysis, I adopted a phonological environment for mid vowels, ___$C_0$i. The utter simplicity of this environment can only be appreciated after scouring the paradigm of (38) in search of some better generalization. There is simply no shorter way to predict the mid vowels. If the problem is turned around and one looks for an environment to predict /i/ from /e/, the difficulties are compounded. Brame and Bordelois (1973) take this approach and are forced into three unrelated environments:

(45)
$$e \longrightarrow i/ \begin{cases} [+\overline{\text{stress}}] & C_0V \\ \rule{1cm}{0.4pt} & C_0iV \\ \rule{1cm}{0.4pt} & C_0a \end{cases}$$

Of course, there are other reasons for rejecting (45) (primarily that /e/ should not be taken as underlying), but the difference in complexity is overwhelming. Compare rule (46).

(46)
$$V \longrightarrow [-\text{high}]/\rule{1cm}{0.4pt}C_0i$$

Despite the elegance of this rule, we cannot construct a synchronic phonological explanation for it. One problem is that this "rule" is restricted to certain verbs and is not a general process at all.

In general, in cases of minor alternations such as those we have been discussing, we cannot claim that something in the environment is *causing* an alternation; the environment is rather a description of the forms in which the alternations take place. The environment ___$C_0$i is suspicious because we do not know whether or not speakers can construct generalizations of this sort. We know that for a phonetically conditioned rule (a P-rule) we can posit or search out some causal relation between the conditioning environment and the change described by the rule. Further, the correctness of the statement of a P-rule can be empirically tested. We also know that at times speakers construct generalizations based on morphological categories. But when we have a case in which a set of morphological categories is coextensive with a phonologically stated environment, how do we know whether the speakers construct a phonological association or a morphological one?

Consider an example from English. Certain verbs whose present tense forms end in /-iyp/, e.g., *creep, weep, sleep,* and *keep,* have past tense forms in /-ɛpt/, e.g., *crept, wept, slept, kept.* The past tense vowel could be predicted on the basis of the following cluster, as in Chomsky and Halle (1968), or could be predicted morphologically, to occur only in the past. In any case the alternation is restricted to certain verbs; *peeped, beeped, heaped, seeped, reaped* have no alternation. In some dialects, and in casual speech, the final /t/ after an obstruent is lost. However, the stem vowel in *crept, lept, slept,* and *kept* does not change but remains [ɛ] in [krɛp], [wɛp], etc. This suggests that the alternation is a function of past tense, not the phonological environment of an obstruent cluster. Without the loss of final /t/, there is no way to decide whether the alternation should be predicted phonologically or morphologically.

On the other hand, among the Spanish alternations we have been discussing, we find a case with a different result. I previously proposed that the diphthongs /we/ and /ye/ be predicted on the basis of stress, a phonological conditioning. The alternative would be to list the morphological environments in which the diphthongs occur: certain persons and numbers of the present tense. In the dialects of New Mexico, the stress on first plural forms of the subjunctive is retracted to the stem vowel (as discussed in Section 3.1). When this occurs, a diphthong emerges in verbs that have diphthongs under stress: *mintámos > miéntanos* (Espinosa, 1946:88). Such a change suggests that stress is in fact conditioning the alternation.

A similar change would help us determine whether or not the environment ____$C_0$i conditions the appearance of a mid vowel. If, for example, there were stress shift on a form such as *mentía* to *\*mentyá,* or a stress shift of *mintyó* to *\*mintío,* any changes in the stem vowels would be of great interest. Unfortunately, this situation is only hypothetical; the independent evidence we need does not exist. Thus there is a possibility that the mid vowels in these alternations are morphologically determined. Let us examine this possibility.

In (29) the mid vowels are predicted before ____$C_0$i. We can replace this environment with a list of the morphological categories that the mid vowels occur in. In finite verb forms, mid vowels occur in the unstressed stems of the indicative with the exception of the third person of the preterite (refer to (28) and (30)). The high vowel occurs in all unstressed stems of the subjunctive. The mid vowel also occurs in the infinitive and the past participle. Using this morphological information, the stem vowel alternations would be predicted by the following revision of (43):

$$(47) \quad \begin{Bmatrix} \text{ye} / \text{we} \\ \text{e} / \text{o} \\ \langle \text{i} / \text{u} \rangle \end{Bmatrix} \longrightarrow \begin{Bmatrix} \text{ye} / \text{we} / [+\text{stress}] \\ \text{e} / \text{o} \langle / \underline{\quad} + \begin{Bmatrix} \text{infinitive} \\ \text{past participle} \\ \text{indicative} \\ \quad \text{except third preterite} \end{Bmatrix} \rangle \\ \langle \text{i} / \text{u} \rangle \end{Bmatrix}$$

It is very obvious that the phonological statement of the rule as in (29) is far simpler, but it is not obvious that the simplest analysis is always the psychologically valid analysis. After all the mid vowel variant is prone to loss and has been lost in some dialects. Perhaps it is lost precisely because the conditioning environment for it is so complex.

I have no answer to the question of the extent to which morphophonemic alternations are conditioned phonologically or morphologically. But I consider it to be an important question that must be answered before we can hope to approach psychological reality with the grammars we write.

Another point that deserves some discussion is the relation between the stem vowel alternation just discussed and the theme vowel alternations discussed earlier. Brame and Bordelois (1973) claim that these alternations are due to one and the same process. In fact they are quite adamant about making the connection:

> The parallelism between the stem vowels and the theme vowels . . . can be no coincidence. This parallelism indicates that the change of *e* to *ie* and the change of *e* to *i* is a single unified process. This parallelism is missed by Harris (1969). Second conjugation theme vowels and third conjugation stem vowels undergo two unrelated rules in Harris's system. . . . Thus, the parallelism is accidental in Harris's approach [p. 142].

According to Brame and Bordelois, my analysis is much more deficient than Harris's because at least Harris derives the stem vowel diphthong and the theme vowel diphthong by the same rule, even if he "misses" the "parallelism" elsewhere. In my analysis stem vowel alternations and theme vowel alternations are treated by two separate and unrelated rules. Thus I claim that they represent two separate and unrelated alternations and that any parallelisms between them are accidental, the result of history.

First, let us examine the alleged generalizations that are missed by treating the two alternations separately. Perhaps the strongest similarity between the alternations is that the same segments participate in both the theme vowel and stem vowel alternations: /i/, /e/, and /ye/. (Of course, stem vowels may also be back vowels.) The similarity of participating segments does not mean much, however, unless these segments appear in the same environments in both alternations. Brame and Bordelois claim a similarity of environment for the alternation of /e/ with /i/, in particular, they begin with underlying /e/ and generate /i/ under stress. That stressed /e/ becomes /i/ is not a very impressive generalization, however, since there are cases of the theme vowel remaining /e/ under stress, as in *comér, comémos*. To account for *comér*, Brame and

Bordelois add an environment to the rule, so that it reads as follows:

(48)  $\qquad$ e $\longrightarrow$ i / [+ stress] $C_0V$

This is only an ad hoc addition to the rule to block it from applying to
*comér*. To block the rule from applying to *comémos*, a condition is added
to the rule. Furthermore, there are cases of both the stem vowel and the
theme vowel showing up as /i/ without stress, as in *pidámos, pidiéra* and
*vivirá, vivirémos* (although Brame and Bordelois consider the subsequent forms to be derived from the infinitive). To account for unstressed /i/ as a stem vowel, Brame and Bordelois generate /i/ in the following two environments (as mentioned above):

(49)  $\qquad$ e $\longrightarrow$ i / $\begin{cases} \underline{\quad}C_0i\acute{V}\rbrace & \text{(a)} \\ \underline{\quad}C_0\acute{a} & \text{(b)} \end{cases}$

Despite the alleged similarity between the alternation of /e/ and /i/ in
stem and theme vowels, the environments (49a) and (49b) are applicable only to stem vowels in verbs. Rule (49b) would in fact generate the
wrong result if it were allowed to apply freely to theme vowels, because
it would change *comerá* (future, third singular) to *\*comirá*. Environment
(49a) does not arise for theme vowels in verbs; Brame and Bordelois
give an example of a "theme vowel" in a noun becoming /i/: *demolér* 'to
demolish' *demolición* 'demolition'. However, if we take non-verbs into
account, other problems arise, since stem vowels in non-verbs do not
undergo (49a): e.g., *recepción* 'reception', *dirección* 'direction'. (See
Harris (1974a) and Brame and Bordelois (1974) for further discussion.)
In short, the similarity between the alternation of /e/ and /i/ in stem
vowels and theme vowels is very weak; I simply do not consider it to
constitute a generalization worth capturing. Now, if we want to EX-
PLAIN the similarities between the alternations, we must examine the
history of the language; but there is no synchronic EXPLANATION.

The parallelism between stem vowel and theme vowel alternations
cited by Brame and Bordelois in the case of the diphthong /ye/ involves
the consonants following the diphthongizing context. Recall now that
the theme vowel alternate /ye/ appears in preterite, third plural
*comiéron, viviéron,* past subjunctive *comiéra, viviéra,* etc., and the
present participle, *comiéndo, viviéndo*. Given these forms, a phonological context may be devised: Diphthongization occurs before /rV/ and
/nd/. In third conjugation stem vowels, there are two-way alternations
of high and mid vowels, as in *pedir,* and three-way alternations of high
vowels, mid vowels, and diphthongs, as in *mentir* and *dormir*. It
happens that all the stems having the three-way alternation, which includes the diphthong, end in /r/, or /r/ or /n/ followed by an anterior con-

sonant, e.g., *hervir* 'to boil', *advertir* 'to advise', *sentir* 'to feel, regret', *morir* 'to die', *prefirir* 'to prefer' (Brame and Bordelois, 1973:138). Stems ending in other consonants and consonant clusters only have the two-way alternation, e.g., *pedir*, *sequir* 'to follow', *concebir* 'to conceive', *sumergir* 'to submerge'. Thus for third conjugation stems the environment for diphthongization is a generalization of the environment /rV/, /nd/, which triggers diphthongization in theme vowels:

$$(50) \qquad e \longrightarrow ye\,/\,[+\overline{stress}] \left\{ \begin{array}{c} rV \\ \left[ \begin{array}{c} -syll \\ -obst \end{array} \right] \left[ \begin{array}{c} -syll \\ +ant \end{array} \right] \end{array} \right\}$$

The parallelism expressed in this rule is somewhat weakened by a few additional facts. First, in order to have rule (50) produce the diphthong in the alternate past subjunctive forms, *comiese*, *viviese*, etc., /s/ must be added as another option in the structural description. Second, the generalization regarding consonants is relevant only for third conjugation diphthongization. In first and second conjugation the diphthong appears before single obstruents, *mover*, *muevo* 'to move', *rodar*, *ruedo* 'to roll', *rogar*, *ruego*, 'to pray'; before a sonorant followed by a nonanterior consonant, *colgar*, *cuelgo* 'to hang'; and before triliteral clusters, *temblar*, *tiemblo* 'to tremble', *mostrar*, *muestro* 'to show'.

In order for Brame and Bordelois to claim that theme vowel and stem vowel diphthongs come from the same source under the same conditions, they must claim that third conjugation stem vowel diphthongization takes place under different conditions from first and second conjugation stem vowel diphthongization, because third conjugation stem vowels require certain following consonants while first and second conjugation do not. It is clear that the phonological environment of (50) cannot be considered a CONDITIONING environment, an environment whose properties CAUSE diphthongization, but rather it is merely a convenient DESCRIPTION of the contexts in which the diphthong appears under certain morphological conditions. Because of this, and because the alleged parallelism is not general in all three conjugations, the linguistic significance of a rule such as (50) is certainly open to question.

The only strong similarity between the stem vowel and theme vowel alternations is that they involve the same set of alternates: a high vowel, a mid vowel, and a diphthong. This similarity must be regarded as coincidental synchronically, a result of the historical fact that these vowels underwent some of the same sound changes. Furthermore, a phonological similarity such as this is easily overridden and obscured by the morphological function of the alternations, particularly in the theme vowels, for it is easy to see that from a language user's point of view a morphological generalization is much more important than a phonological one. The different directions of analogical change for theme vowels and stem vowels bears out the morphological function of the theme vowel alternations and, further, shows the two alternations to be unrelated. In stem vowels leveling is taking place; one alternate, the mid vowel, is consistently replaced by one of the other alternates. The only analogical change among theme vowels is the EXTENSION of /e/ in the first plural present indicative form of third conjugation, to give *vivémos* for *vivímos*. If stem and theme vowel alternations were as closely related as Brame and Bordelois claim, we would expect analogical changes to affect them in a parallel manner; yet the facts show quite a divergent development for theme vowels and stem vowels.[6]

## 8.7 Conclusion

To conclude this chapter, let us review the theoretical points that arose in the course of the analysis. Linguists are always interested in "capturing generalizations" about the languages they describe. But, of course, there are many generalizations, and we must distinguish between those that are significant and those that are not. Because of the nature of linguistic change, many historical relations or generalizations leave a residue in the synchronic grammar. Often in generative phonologies there has been an attempt to revive these historical relations and present them as synchronic generalizations. Thus, as they pursued fossil generalizations, phonologists have been lead far afield of their goals of describing competence. Instead we should attempt to distinguish between residual generalizations and synchronically viable generalizations. The True Generalization Condition is an attempt to constrain grammars so that they make just this distinction.

We should also explore different methods of capturing generalizations. For the most part generative phonology provides us with only one way of expressing a generalization: by giving a rule. These rules are all the type of rule that changes one item into another so that, if two

---

[6] Another putative generalization proposed by Brame and Bordelois (1973) that my analysis does not capture is the phonological relatedness of raising (e ⟶ i) and breaking (diphthongization). Brame and Bordelois collapse these two alleged processes into one rule. I will not discuss this problem here because Harris (1974a) has adequately pointed out the weakness of the arguments in favor of this relation. Notice, however, that such a relation could not be made in our analysis, since we do not take the mid vowels to be underlying.

forms are related, an attempt is made to derive them from the same underlying form. Thus if a morpheme has several allomorphs, all of these are traced back to a single underlying form. In this chapter we have seen that the relations among allomorphs and the generalizations about their distribution can be expressed in a different sort of underlying form and rule. We have also seen that this method is more direct and less problematic than the method of trying to relate all forms to a single underlying form.

There are certainly other types of generalizations that we have not explored, but that might turn out to be significant. For example, we might want to account for the fact that third conjugation verb stems exhibiting a three-way alternation all end in /r/, or /r/ or /n/ plus an anterior consonant. If it could be shown that this generalization is real at least for some speakers, then it could be expressed as a redundancy condition on lexical items (much as Brame and Bordelois suggest). There is, perhaps, yet another type of relationship between third plural preterite forms and past subjunctive forms, e.g., *comiéron, comiéra, pidiéron, pidiéra.* The forms always have the same theme vowel and the same stem vowel; further, the C following the ThV is an /r/. (A common heuristic device in Spanish language classes is to teach the students to derive the past subjunctive from the third plural preterite form.) If this is a native-speaker-type generalization, we would have to ask if our expression of it is adequate. In the analysis I proposed, this relationship is expressed by the two form types being treated by the same case in each of two rules, the ThV rule and the stem vowel rule. The adequacy of this representation should be investigated further.

Another point must be emphasized. In natural generative theory all P-rules are phonetically natural because they are phonetically motivated; on the other hand, phonological naturalness CANNOT be used as a criterion in expressing nonphonetic generalizations. Rules with morphological information are not phonetically natural; in fact, Vennemann (1971) states that morphosyntactic processes "are better the less 'natural', the less predictable they are, because symbolicness, i.e., informational value, is reciprocally related to predictability" (ms, p. 4). It is perhaps possible to develop some notions of morphosyntactic naturalness that can guide the description of morphosyntactically motivated alternations. Furthermore, some principles regarding simplicity and generality will clearly be necessary for evaluating morphological analyses. Natural generative theory provides a framework in which these empirical problems can be investigated.

# II

## NATURAL
## PHONOLOGICAL
## STRUCTURE

# 9

# Constraints on Phonological Structure

In the foregoing chapters we have discussed the dynamic rules and processes of morphophonology, comparing their representation in previous theories of generative phonology to their representation in natural generative phonology. We turn now to an examination of what are considered static conditions in TGP—constraints on possible segments and constraints on possible sequences of segments. In this chapter we take up two problems: the viability of the distinction between morpheme structure conditions and phonological rules and the correct formulation of phonotactic constraints. I will argue in the first case that there should be no separate class of rules designated as morpheme structure conditions and for the second case that phonotactic constraints should be stated in terms of the syllable rather than the morpheme. In subsequent chapters the form and content of syllable structure conditions are examined in detail.

## 9.1 Morpheme Structure Conditions

In TGP morpheme structure conditions (MSC) state the redundancies at the systematic phonemic level (Stanley, 1967). MSC's designate the feature values that are predictable or redundant in the lexical entries. There are two types of MSC's: segment structure conditions and sequence structure conditions. Segment structure conditions state the redundant feature values for segments regardless of their environment. A typical segment structure condition for vowels is the following:[1]

(1)
$$\begin{bmatrix} V \\ -low \\ \alpha back \end{bmatrix} \longrightarrow [\alpha round]$$

This rule is applicable to the Spanish vowel system (/a, i, e, o, u/), in which all non-low back vowels are round and all front vowels are non-round. The rule tells us that roundness is predictable, redundant, or nondistinctive for this underlying system.

A typical sequence structure condition is the following one for English that says a consonantal segment preceding a true consonant at the beginning of a morpheme must be /s/. All the features of /s/ except [+consonantal] are redundant.

(2) $[+consonantal] \longrightarrow$
$$\begin{bmatrix} -vocalic \\ +anterior \\ +coronal \\ +strident \\ +continuant \\ -voice \end{bmatrix} / + \underline{\hspace{1cm}} \begin{bmatrix} +consonantal \\ -vocalic \end{bmatrix}$$

MSC's have two basic functions. First, they create lexical economy by rendering a large number of lexical feature values redundant. Second, they express the constraints on the phonological system as a whole. Segmental conditions define the inventory of consonants and vowels, stating what the inadmissible segments are. For instance, MSC (1) rules out all front rounded or back unrounded non-low vowels. Sequential conditions state the phonotactic constraints: They are statements concerning which segments may follow and precede other segments. Thus

[1.] Stanley (1967) would give the rule in the following form:

$$I(C): \begin{bmatrix} V \\ -low \\ \alpha back \end{bmatrix}$$
$$\downarrow$$
$$T(C): [\alpha round]$$

where I stands for "if" and T stands for "then."

There is no great significance attached to this difference in format. In the text I use the same format for MSC's as for P-rules only for convenience.

MSC (2) rules out initial clusters such as */zp/, */rb/, */dn/, and so on. Together the two types of MSC define a possible morpheme for the language (Chomsky, 1964; Halle, 1964; Chomsky and Halle, 1968).

MSC's are distinguished from P-rules by definition. MSC's state the redundancies at the systematic phonemic level; P-rules map the systematic phonemic level onto the systematic phonetic level (Stanley, 1967). NGP does not make such a distinction. In NGP, since there is no separation of levels of representation and a rule applies to any string that meets its SD, there is no distinction made between MSC's and P-rules (Vennemann, 1972c:111). Because this is an important difference between the two theories, it is necessary for us to ask if the distinction between MSC's and P-rules is empirically motivated. This is equivalent to asking whether or not there is empirical evidence for the existence of a systematic phonemic level. I will be arguing briefly that the differentiation between constraints at the systematic phonemic level and the surface phonetic level is difficult to enforce on a principled basis and brings contradictory results.

A functional difference between the two types of rules in TGP is that P-rules change feature values but MSC's do not. If a rule must ever change a feature value, it must be a P-rule and not an MSC. Consider an example. In Spanish all syllable-final nasals before consonants are homorganic. This generalization holds within a morpheme:

(3)     [ambos]   'both'
        [onda]    'wave'
        [taŋgo]   'tango'

Thus there is a rule of nasal assimilation in Spanish. Now we must ask if it is an MSC or a P-rule.

$$
(4) \quad [+\text{nasal}] \longrightarrow \begin{bmatrix} \alpha\text{anterior} \\ \beta\text{coronal} \\ . \\ . \\ . \end{bmatrix} \Big/ \underline{\quad}\$ \begin{bmatrix} C \\ \alpha\text{anterior} \\ \beta\text{coronal} \\ . \\ . \\ . \end{bmatrix}
$$

The nasals in the words in (3) never alternate: Their features do not have to change. But there are cases for which nasal assimilation must change features. Nasal assimilation takes place across word boundaries (#). For example, the indefinite article is *un* /un/. The alveolar nasal is considered underlying because it occurs before vowels; in all other positions, the /n/ assimilates (Harris, 1969:16):

(5)  *un arbol*  [unarβol]  'a tree'   *un saco*   [unsako]   'a sack'
     *un peso*   [umpeso]   'a peso'   *un chico*  [uṅčiko][2] 'a boy'
     *un tio*    [uñtio][2]  'an uncle'  *un gato*   [uŋ gato]  'a cat'

To generate these variants of /un/, the nasal assimilation rule must change feature values; therefore it is a P-rule, not an MSC. But what about the generalization that could be made about the lexical items in (3)? Considerable lexical economy could be gained if all the features of such nasals were stated in an MSC. If we insist upon capturing the facts of nasal assimilation evidenced in (3), we would have to state rule (4) twice, once as an MSC and once as a P-rule. Clearly a loss of economy results. Thus, although nasal assimilation changes feature values, it is not at all clear that it is a P-rule and NOT an MSC.

Another criterion for differentiating between MSC's and P-rules brings the same confusing results. Chomsky and Halle (1968:171) state that "we cannot in all cases determine from the form of a rule whether it is a lexical redundancy rule or a rule of the phonology." They go on to give one possible criterion: "If . . . a rule . . . were to apply across a formative boundary, it could not be a lexical redundancy rule." Using the nasal assimilation case again, we see that, applying this criterion, nasal assimilation must be a P-rule because it may apply across formative and even word boundaries. Yet, for the reasons stated above, we would like a nasal assimilation to be an MSC. We might conclude that there are some phonological generalizations that have the characteristics of both MSC's and P-rules.

This is exactly the prediction that NGP makes about phonetically motivated rules such as nasal assimilation. Such rules express phonological constraints that hold at any level. In an NGP, the forms in (3) are listed in the lexicon with their nasal C's unspecified for point of articulation features. Rule (4) applies to fill in these features, and it applies also to the forms in (5), changing the features of the nasal to match those of the following consonant.

Furthermore, we should consider carefully the statement that MSC's define the notion "possible morpheme." Chomsky and Halle (1968) have claimed that it is the MSC's that make it possible for a speaker of English to differentiate between nonsense words on the basis of whether or not these words are possible English words. Shibatani (1973:94–95) has quite correctly observed that a possible morpheme is not completely definable on the systematic phonemic level, but that an acceptable form in a language is defined by the phonological rules of

---

[2] The nasal in [uñtio] is dental, while the [n] is alveolar; in [uṅčiko] the nasal is alveopalatal. The palatal nasal [ñ] does not occur in syllable-final position (see Chapter 11, note 2).

the language (or the surface phonetic constraints), in addition to the underlying phonotactic constraints. The example Shibatani uses to prove this point is from German, where all word-final obstruents are devoiced.[3] However, the devoicing occurs at the phonetic level, and there is nothing to prevent lexical forms from ending in voiced obstruents. Shibatani argues that, since /bund/, /rād/, /līb/ are possible lexical forms, the speaker of German should accept them as possible German forms. But Shibatani reports that native speakers of German reject these forms "ON THE GROUNDS THAT THEY END IN VOICED OBSTRUENTS, about which the German MSCs say nothing" (Shibatani 1973:95 [emphasis in original]). This and many similar examples argue against the psychological reality of abstract lexical representations; constraints on abstract forms, forms to which the phonological rules have not applied, do not capture the speaker's intuitions about what is a possible morpheme in his language.

Consider another related problem. In Spanish initial clusters of /s/ plus a [ + consonantal] segment are not allowed. When foreign words are borrowed that have such a cluster, an epenthetic /e/ is inserted before the cluster to render the form acceptable for Spanish.

(6)  esnob      'snob'
     esmoking   'tuxedo (smoking jacket)'
     eslavo     'Slav'

Thus a rule of epenthesis is necessary to derive a "possible morpheme." Yet in the standard TGP treatment of Spanish, Harris (1969) considers the rule of epenthesis to be a P-rule, since in his analysis it must apply AFTER the stress assignment rule (still another criterion for differentiating MSC's and P-rules). For Harris, the underlying form of the verb *estar* 'to be' is /stare/. The present tense forms of this verb are stressed on the desinence. Ordinarily a bisyllabic verb receives stress on the penultimate syllable in the present tense. But Harris considers *estar* to be monosyllabic at the point where stress is assigned, which accounts for its irregular stress.

stress  epenthesis

(7)  1 sg.  stoy ⟶ stóy ⟶ *estóy*
     2 sg.  stas ⟶ stás ⟶ *estás*

If the epenthetic vowel is added by a P-rule, lexical items in Spanish may begin with the cluster /s/ plus a consonant. The MSC's of Spanish would

---

[3] Venneman (1972d) shows that this is syllable-final devoicing, rather than word-final devoicing. The distinction is not crucial to the present argument.

have to be written to ALLOW such clusters, even though Spanish speakers know quite certainly that they are not possible initial clusters in Spanish. This MSC gives the wrong definition of "possible morpheme" of Spanish, and it is the P-rule of epenthesis that makes the form acceptable. In this analysis, which is allowed by TGP, the MSC and the P-rule contradict each other. The NGP analysis of epenthesis is given in Chapter 13, but for now it is enough to note that it is not possible to distinguish MSC's from P-rules by claiming that only MSC's may express phonotactic constraints, because this is precisely the function of epenthesis and even this rule may be considered a P-rule.

It seems, then, that the claim that there is a systematic distinction between MSC's and phonological rules is based on scanty empirical evidence. Without evidence to the contrary, one must assume that the lack of such a distinction in NGP is a point in that theory's favor.

Just above I mentioned that in the epenthesis case the generalization expressed by the MSC contradicts the generalization of the phonological rules. That is, the MSC's define one type of unit (in the epenthesis case, a unit that may have initial #sC) and the phonological rules define another unit (one that may NOT have initial #sC). Such cases are quite common in TGP analyses due to the separation of the systematic phonemic level from the systematic phonetic level. The more abstract the systematic phonemic level, the greater the possibility for contradictory generalizations at the two levels.

To see how this is so, consider now segment structure conditions. Stanley (1967:403) suggests that segment structure conditions should apply at the systematic phonemic level AND after the application of certain P-rules. I will give a real language example that is of the same type as one of Stanley's hypothetical examples.

As I mentioned above, Spanish has five vowels, /a, i, e, o, u/. As we saw in (1), a generalization about the feature specification of these vowels is that non-low vowels agree in the feature values for back roundness. MSC (1) is repeated here for convenience:

$$(1) \qquad \begin{bmatrix} V \\ -\text{low} \\ \alpha\text{back} \end{bmatrix} \longrightarrow [\alpha\text{round}]$$

MSC (1) is a segment structure condition operating at the systematic phonemic level. An epenthetic vowel, added after the systematic phonemic level, will also meet the conditions stated in (1). The epenthesis rule we discussed above inserts /e/ before clusters of /s/ followed by a consonant. The epenthetic vowel conforms to condition (1), as it is both [−back] and [−round]. If the redundant feature [−round] had to be specified in the epenthesis rule, a generalization would be missed. Stanley proposes that the redundant feature need not be included in the P-rule, but rather that the MSC (1) could apply again after the epenthesis rule to supply the redundant feature.

Stanley's suggestion that the output of some P-rules be subjected to the segment structure rules seems to be a good one and one that should be extended to all P-rules. The trouble is that for many TGP analyses, the reapplication of the segment structure conditions would produce the wrong results, because these analyses postulate a segment inventory for the systematic phonemic level that does not correspond to the inventory at the phonetic level. Consider the underlying consonant inventory that Harris (1969:166) posits for Spanish, and compare it to a partial inventory for the systematic phonetic level. All cases of systematic phonetic [x] are derived from underlying /ǰ/.

(8)                      Underlying consonants

| p | t | č | k |
|---|---|---|---|
| b | d | ǰ | g |
| f | s |   |   |

(9)                      Systematic phonetic

| p | t | č | k |
|---|---|---|---|
| b | d |   | g |
| f | s |   | x |

A segment structure condition for (8) could capture the generalization that voiceless fricatives are redundantly [ + anterior]; that is, /f/ and /s/ exist, but /x/ does not:

(10)     $\begin{bmatrix} +\text{continuant} \\ -\text{voice} \end{bmatrix} \longrightarrow [+\text{anterior}]$

If (10) could reapply after each P-rule, it would make the derivation of [x] from /ǰ/ impossible. Harris's analysis may be maintained either by not stating (10) as an MSC, or by not allowing (10) to reapply after the P-rules. If (10) is not stated, the economy that Harris hoped to obtain by positing the "somewhat more symmetrical" system (8) would be lost. If (10) is not allowed to apply after the P-rules, then we must find some way to constrain (10) while still allowing (1) to reapply. Such a constraint is possible, but any attempt at it is certain to be ad hoc.

This problem arises because of the decision to posit different segment inventories at the abstract and surface levels. The condition (10) holds only at the abstract level, not at the surface level. It is not clear how a constraint that is incompatible with the surface segment structure can be considered part of a speaker's competence. The burden of proof for the psychological reality of such constraints is surely on those who propose them.[4]

In NGP such a problem cannot arise. Because all statements in the grammar are true generalizations about surface forms, any constraint that holds on one "level" also holds on any other. NGP has segment structure conditions of the same type as those proposed for TGP, and these conditions, like all rules in NGP, may reapply after other rules if their SD's are met. Segment structure conditions may be used throughout a derivation to fill in redundant feature values and to express constraints on segment structure. On the other hand, the sequence structure conditions of TGP are not suitable for NGP. We turn now to a discussion of sequence structure conditions.

## 9.2 The Basic Unit for Phonotactic Constraints

As we noted above, constraints on sequences of segments (phonotactic constraints) are expressed on the systematic phonemic level by MSC's of the following form:

$$(11) \; [+\text{consonantal}] \longrightarrow \begin{bmatrix} +\text{anterior} \\ +\text{coronal} \\ +\text{continuant} \\ +\text{strident} \\ -\text{voice} \end{bmatrix} / + \underline{\quad} \begin{bmatrix} -\text{vocalic} \\ +\text{consonantal} \end{bmatrix}$$

Rule (11) captures the generalization for English that only /s/ may precede a true consonant at the beginning of a morpheme. The form of such rules may be criticized from two points of view. In this section I will consider the validity of the claim that the morpheme should be taken as the basic unit for the statement of sequential constraints. In Section 9.3, I will discuss the directionality of such rules. In following chapters, I will propose an alternate method of expressing phonotactic constraints.

I will assume that the purpose of the sequential MSC is to express the generalizations about how segments may be combined to form larger units. We know that all languages have very rigid constraints on sequence structure. For instance, a language such as Japanese has the following restrictions: (i) no more than one C may occur at the beginning or end of a sequence; (ii) no more than two C's may occur together in a

---

[4] See also Hooper (1975) and Clayton (1976) for further arguments against the notion of morpheme structure conditions.

sequence; and (iii) there are rigid constraints on which two C's may occur together: specifically, the two C's must be identical voiceless stops or clusters of nasal plus consonant. On the other hand, English allows clusters of up to three C's in initial and final position. But even so, the possibilities for segment sequences in such clusters are severely restricted. Consider initial clusters of two C's: #pr is allowed, but not #rp. In initial clusters of three C's, #str is allowed, but all other combinations of these three segments are ruled out: #trs, #rts, #srt, #tsr, and #rst. Even in the languages that allow relatively complex consonant clusters, the occurring clusters represent only a very small percentage of all theoretically possible consonant clusters. A metatheory of language should be able to define the possible segment sequences in a natural language and should supply a mechanism for defining language-specific constraints on segment sequences.

In TGP the MSC's coupled with a theory of markedness are supposed to serve this function (Chomsky and Halle, 1968, Chapter 9; Cairns, 1969). Because MSC's are stated in terms of morphemes, for most languages they cannot capture all the generalizations about sequence structure. This is because the morpheme is by definition a syntactic unit. Although a morpheme may be meaningful in itself, it is not necessarily pronounceable in isolation and does not necessarily have an acceptable phonological structure unless it is combined with other morphemes. The most striking example is a zero allomorph, Ø, which has no phonological manifestation at all. For example, the English past tense morpheme in *put* and *hit* is null; the plural morpheme in *fish* and *sheep* is also null or zero. A similar example is the past tense morpheme in *sang* or *brought,* which is realized as a change in the stem. It does not seem possible to characterize the phonological structure of such morphemes in terms of MSC's.

Consider a different sort of example from Spanish. The progressive morpheme in Spanish is +*ndo.* It is added to a sequence of stem plus theme vowel as the following examples illustrate (orthography):

(12)

| Stem | | Theme | | Progressive | |
|------|---|-------|---|-------------|---|
| *habl* | + | *a* | + | *ndo* | *hablando* 'speaking' |
| *com* | + | *ie* | + | *ndo* | *comiendo* 'eating' |
| *viv* | + | *ie* | + | *ndo* | *viviendo* 'living' |

Although the morpheme +*ndo* is an acceptable morpheme, it is not an acceptable or pronounceable initial cluster. The MSC's of Spanish must be stated to allow clusters such as +*nd* in morpheme initial position.

Therefore they cannot express the stronger constraint that such clusters are not allowed in word initial position. And they cannot account for the significant fact that morphemes with such clusters must always be combined with other morphemes in such a way that they are preceded by a vowel.

It does not help to try to meet these objections by distinguishing between lexical and grammatical morphemes and claiming that only lexical morphemes are subject to MSC's.[5] For the most part such an approach would work when dealing with the BEGINNINGS of morphemes, but we encounter trouble again when we examine the ENDS of morphemes. There are strict constraints on sequences at the ends of phonological structures, but lexical morphemes do not obey these constraints. Consider the final clusters in the following Spanish verb stems:

(13)

| Stem (phonemic) | Infinitive | |
| --- | --- | --- |
| abl+ | ablar | 'to speak' |
| kompr+ | komprar | 'to buy' |
| kans+ | kansar | 'to tire' |

None of these final clusters (/bl/, /mpr/, /ns/) are acceptable as word or utterance-final clusters; in fact, these stems are not pronounceable in isolation. Yet strictly formulated MSC's would have to state that such phonological sequences are acceptable.

Another possible suggestion is that these problems will not arise if MSC's for stems are separate from the MSC's for affixes. For instance, initial +nd would be allowed only for suffixes and final bl+ only on stems that will be followed by a vowel. This suggestion, however, does not provide an explanatory account of the fact that +nd is allowed only on suffixes and further must be preceded by a V in the output combination, and that all stems that end in C clusters are always followed by suffixes that have initial V's. The theory of phonotactics to be presented below provides an explanatory account of all such constraints.

It is clear, then, that constraints on sequence structure that are stated in terms of the morpheme cannot make the strongest possible nor the most explanatory generalizations about phonotactic structure. Instead of using a unit of syntax, the morpheme, as the basic unit for expressing constraints on phonological structure, we should use a unit that is purely phonological. The smallest phonological unit that may be multi-

---

[5] This is apparently what Cairns (1969) had in mind when he phrased his discussion in terms of "stems."

segmental (i.e., the smallest pronounceable unit) is the syllable. If the constraints on sequence structure are to represent what is pronounceable in a specific language, then they should be stated in terms of the smallest pronounceable unit.

To see why the syllable must be used to express phonotactic constraints, consider the famous unacceptable English sequence *bnik*. Initial clusters of *bn* must be ruled out. There are also some internal occurrences of *bn* that must be ruled out. But there ARE some internal occurrences of *bn* that are acceptable.[6]

(14)    *bnik*
        stabnik (cf. *sputnik, beatnik, Abner*)
        *stambnik*

We can exclude *bnik* and *stambnik* but allow *stabnik*, if the constraint is stated in terms of the syllable. The constraint is that *bn* is not a possible syllable-initial cluster. The items in (14) are syllabified as in (15).

(15)    *$bnik
        stab$nik
        *stam$bnik

The form *stabnik* is acceptable because the consonants *b* and *n* occur in separate syllables. The cluster *mb* is not an acceptable syllable-final cluster; there is no acceptable syllabification of *stambnik*. The best way the unacceptability of *bnik* and *stambnik* can be accounted for in a single generalization, while still allowing *stabnik*, is by stating that generalization in terms of the syllable.

Another reason for choosing the syllable instead of the morpheme or word as the basic phonological unit is that morphemes and words may be made up of more than one syllable. Recurring sequences must be accounted for under two descriptions. For instance, one part of the marking convention for the feature consonantal proposed by Chomsky and Halle (1968:404) is (16).

(16)    [u consonantal] $\longrightarrow$ [+consonantal] / $\begin{bmatrix} + \\ +\text{vocalic} \\ -\text{consonantal} \end{bmatrix}$___

In prose, the unmarked value for consonantal is plus in two environments: after a morpheme boundary and after a vowel. What Chomsky and Halle intend here is to make the C's in a sequence +CVCV unmarked. But their rule misses the generalization. It claims, in effect,

[6] This observation is due to Larry Hyman.

that there are two unmarked positions for C's. However, both C positions in + CVCV are syllable initial; there is only one unmarked position for a C, and that is syllable-initial position.

A more serious difficulty with (16) is that it claims that a C after a V is unmarked for consonantality (and another marking convention states that such a C is unmarked for vocalic as well), independent of what segment follows the C. That is, $C_2$ in each of the following sequences is unmarked for both consonantal and vocalic.

(17)     a.   + $C_1VC_2V$
         b.   + $C_1VC_2$ +
         c.   + $C_1VC_2C_3V$

Although it is universally assumed that the unmarked syllable is open (\$CV\$), the Chomsky and Halle marking conventions fail to distinguish between an open syllable and a closed one (\$CVC\$). They do not represent the fact that a syllable-final C (as in (b) and (c)) is more marked than a syllable-initial C.[7] I will present considerable evidence in the following chapters to the effect that the only unmarked position for a C is syllable-initial position. The marking conventions of Chomsky and Halle fail to capture this generalization: On the one hand, their convention must state in two different ways a single generalization, and on the other hand, the convention actually produces results that are at variance with the well-known facts about segment sequences. Both of these problems can be solved by stating sequential constraints in terms of the syllable, rather than in terms of syntactic or semantic units.[8]

The use of the syllable to define basic sequence structure conditions does not exclude any reference to be morpheme or word in stating constraints. Some languages do have constraints on the shape of words or morphemes. For example, in Akan (Schachter and Fromkin, 1968) root morphemes (stems) may consist of a maximum of three syllables. A valid generalization may be stated in terms of the root morpheme to the effect that such morphemes may consist of from one to three syllables. It is interesting to note that even this type of generalization does not refer to all morphemes, but only root morphemes. It seems, in fact, that there are no phonotactic constraints that are applicable to morphemes and

---

[7] This observation is due to Sandra Thompson.

[8] Stating phonotactic constraints in terms of the syllable is certainly no new idea. Jakobson and Halle (1956:31) observe "the elementary pattern underlying any grouping of phonemes is the SYLLABLE" [emphasis theirs]. See Pulgram (1970:41) for references to the numerous other scholars who have made the same observation in recent years. The only reason the point has to be argued again here is that TGP made the false assumption that phonotactic constraints could be stated in terms of the morpheme.

that apply to all morphemes, regardless of function or type, except in languages in which the unit morpheme always corresponds to the syllable. For instance, in Mandarin MSC's would in effect be syllable structure conditions, since all morphemes are monosyllabic. A different sort of relation obtains in Desano, where, according to Kaye (1971), all segments of each morpheme agree in nasality and all morphemes consist of complete syllables.

In a limited number of cases there are constraints that apply to the word as a unit. For instance, in English the phoneme /ž/, as in *pleasure*, may not appear in word-initial position. Another type of constraint on word structure is discussed in Section 10.3.

## 9.3  Directionality

Stanley (1967) proposed three types of MSC: the if–then condition (such as (1) and (2) of this chapter), the negative condition (which we will not be discussing), and the positive condition. Stanley used the positive condition to state phonotactic constraints on sequences of vowels, consonants, and liquids. For instance, in the simplest case, and, unlike Stanley, using the syllable as a base, a language that has only CV syllables would have the following condition:

$$P(C): \quad \$CV\$$$

(P stands for positive; (C) for condition.) Any syllable that does not meet this condition would not be judged a well-formed syllable for this language. This type of condition, rather than the if–then condition, is particularly appropriate for such a phonotactic constraint because, to use an if–then condition, one must decide whether the features of the C are predictable from the following V or if the features of the V are predictable from the preceding C. Such a decision is purely arbitrary.

To illustrate this, consider the problem that arises in markedness theory as a result of the use of if–then conditions to predict markedness. There have been two marking conventions proposed for assigning feature values to sequences of the shape + VC. They are from Chomsky and Halle (1968) and Cairns (1969).

| (18) | | Chomsky and Halle<br>+VC | Cairns<br>+VC |
|---|---|---|---|
| | consonantal | MU | UM |
| | vocalic | MU | UU |

Chomsky and Halle claim that a vowel in initial position is fully marked, while a C after a V (as we noted above) is fully unmarked. Cairns bases his marking convention for the initial vowel on the following consonants; he claims that a V is unmarked if a consonant follows and that a segment is [m consonantal] after any other segment. There are no substantive arguments for one marking convention or the other for this particular sequence. No empirical issue is involved. The fact that there is more than one analysis of this sequence is a consequence of the formal decision to predict the features of one segment on the basis of the features of another.

A similar problem is encountered in any attempt to incorporate syllable boundaries into the phonological string using if–then conditions. The question is, are the occurrences of $'s predictable on the basis of existing segments, or are the segments predictable on the basis of existing $'s? Both approaches have been proposed. Fudge (1969) proposed rules that generate syllables or predict the occurrence of certain segments by the position in the syllable. In Hooper (1972c), I proposed the alternate approach: to insert $'s on the basis of existing strings of segments.

Actually, there is evidence that a comprehensive treatment of syllable structure should be able to move in both directions. We know that speakers can, more or less consistently, break words in their language up into syllables. This ability is equivalent to inserting $'s into existing strings. At the same time, speakers can take foreign words and modify their syllable structure by inserting or deleting segments to produce strings with syllable structure consistent with that of the native language. A simple example of this process is the adaptation of English loan words into Japanese. Consider the English word *beer*. Since Japanese does not allow syllable-final consonants (except for nasals and C's identical to following C's), the Japanese version of *beer* cannot end in /r/. Instead of dropping the /r/, an acceptable syllable is produced by adding a V after /r/. The result is *biiru* [bi:rɯ]. This type of process seems to show that syllable-formation is productive and that there is very possibly a rule that inserts V's into syllables in the correct position. Thus there is evidence that syllable division may be predicted on the basis of existing segments and that the occurrence of segments may also be predicted on the basis of existing syllable division.

In order to account for the evidence in the previous paragraph, and to avoid any problems of directionality, I propose that syllable structure conditions (SSC) be stated as positive conditions on sequences of $'s and segments. Thus for a strict CV language, the syllable structure condition would be:

(19)                              P(C):   $CV$

This condition has two functions. As a positive condition, it merely captures the generalization that all of the syllables of this language have the shape CV. Second, it functions as a generative rule. And in this respect it is different from the positive conditions of Stanley (1967). As a rule that may change or add feature values, the condition is understood as an abbreviation for the following three if–then conditions.

(20)      a. I(C):  C(V)
             ↓
        T(C):  $

      b. I(C): $C
               ↓
        T(C):  V

      c. I(C): $  V$
             ↓
        T(C):  C

Notice that these conditions overlap (unlike the if–then conditions of markedness theory) so that given a string of segments, $'s may be inserted; or given a string of C's and $'s, V's may be inserted; or, finally, given a string of $'s and V's, C's may be inserted. If these conditions were rendered in terms of binary distinctive features, it would be possible to predict the values of the features consonantal and vocalic of a segment following a C. However, I do not intend that phonotactics should be stated as a matter of redundancy. The conditions overlap so that they also allow the values of consonantal and vocalic to be predictable in a segment preceding a V. The SSC applies at the level of word formation to organize the string into syllables. It may then reapply if the insertion of a $ or a segment becomes necessary in the course of a derivation.

 Furthermore, the SSC can be used to account for cases of loan word treatment in the following manner. A Japanese speaker substitutes a long V for the English diphthong [iy] in *beer:* *[biːr]. Part (a) of the SSC will apply to assign S's: $bi:$r$ ($'s also replace all syntactic boundaries; see immediately below). The second syllable of the sequence is unacceptable because there is no V. Part (b) of the SSC can remedy this situation by inserting a V: $bi:$rV$. The string now consists of acceptable syllables. All that remains to make this an acceptable Japanese word is to determine the quality of the inserted V. We will see in Chapter 13 that even the quality of the vowel can be determined automatically on the basis of universal principles.

Besides the language specific SSC, $'s are also assigned by a universal rule that places $'s at the beginning and ends of words. (See Hoard (1971) and Hooper (1972c).) Sometimes such $'s are moved when resyllabification takes place around #'s, but in many cases the $'s must remain to mark the word boundaries. For instance, in English the pairs *nitrate* and *night rate* are distinguished phonetically by the occurrence of a $ between the *t* and *r* in the latter, which is there to mark the place of the #. No such # occurs in *nitrate*, so the $ falls before the cluster *tr*.

It is important to note that the SSC is a positive condition and does not predict the features of one segment on the basis of feature values of other segments. None of the +'s or −'s for the features consonantal and vocalic are considered redundant. This particular proposal is not directed toward achieving lexical economy. Thus the problem of multiple analyses such as those proposed by Chomsky and Halle and Cairns does not arise. More important, however, is the claim implicit in the SSC that the values of features such as consonantal and vocalic do not stand in any unidirectional relation of predictability. The parts of (20) show that the various parts of the syllable are predictable from one another depending on the situation, but there is no static unidirectional relation in which it can be said that the feature values for the V are predictable from the preceding C, or the C is predictable from the following V.

This does not mean that there are not some relations in which the feature values of one segment are predictable from another segment. In fact, there is an important distinction to be made here. Conditions on sequence structure should be distinguished from assimilation rules in which the value of a feature is truly predictable from its environment. A good example of a rule of this type is nasal assimilation:

$$
(21) \quad \begin{bmatrix} C \\ +\text{nasal} \end{bmatrix} \longrightarrow \begin{bmatrix} \alpha\text{anterior} \\ \beta\text{coronal} \\ \cdot \\ \cdot \\ \cdot \end{bmatrix} / \underline{\quad} \begin{bmatrix} C \\ \alpha\text{anterior} \\ \beta\text{coronal} \\ \cdot \\ \cdot \\ \cdot \end{bmatrix}
$$

In this case we can truly claim that the features of the nasal are redundant or predictable from the environment and that the relation moves in one direction only, i.e., that it is the nasal C that assimilates, and not the following consonant.

# 10

# Strength Relations
# in Syllable Structure

## 10.1. Strength Relations

To this point I have discussed only the very simplest type of syllable structure condition (SSC), that of a CV language. There are many more complex syllable types that must be described. Many languages allow consonant clusters in syllable-initial and syllable-final positions, yet the composition of these clusters is restricted, and these restrictions must also be described and explained. In this chapter I introduce a theory of syllable structure that provides a simple description of language-specific and universal syllable structures and an explanation for the constraints on syllable structure. To begin, let us examine a language with syllable structure of moderate complexity. The following chart shows the possible distribution of consonants in a syllable of modern Spanish.[1]

[1] Although other obstruents besides /s/ appear orthographically in syllable-final position, in casual speech such C's are systematically omitted. On the other hand, only a few dialects delete /s/ in this position, and the sonorants are quite stable here. All of these phenomena are discussed in detail in Chapter 11. Other nasals occur in syllable-final position, but they are predictable from the nasal assimilation rule. For simplicity, I will not include these in the general discussion, but see Chapter 11, notes 2 and 3.

(1)               $\$C_mC_nC_pVC_qC_r\$$
                  m1 = /f, p, t, k, b, d, g/
                  m2 = /s, m, n, ñ, l, r, r̄, č, x/
                  n = /r, l/
                  p,q = /y, w/
                  r = /s, m, n, l, r/

The C's in $C_m$ position (initial position) are divided into two groups. Group m1 are those C's that may be followed by another consonant. Notice that all members of group m1 are obstruents. Group 2m consists of those C's that may not appear in a cluster. Notice that group m2 includes all the sonorants, and that group r is a subset of group m2. The C's that may occur after obstruents in $C_n$ position are also included in groups m2 and r. What the chart in (1) shows is that the occurrence of a segment seems to depend on whether it is an obstruent, nasal, liquid, glide, or vowel. In fact, in Hooper (1972c) I pointed out that there is a rough hierarchy of suitability for initial and final positions that is illustrated in (2).

(2)   Optimal syllable-initial   obstruents       ↑
                           |   nasals
                           |   liquids
                           |   glides
                           ↓   vowels     Optimal syllable-final

The significant fact is that the hierarchy for final position is the exact converse of the hierarchy for initial position. It is reasonable to expect the SSC to be able to capture this relation.

Vennemann (1972d) has proposed a method of capturing this relation between segment type and syllabification. He has proposed that syllabification rules be stated in terms of consonantal strength. For Modern Icelandic Vennemann proposes a strength scale for consonants such as (3).

(3)

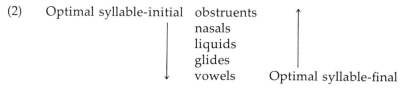

                              f
                              b
       j          m   d       p
      v   r   l   n   g   s   k   t
      1   2   3   4   5   6   7   8 →

In Section 10.3 I will discuss the way Vennemann justifies such a strength scale, but for now it is sufficient to note that the obstruents are assigned higher numbers (indicating their greater strength), while nasals have relatively lower numbers and liquids and glides have the lowest numbers. Vennemann offers two alternate formulations of a $-

insertion rule for Modern Icelandic. One, (4), must mention the individual segments or the features of the segments:

(4)    $\varnothing \longrightarrow S/V \underline{\hspace{1cm}} \begin{Bmatrix} p \\ t \\ k \\ s \end{Bmatrix} \begin{Bmatrix} r \\ j \\ v \end{Bmatrix} V$

The other makes use of the strength scale (3) and refers to C's by their relative strength instead of by their distinctive feature values.

(5)    $\varnothing \longrightarrow S/V \underline{\hspace{1cm}} \begin{bmatrix} C \\ m \text{ strength} \end{bmatrix} \begin{bmatrix} C \\ n \text{ strength} \end{bmatrix} V$
Condition:  m $\geqslant$ 6, n $\leqslant$ 2.

The reason for preferring a treatment of syllabification in terms of strength over one in terms of distinctive features of segments is that by correlating a cover feature strength of consonants with the strength of syllable position, we can develop an EXPLANATION for phonotactic constraints on segments, provided, of course, that the strength hierarchy can be independently motivated. We shall see below that this is possible. Vennemann's proposal captures the relationship between the universal intrinsic structure of the syllable and the distribution of segment types in the syllable. Specifically, there are weak and strong positions in the syllable, and consistently the weak positions are occupied by the weaker C's, while the strong positions are occupied by the strong C's.

The explanatory value of such a view of syllable structure also seemed attractive to earlier phoneticians and phonologists. Jespersen (as reported in Malmberg, 1963) proposed that sounds group themselves in a syllable according to their sonority or audibility. The most sonorous segment occupies the nucleus, and the farther from the nucleus on either margin the least sonorant the sounds will be. Jespersen proposed the following ranking on the basis of sonority. The least sonorant are listed first.

(6)    1. Voiceless consonants:
       a.  stops (p, t, k)
       b.  fricatives (f, s)
    2. Voiced stops (b, d, g)
    3. Voiced fricatives (v, z)
    4. Nasals and laterals (m, n, l)
    5. Trills and flaps (r)
    6. Close vowels (y, i, u)

7.   Mid vowels (e, o, ε, ɔ)
8.   Open vowels (a)

(Note the striking correspondence with Vennemann's rankings.)

A similar proposal was made by Saussure (1915[1959]), who formulated a definition of the syllable on the basis of the degree of opening of the sounds. The most open sounds occur at the syllable nucleus, the least open at the margins. A classification of segments on the basis of opening yields results similar to a classification on the basis of sonority. Vowels are at once the most open and the most sonorant. Stops are the least open and the least sonorant.

For Jespersen and Saussure, C's occupy one end of the scale and V's the other. This is understandable in view of Jakobson's and Halle's (1956:31) explanation of syllable structure: "The pivotal principle of syllable structure is the contrast of successive features within the syllable." The dominant part of any syllable is the nucleus, which usually consists of a vowel. The margins of the syllable (the onset and the coda) provide a contrast with the nucleus: The consonantal release produces the minimum amount of energy and the vocalic nucleus the maximum amount of energy. In this view, in which the prime function of the successive segments is to CONTRAST, the optimal segment for syllable-initial position is the least vowel-like segment. Thus in our terms "strongest" (or optimal) consonant is defined as the least vowel-like consonant, whether the particular parameter is sonority or openness.

By discussing the physical parameters of strength and syllabicity, I do not intend to give the impression that there is some absolute physical correlate to strength or to the syllable. In fact, all attempts to establish consonantal strength hierarchies on a single phonetic parameter have been less than successful, and all attempts to locate syllable boundaries on a purely physical basis have also failed. As Pulgram (1970) points out, this failure of phonetics does not deny the existence of a functional linguistic unit, for, after all, it is also impossible on a purely physical basis to indentify the boundaries between individual segments. Yet no one would claim that segments, consonants, and vowels do not exist as functional units of language. With Pulgram, then, I am viewing the syllable, and for that matter the cover feature strength, as theoretical constructs, not entirely divorced from physical reality, but abstract in that their importance is seen only in their function in a linguistic system.

In the remainder of this chapter I will present a wide variety of evidence to support the following three claims: (i) Strength hierarchies can be determined on various phonological grounds; (ii) syllable structure follows a definite pattern; and (iii) the pattern of consonantal strength and the pattern of syllable structure are related.

## 10.2. The Intrinsic Structure of the Syllable

If the syllable is viewed as a unit whose center is the most vowel-like and whose outer margins are the least vowel-like, then it is reasonable to speculate further that any intervening segments will be intermediate between least and most vowel-like. This structure is exactly what occurs in consonant clustering:

| MARGIN | NUCLEUS | MARGIN |
|---|---|---|
| obstruents nasals liquids glides | vowels | glides liquids nasals obstruents |
| Least vowel-like | Most vowel-like | Less vowel-like |
| STRONG | WEAK | WEAK |

Consonantal strength is crucial, not merely to the determination of the placement of C's around the nucleus, but also to the difference between syllable-initial position and syllable-final position. A great deal of phonological evidence indicates that syllable-initial position is universally stronger than syllable-final position.[2]

On a universal level, the CV syllable is the optimal syllable. There is no language that does not allow a syllable type CV, and there are some languages that allow this type and no other.[3] This means that a C in initial position is favored over a C in any other position, e.g., CCV or CVC, and that in initial position a C is favored over a V, as in V or VC. It has also been observed that the CV syllable is the first syllable type learned by children (Jakobson, 1941 [1972]; Jackobson and Halle, 1956).

Phonological processes also show that syllable-initial position is the strongest position. Processes generally known under the name "strengthening" always occur in syllable-initial position and never in syllable-final or second position. For example, there is an optional rule in Spanish that changes glides /y/ and /w/ into obstruents (fricatives) in syllable-initial position. The following words have two alternate pronunciations:

(7)
| | hielo | huevo | haya | agua |
|---|---|---|---|---|
| | 'ice' | 'egg' | 'there is' | 'water' |
| | [yelo] | [weβo] | [aya] | [awa] |
| | [ŷelo] | [gʷeβo] | [aŷa] | [aɣʷa] |

---

[2] This observation has been made recently by Vennemann (1972c:109; 1972d:9).

[3] Sommer (1970) has claimed that Kunjen is a language with no CV syllables. However, this claim is applicable only to the underlying level he posits, since CV syllables do occur in the surface.

The rule may be stated informally as:

(8)
$$\begin{bmatrix} y \\ w \end{bmatrix} \longrightarrow \begin{bmatrix} \hat{y} \\ g^w \end{bmatrix} / S\underline{\phantom{xxx}}$$

Similarly, in English the environment for aspiration of voiceless stops is syllable-initial position. Thus we have *pin* [pʰɪn], *open* [owpʰən]. But in second position, after syllable-initial /s/, the /p/ is unaspirated: *spin* [spɪn]. And in syllable-final position, the voiceless stop is unreleased: *top* [tʰapᵖ], *topnotch* [tʰapᵖnač]. Both the unaspirated and released variants are weaker than the aspirated consonant.

The strong and weak consonantal positions in the syllable are distinguished by the number of contrasts that are possible in the position. As we saw in (1), all C's of Spanish may occur in syllable-initial position; thus all contrasts are possible in that position. The chart in (1) also shows that second position and syllable-final position have a much smaller inventory of occurring segments. What is not evident in (1) is that some contrasts are actually neutralized in syllable-final position. In syllable-final position the nasal consonants do not contrast. When they occur before a C in the next syllable, the nasal assimilates all point of articulation features to the features of the next C. In word or utterance final position, there is no assimilation, but the nasal C's do not contrast. In some dialects, only /n/ occurs word-finally, while in other dialects all word-final nasals are realized as velars, /ŋ/ (Malmberg, 1948).

Similarly, we find assimilation occurring more readily and more commonly at the end of the syllable than at the beginning. As syllables are strung together, the end of one syllable (its weak position) immediately precedes the beginning of the next (the strong position). Given the theory of the syllable presented here, it is reasonable to expect that the C in the stronger position will influence the C in the weaker position, but it is not reasonable to expect the opposite relation will hold. Indeed, the facts bear out this projection. Nasal assimilation in Spanish occurs before the glides /y/ and /w/, but only if the nasal is syllable-final and the glide is syllable-initial. If the nasal and the glide are tautosyllabic, no assimilation takes place. The difference in syllabification in the following examples is due to the influence of the word boundary ([ñ] is a palatoalveolar nasal):

(9) *un hielo* [uñyelo] 'an ice' *nieto* [nyeto] 'grandson'
    *un huevo* [uŋweβo] 'an egg' *nuevo* [nweβo] 'new'

Notice that the assimilation evident in the first column takes place even if the optional glide strengthening rule (8) has not applied. Thus the only relevant difference between the glides in the first column of (9) and the glides in the second column is their position in the syllable (Hooper, 1972c). Vennemann (1972d:15) explains further that assimilation in syllable-final position is entirely natural because assimilation is a weakening process. We return to this concept in Chapter 13.

Diachronic evidence also attests the relative weakness of syllable-final position. The loss of consonants in syllable-final position is extremely common. Correspondences between Latin and Modern Spanish illustrate this loss.[4]

(10)      Latin    > Spanish
          *septem*  > *siete*    'seven'
          *ursum*   > *oso*      'bear'
          *pulsum*  > *poso*     'rest'
          *sponsum* > *esposo*   'spouse'

These same consonants in syllable-initial position are never deleted. Similar processes of syllable-final attrition are attested in nonrelated languages. See Chen (1972) for a duscussion of this process in Chinese dialects.

The evidence presented in this section both clarifies and substantiates the claim that syllables have inherently weak and strong positions. In the next sections I will try to clarify the terms weak and strong as applied to consonants and exemplify the kinds of evidence that can be used to establish universal and language-specific strength relations among consonants.

## 10.3. Consonantal Strength Hierarchies

The cover feature strength corresponds inversely to the rough phonetic correlates of degree of sonority (as Jespersen observed) and degree of opening (as Saussure observed). To date, these phonetic parameters have not been made more precise. However, there is considerable phonological evidence, both in syllable structure and independently of syllable structure, that points to the significance of a hierarchy among consonants. In this section, we will present phonological evidence for the strength hierarchy that is completely independent of syllable structure.[5] This evidence shows that voiceless C's are ranked higher than

---

[4] Romance nouns are derived from the Latin accusative. The loss of final [m] is also a case of syllable-final weakening, but this loss only occurs when a homorganic obstruent does NOT follow, i.e., at the end of the word.

[5] Zwicky (1972) discusses the consonantal hierarchy in English. However, his examples relate directly to syllable structure, as I show in Hooper (1976a).

voiced C's in terms of strength, stops higher than spirants, nonnasals higher than nasals, and nasal consonants higher than liquids and glides.

The goal in the following discussion is to establish consonantal strength rankings for classes of consonants such as /p, t, k/ in relation to /b, d, g/ or /m, n, ŋ/. It is also possible to rank consonants by relative strength according to point of articulation as well as manner of articulation (Jakobson and Halle, 1956:50–58; Foley, 1970). Such details will be ignored here, except where they are necessary to the statement of the specific syllable structure condition for Spanish to be presented in Chapter 11.

Foley (1970) shows that a system of strength rankings can be justified on the basis of historical sound changes. He notes that in several Indo-European languages there have been consonant shifts in which a group of related changes took place. Consider the following example of the Spanish consonant shift. Long C's become short, short C's become voiced, voiced C's become continuants, and subsequently some continuants are lost.

(11)     a.  tt ⟶ t
         b.  t ⟶ d
         c.  d ⟶ ð
         d.  ð ⟶ Ø

The last two developments in (11) have taken place twice. First Latin voiced stops spirantized and were deleted (Otero, 1971:304–05).

(12)     Latin    Medieval    Modern
         *radice* > raðice    > *raiz*     'root'
         *legale* > leɣale    > *leal*     'loyal'

The second stage (11b) produced a new group of voiced obstruents from voiceless ones. After many centuries the voiced stops also spirantized (Otero, 1971:315), and the interdental voiced spirant is now lost in some dialects.

(13)     Latin      Medieval      Modern
         *lupu*    > lobo        > loβo       'wolf'
         *sakrato* > sagrado     > saɣraðo    'sacred'
                     Dialectal:    sagrao

Examples of the degemination (11a) are (Menéndez Pidal, 1968:134):

(14)     Latin     Modern Spanish (orthography)
         *cuppa* > *copa*    'cup'

> *gutta* > *gota*   'drop'
> *bucca* > *boca*   'mouth'

This consonant shift is considered a weakening process, since each stage brought the consonant closer to zero. Thus the following strength hierarchy is established:

(15) 
$$\overrightarrow{\frac{\eth \quad d \quad t \quad tt}{1 \quad 2 \quad 3 \quad 4 \quad \text{strength}}}$$

These changes suggest that voiceless obstruents are stronger than voiced, that geminate stops are stronger than simple stops, and that stops are stronger than fricatives. As Foley (1970) argues, these relations are paralleled in other sound shifts, notably the Germanic consonant shifts, which Foley considers a strengthening.

Synchronic rules of assimilation give indications about relative strength of consonants for a particular language. If all C's assimilate in a certain position, then we can attribute the assimilation to the particular position, which would be considered a weak position. However, if some C's assimilate in a certain position and some do not, then the difference must be among the C's and that difference is one of strength. Some examples from Vennemann (1972d) illustrate how assimilation rules give indications about relative strength. For instance, Vennemann reports that in Modern Icelandic /s/ never voices in a voiced environment but the other spirants do. This means that /s/ is stronger than other spirants. Or consider some indications of the weakness of /r/ relative to the other sonorants, /l, m, n/. The /r/ is always devoiced by a following /p, t, k/, but the other resonants are devoiced only optionally. For a more complete list of synchronic evidence for strength rankings in Icelandic, see Vennemann (1972d).

Hankamer and Aissen (1974) report on a consonantal hierarchy that functions in the consonant assimilation rules of Pali, a middle Indic dialect. They refer to this hierarchy as the "sonority hierarchy," but it is, for the most part, just an inverse of the strength hierarchy. We will discuss it in terms of strength.

In Pali, there are no consonant clusters, only geminates and clusters of nasal followed by homorganic obstruents. However, potential clusters are created by the combination of consonant-final morphemes with consonant-initial morphemes. To avoid these clusters, assimilation takes place, and these assimilations are governed by the strength hierarchy. If the two consonants that come together are of the same strength, the first, the syllable-final C, assimilates to the second, the syllable-initial C, as predicted by the general theory of syllable structure presented above. Of course, the same result obtains if the first C is weaker than the second. The cases that are of interest, however, are those in which the first C is stronger than the second. In these cases general syllable structure considerations are overridden by the pressure of the stronger C to dominate, and the syllable-initial C assimilates to the syllable-final C. In these cases, then, syllable position is not relevant; the inherent strength of the C determines the assimilation. These assimilations reveal the following strength relations.

(a)   The stops are stronger than /s/; /s/ assimilates to a preceding consonant.

(16)      vak + ssa      *vakkha*      (future) *vak*      'to speak'

(/s/ causes aspiration of a neighboring stop.)

(b)   The stops are stronger than nasals; nasals assimilate to preceding stops.

(17)      lag + na      *lagga*      (past participle) *lag*      'to attach'

(c)   /y/ assimilates to stops, /s/, and nasals.

(18)      pac + ya      *pacca-*      (passive) *pac*      'to cook'
          arabh + ya    *arabbha*     (gerund) *arabh*     'to begin'
          dis + ya      *dissa-*      (passive) *dis*      'to see'
          kas + ya      *kassa-*      (passive) *kas*      'to farm'
          gam + ya      *gamma*       (gerundive) *gam*    'to go'
          khan + ya     *kanna*       (passive) *khan*     'to dig up'

(d)   Historically, /y/ assimilates to /l/ and /v/.

(19)      Skt. *kalya*       Pali *kalla*       'ready'
               *parivyaya*        *paribbaya*    'reward'
               *bhavya*           *bhabba*       'in condition to'

(e)   Historically, /v/ assimilates to /l/.

(20)      Skt. *bilva*       Pali *billa*       'a fruit'
               *khalvata*         *khallata*     'bald'

(f)   In other Prakrits, nasals assimilate to /s/.

(21)      Pali *rasmi*      Prk. *rassi*      'rope'

This evidence suggests the following strength hierarchy:

(22)      $\dfrac{\begin{matrix} \text{y} & \text{v} & \text{l} & \text{nasals} & \text{s} & \text{stops} \end{matrix}}{\begin{matrix} 1 & 2 & 3 & 4 & 5 & 6 \end{matrix}} \longrightarrow$

Hankramer and Aissen also propose a position for /r/ on the scale, i.e., at the lowest point. However, in all their examples involving /r/, it is in syllable-final position, where we would expect it to assimilate because of its position. In these examples /r/ assimilates to /y/ and historically to /v/.

| (23) | kar + ya | *kayya* | (passive) *kar* | 'to make' |
|------|----------|---------|-----------------|-----------|
|      | udir + ya | *udiyya* | (passive) *udir* | 'to utter' |
| Skt. *sarva* | | Pali *sabba* | 'all' | |
|      | *kurvanti* | *kubbanti* | 'they make' | |

These examples show only that /r/ is not substantially stronger than the glides; unlike /l/, to which /v/ and /y/ assimilate, /r/ is not strong enough to cause a progressive assimilation.

Thus Pali presents another example of the functioning of a consonantal hierarchy, which, although unrelated to syllable structure, is basically the same hierarchy relevant to syllable structure.

It is interesting that at least one language makes another use of the cover feature strength. Williamson (1972) reports that in Ijo (a cluster of dialects spoken in Nigeria), constraints on the distrition of syllable-initial consonants require the following classification of consonants:

(24) Obstruents
    voiceless

| | | | | | |
|---|---|---|---|---|---|
| non-stop | f | s | | | ] STRONG |
| stop | p | t | k | kp | |

    voiced

| | | | | | |
|---|---|---|---|---|---|
| non-implosive | b | d | g | gb | ] MEDIUM |
| implosive | ɓ | ɗ | | | |

    sonorants

| | | | | |
|---|---|---|---|---|
| non-approximant | m | l | | ] WEAK |
| approximant | w | r | y | |

Given this classification, it may be said that within a word, a consonant may not be stronger than a preceding consonant. Thus in a bisyllabic word, $\#C_1VC_2V\#$, if $C_1$ is strong, $C_2$ may be strong, medium, or weak; but if $C_1$ is medium, $C_2$ can only be medium or weak, never strong. The interesting point for our purposes is that the classification of consonants arrived at by Williamson fits nicely the classification by strength that we have established on the basis of other data.

## 10.4 The Cover Feature Strength

The strength relations discussed so far are assumed to be universal but not absolute. There are language-specific strength relations that may violate these universal tendencies in minor ways, but I would expect that phonetic explanations for such violations can be found.

Compiling all the evidence presented so far, we can establish the following universal strength hierarchy:

(25)

| glides | liquids | nasals | voiced continuant | voiceless voiced stop | voiceless stop |
|--------|---------|--------|-------------------|----------------------|----------------|
| 1 | 2 | 3 | 4 | 5 | 6 |

$\longrightarrow$

On the basis of the evidence I have examined, I have not been able to discover a universal strength relation of voiceless continuants to voiced stops. It is possible that the difference between the two classes is never significant. Or the relation between these two C types may be always determined by language-specific phonetic and historical factors.

There is one important C type that has not been ranked on the strength scale. There is very little evidence that bears on the position of affricates in the hierarchy. Foley (1970) ranks affricates as quite high, since the Old High German consonant shift which he considers to be a case of strengthening includes the shift of voiceless stop to affricate. Because of the complexity of the affricate, it is reasonable to assume that voiceless affricates are the strongest of the consonants. Voiced affricates must be somewhat weaker, but lacking pertinent evidence it seems pointless to speculate on their exact position on the scale. We should also recall that the relative strength of affricates will depend upon their language-specific phonetic properties and their relation to the other consonants in the language system. The clustering behavior of affricates is discussed in Chapter 11.

Vennemann and Ladefoged (1973) propose that the cover feature strength be assigned to segments on the basis of the feature values for the binary distinctive features. They give an example of the way the features stop and fricative relate to strength:

(26)       [3 strength] $\longleftrightarrow$ $\begin{bmatrix} +\text{stop} \\ -\text{fricative} \end{bmatrix}$

           [2 strength] $\longleftrightarrow$ $\begin{bmatrix} -\text{stop} \\ +\text{fricative} \end{bmatrix}$

           [1 strength] $\longleftrightarrow$ $\begin{bmatrix} -\text{stop} \\ -\text{fricative} \end{bmatrix}$

The bidirectional arrow reads "is equivalent to" (pp. 18–19). Rules of this form are called "feature redundancy rules."

Professor Vennemann (personal communication) has suggested that if we wish to formalize the universal strength relations explained in the preceding pages, a formalization better than that of (11) would express statements of the following sort: If A is an archisegment specified for all features except VOICE, B is the voiceless realization of A and C is the voiced realization, and if B is [m strength] and C is [n strength], then m is larger than n for all languages. In a formula (again, proposed by Vennemann):

$$\text{strength}\left(\begin{bmatrix} A \\ -\text{voice} \end{bmatrix}\right) > \text{strength}\left(\begin{bmatrix} A \\ +\text{voice} \end{bmatrix}\right)$$

Similarly, formulas can be given for the other strength relations discussed above:

(27)  $$\text{strength}\left(\begin{bmatrix} A \\ -\text{sonorant} \end{bmatrix}\right) > \text{strength}\left(\begin{bmatrix} A \\ +\text{sonorant} \end{bmatrix}\right)$$

$$\text{strength}\left(\begin{bmatrix} A \\ -\text{continuant} \end{bmatrix}\right) > \text{strength}\left(\begin{bmatrix} A \\ +\text{continuant} \end{bmatrix}\right)$$

$$\text{strength}\left(\begin{bmatrix} A \\ +\text{tense} \end{bmatrix}\right) > \text{strength}\left(\begin{bmatrix} A \\ -\text{tense} \end{bmatrix}\right)$$

And where A is [+sonorant]:

$$\text{strength}\left(\begin{bmatrix} A \\ +\text{nasal} \end{bmatrix}\right) > \text{strength}\left(\begin{bmatrix} A \\ -\text{nasal} \end{bmatrix}\right)$$

# 11

# A Strength Scale and Syllable Structure Condition for Spanish

The following is a tentative strength scale proposal for American Spanish, a casual style of speech:

(1)

| | | | | | | | f | | | |
|---|---|---|---|---|---|---|---|---|---|---|
| | | m | | $\beta$ | $\hat{y}$ | | b | p | | |
| y | | n | s | ð | | $\tilde{r}$ | d | t | č | |
| w | r | l | ñ | x | $\gamma$ | $\gamma^w$ | | g | k | |
| 1 | 2 | 3 | 4 | 5 | 6 | | | 7 | 8 | → |

This strength scale and the related SSC (2) will be discussed in detail in this chapter.

(2) $\quad\quad$ P(C): $\$C_m C_n C_p V C_q C_r\$$ $\quad$ where $n \leqslant 3$
$\quad\quad\quad$ If $n > 1$, then $m \geqslant 6$
$\quad\quad\quad$ $m > n$
$\quad\quad\quad$ p, q = 1
$\quad\quad\quad$ $r \leqslant 5$
$\quad\quad\quad$ $n > p$
$\quad\quad\quad$ $r > q^1$

## 11.1  The Conditions on Syllable-Initial Position

The lack of a condition on $C_m$ implies that syllable-initial position may be filled with a C of any strength value. It is also possible for this C position and any other C position to be empty. The strength scale value [0 strength] indicates that the C position is empty or Ø. Thus the conditions m > n and n > p imply that positions $C_n$ and $C_p$ may not be filled if $C_m$ is empty. If there is only one C at the beginning of the syllable, no matter what its strength scale value, it will occupy the $C_m$ or first C position.

The conditions m > n, n > p, and r > q describe clustering behavior of C's in a Spanish syllable. Furthermore, the conditions m > n and n > p make it necessary to analyze a syllable of glide plus vowel (/ya/) as having the glide in $C_m$ position, with $C_n$ and $C_p$ empty, rather than having the syllable /ya/ analyzed as having the glide in $C_p$ position, with $C_m$ and $C_n$ empty. There are several reasons for considering the former analysis preferable. First, the simple conditions m > n, n > p, and r > q are universal and follow naturally from the theory of syllable structure developed here (see Chapter 12). Second, if a single syllable-initial glide occupies the $C_p$ position, and p = 1, then there is no way to explain or even account for the glide strengthening process (described in Section 10.2) by which the glides /y/ and /w/ become obstruents [ŷ] and [γʷ] in syllable-initial position. The exact account of this process within the present framework is found in Section 11.10.

I have repeatedly claimed that syllable-initial position is a strong position, a position of consonantal strengthening. There is one common phonological process that might appear to be a counter-example to that claim. The process of spirantization of voiced C's in Spanish, which is a weakening process, may occur in syllable-initial position, e.g., *padre* [paðre] 'father', *lago* [layo] 'lake', *huevo* [weβo] 'egg'.

This process is not a true counter-example to the claims made here. Instead, it is evidence that even though syllable structure is an important conditioning factor for many phonological processes, it is not the ONLY conditioning factor for such processes. Although the internal structure of the syllable is extremely important, contact between segments in contiguous syllables also may condition phonological rules. To

---

[1] The condition r > q unquestionably holds for the Spanish syllable, but its universal status may be questioned. Theo Vennemann (personal communication) has reminded me that English syllables may end in /st/ or /ts/, *past, pats*. I am using the SSC to predict allophonic variation governed by position in the syllable. The claim that r > q for all languages predicts that the phonetic realization of, e.g., /s/ in Vst$ and Vts$, is different, the syllable-final version being stronger than the other (see Section 11.6 and Chapter 12).

see that factors other than syllable structure condition spirantization, consider the following facts:

(i) Spirantization also occurs in syllable-final position:

At the end of a word or utterance: *ciudad* [syuðað] 'city'
At the end of a word-internal syllable: *admirable* [aðmiraβle] 'admirable'

(ii) Spirantization is blocked in syllable-initial position:

At the beginning of a breath group: *Bueno, vamos!* [bweno // bamos] 'Good, we go!'
After a nasal: *onda* [onda] 'wave', *ambos* [ambos] 'both'
And spirantization of /d/ is blocked after /l/: *aldea* [aldea] 'village'.

Thus it would be impossible to attribute spirantization to syllable structure; i.e., the spirantization rule could not be stated in terms of Ṣ's. It appears instead that spirantization occurs in all positions except those in which the vocal tract is obstructed by a closure just prior to articulation. In utterance-initial position we assume that the mouth was closed just before speaking. Nasal C's require complete closure of the vocal tract. As Harris (1969:39) points out, the significance of the preceding segment is that in each case where spirantization is blocked, the preceding sonorant is homorganic with the stop. All syllable-final nasals are homorganic with the following C and /l/ is homorganic with the /d/, which accounts for the fact that /b/ and /g/ spirantize after /l/ but /d/ does not. This explanation has nothing to do with syllable structure; apparently spirantization does not either.

There is one C that does not occur in syllable-initial position, the velar nasal [ŋ]. The reason is that the velar nasal is not phonemic: Its only source is neutralization in syllable-final position (the nasal assimilation rule). Its absence in syllable-initial position should be accounted for by a neutralization rule to the effect that a nonanterior nasal in syllable-initial position must be palatal.[2] Thus I am claiming that this particular constraint is not due to strength relations.[3]

[2] Actually seven nasals may be distinguished phonetically. Harris (1969:12) gives the following feature matrix for these seven nasals:

|  | m | m̃ | ň | n | ṅ | ñ | ŋ |
|---|---|---|---|---|---|---|---|
| coronal | − | − | + | + | + | − | − |
| anterior | + | + | + | + | − | − | − |
| back | − | − | − | − | − | − | + |
| distributed | + | − | − | + | + | + | + |

## 11.2  Second Position

The second C position in the syllable is extremely restricted. The condition, n = 3, states that only /r/, /l/, /y/, and /w/ may occupy this position. Thus clusters such as $pt, $sk, $ks, $rb, $bm are ruled out. The condition "if n > 1, then m ≥ 6" expresses the fact that only the stronger C's may be the first member in a cluster with a liquid. This condition excludes $mr, $sr, $lr, $rl. This condition is probably only a part of a more general condition to the effect that the first member of a syllable-initial cluster must be considerably stronger than the second member. Here "considerably" could mean three points on the strength scale, and the constraint could be stated as m > n + 3. If this general condition were valid and expressed a true generalization, then it would be necessary to locate the glides three points below the liquids on the strength scale because syllable-initial clusters of liquid plus glide are possible. The scale would look like (3):

(3)

| y | | | | | m | | |
|---|---|---|---|---|---|---|---|
| w | | | r | l | n | | |
| 1 | 2 | 3 | 4 | 5 | 6 | 7 . . . . | →|

That is, one would have to claim that the glides are more than just one step below liquids. In fact, it may very well be true that glides are much weaker than any other consonants, but without independent evidence a revision of the strength as in (3) would be unjustified.

Before considering other restrictions on initial C clusters, it is necessary to digress briefly to an explanation of the placement of the individual liquids on the strength scale. There are three liquids in American Spanish: /r/, /r̄/, and /l/. The placement of the trilled /r̄/ is problematical, because this sound is so different from any other in the language. Although classified as a liquid, it is obviously much stronger than the other liquids, because its articulation consists of multiple consecutive vibrations of the tip of the tongue against the alveolar ridge. The distribution of /r̄/ indicates the strength of an obstruent: It occurs only in syllable-initial position and never occurs in clusters. A weakened ver-

---

The variants [m̃, ñ, ṅ, ŋ] are the result of the nasal assimilation rule. [m̃] is labiodental and occurs before /f/. [ñ] is dental and occurs before /t/ or /d/. [ṅ] is alveopalatal, occurring before /č/, and [ŋ] is velar, assimilating to /g/ and /k/. Only /n/, /m/, and /ñ/ contrast in syllable-initial position. The other nasals may be excluded from syllable-initial position by a redundancy rule.

[3] It could be argued that the velar nasal is the weakest nasal, Foley (1970) claims that velars are weaker than bilabials or alveolars. But even if we excluded [ŋ] on the basis of strength, we would still have to account for the nonoccurrence of [m̃, ñ, and ṅ] in syllable-initial position. See note 2.

sion of /r̄/, that heard in fast, nonenergetic speech, is a voiced strident fricative, pronounced with the tongue retracted (Harris, 1969:47; Navarro Tomás 1957:116–117). The weakened version of /r̄/ is clearly an obstruent and would be placed at 6 on the strength scale. We can conclude from this that the stronger version of /r̄/ must belong higher up on the scale, even though this is an odd position for a "liquid."

The liquids /r/ and /l/ are very much liquids in pronunciation and behavior, and their positions on the strength scale are predictable on universal principles. There is evidence in Spanish (and in other languages, e.g., Icelandic (see Vennemann, 1972d)) that the lateral liquid is stronger than the nonlateral liquid. In Spanish, sequences of /l$r/ require the /r/ be strengthened to /r̄/. I will attribute this strengthening to a general principle requiring that the first C of a syllable be stronger than the last C of the preceding syllable (see Section 11.8). While /r/ requires strengthening after /l/, /l/ does not require strengthening after /r/. The /l/ in /perla/ is, for all practical purposes, identical to any other occurrence of /l/.

The difference between /r/ and /l/ may explain the fact that syllable-initial clusters of /tr/ and /dr/ are allowed in Spanish (and in many other languages) while syllable-initial clusters of */tl/ and */dl/ are not.[4] Since I have not classified the stops for strength according to point of articulation, it is not possible to account for this restriction formally at this point. Briefly, the solution involves claiming that dental stops are weaker than labial and velar stops and, as above, that /l/ is stronger than /r/. The clusters */tl/ and */dl/ do not occur, then, because the difference in strength between /t/ and /d/ on the one hand and /l/ on the other is not enough to allow these C's to cluster together. In the next section we will see more evidence that the coronal series of C's in Spanish is weaker than the labial series (and possibly the velars as well).[5]

## 11.3 Strong Consonants That May Not Cluster

Other impossible clusters are not so easily accounted for. The segments [č, ŷ, gʷ] are not permitted in clusters. There are three possible

---

[4] This observation is due to Theo Vennemann (personal communication).

[5] For other languages that allow $pl and $kl, but not *$tl, this explanation is not available. For instance, in Icelandic, /t/ is stronger than /p/ or /k/ (see Section 7.1), yet $tl is not allowed, while $pl and $kl are. A possible account of this restriction that applies to Spanish and Icelandic (and any other language that distinguishes between /p/, /k/, and /t/ in this regard) has nothing to do with strength. By this account the neutralization of the distinction between /r/ and /l/ after /t/ or /d/ is merely a dissimilation: The articulation of /l/ is too much like that of /t/ and /d/ for /l/ to occur after these C's.

avenues to pursue for an explanation of these restrictions:

(4)  (i)  The nonoccurrence of these segments in clusters could be due to accidental gaps, resulting from the fact that their historical sources either were not clustered or could not cluster.

  (ii)  The prohibition against these segments in clusters could be due to their strength rankings.

  (iii)  The restriction against clusters with these segments could be due to other phonetic factors.

There is no historical source for these consonants in clusters. None of them existed in Latin. The modern palatal affricate was derived from clusters of /kt/: Latin *lacte* /lakte/, Modern Spanish *leche* /leče/ 'milk'; Latin *nocte* /nokte/, Modern Spanish *noche* /noče/ 'night'. The process began with syllable-final weakening of the obstruent to a glide (k ⟶ y/___t), /lakte/ > /layte/, /nokte/ > /noyte/. Then the palatal glide preceding the stop palatalized it: /layte/ > /lače/, /noyte/ > /noče/. If any forms existed in which an /r/ followed the /kt/ cluster, the palatalization would have been blocked; the hypothetical cluster ?/ktr/ would give in Modern Spanish ?/ytr/, not */čr/.

The consonants [ŷ] and [g^w] are derived historically and synchronically from the glides /y/ and /w/. Of course, glides may never be followed in syllable-initial position by liquids, since glides are much weaker or more vowel-like than liquids. One source of [g^w] is a cluster itself: /gw/ as in *guapo* and *guante*. Such a cluster of velar plus glide cannot be followed by a liquid, once again, because the glide is weaker than the liquid. Thus there are no sources for clusters of [ŷ] and [g^w] plus liquid.

Thus it is possible to give historical explanations for the gaps in the clustering pattern of Modern Spanish. The question still remains as to whether the gaps are accidental or systematic. That is, are the following acceptable syllables in Spanish: \$črV, \$člV, \$yrV, \$g^wlV? The answer seems to be negative. Although dialects of English have [č] before a retroflex liquid, *tree* [čriy], languages with trilled or tap /r/ often do not have coronal affricates (or even coronal fricatives) before /r/, as Theo Vennemann (personal communication) has pointed out. Professor Vennemann has also given me the following example: In Old High German when the voiceless aspirated stops shifted to affricates (t^h ⟶ t^s, p^h ⟶ p^f, and k^h ⟶ k^x), /t^h/ failed to affricate before /r/. In this case the historical gap is clearly systematic. Thus it is probably not a mere idiosyncrasy of Spanish that such clusters are forbidden, but rather a universal principle that such clusters are highly marked. Thus we would not want to claim that their absence in Spanish is merely accidental; instead we would want to find a universal basis on which to count such clusters as highly unusual or marked.

Now we should consider the next two candidates for an explanation of (4ii) and (4iii) for the prohibition of these clusters. The second suggestion is that these segments may not cluster because of their strength value. According to the theory of syllable structure I have developed so far, this would mean that [č, ŷ, gᵂ] would have to be considered too WEAK to cluster and must all be positioned at 5 or below on the strength scale. I do not consider this to be a viable solution for several reasons. (i) If they were indeed as weak as 5 or even weaker, we would expect them to be acceptable in syllable-final position. Yet clearly syllables ending in [č, ŷ, gᵂ] seem even less acceptable than syllables ending in full stops [p, t, k]. (ii) There is evidence at least in some languages that affricates are even stronger than plain stops, since strengthening processes in some languages (e.g., Old High German, as mentioned above (Foley, 1970)) shift plain stops to affricates. Intuitively, at least, affricates seem in some sense stronger than plain stops since their articulation involves two steps, a full closure and a constricted release, instead of only one. Although [gᵂ] is not an affricate, it also has a double articulation—one velar and one labial.

This suggests that we might account for the clustering restrictions on [č, ŷ, gᵂ] by classifying them as the strongest consonants (at a new level 9) and claim that they are too strong to cluster. Although this solution may be correct, in the context of my whole proposal it has a rather ad hoc flavor. Therefore I would like to offer one more alternative, which could be classified under (4iii), other phonetic factors.

Since [č, ŷ, gᵂ] have a complex, double articulation, a cluster of one of these consonants plus a liquid will be even more complex than the clusters /pr/, /pl/, etc. Since Spanish has only two C positions at the beginning of a syllable, it is perfectly reasonable that such clusters would be prohibited. It is as though [č, ŷ, gᵂ] occupy two C positions instead of only one. That is, [č] would take up BOTH the $C_m$ position AND the $C_n$ position, leaving no C position for another C to form a cluster. However, I would not want to suggest that [č, ŷ, gᵂ] be analyzed as two segments each. It seems, in fact, that in spite of the lengthy discussion, I must leave the problem of clustering behavior of affricates having only made suggestions and without a definite solution.

## 11.4 The Nucleus: Vowels and Glides

The nucleus of the syllable is the only obligatory part: If there is no nucleus, there is no syllable. In Spanish the nucleus must contain a vowel and may contain only one vowel.

It is not absolutely clear whether the glides that optionally surround the V should be analyzed as part of the nucleus or a part of the consonantal margin of the syllable. In Spanish glides function like V's in that they do not affect the choice of surrounding consonants. But they are like C's in that they may strengthen in syllable-initial position, and here they actually become obstruents.

If glides are considered consonants, they must be the weakest consonants on the strength scale. The fact that they occur closest to the vowel in relation to the other C's and that they strengthen in syllable-initial position supports the general hypothesis developed here concerning the relation between consonantal strength and syllable structure. Thus there is no reason why we should not account for their occurrence in the syllable as though they were consonants.

## 11.5  Syllable-Final Position

We have noted above that syllable-final position is a relatively weak position, so it is not surprising to find limitations on the strength of consonants that may occur in this position. The condition r < 5 allows only glides, liquids, nasals, /s/, and /x/ in syllable-final position. The fricative /x/ does not commonly occur in this position; these fricatives are discussed separately in Section 11.6.

The only stronger obstruent that commonly occurs in syllable-final position is [ð], as in the suffix /dad/: *ciudad* [syuðað] 'city'. This [ð] is often deleted entirely in many dialects. The occurrence of [ð] here and the absence of [β] and [γ] may, however, be attributed to strength. We mentioned above that the fact that /t/ and /d/ do not cluster with /l/ could be due to the weakness of dental stops relative to the labials and velars. In addition, it is the [ð] that is most commonly deleted intervocalically: *soldado* [soldao] 'soldier'. We can also note that among the nasals, the coronal position is favored for word-final nasals in the standard dialect. All of these facts are clues to the relative weakness of the coronal C's as opposed to the noncoronal C's. And this relative weakness explains the occurrence of [ð] in syllable-final position.

Even though some of the stronger C's occur in syllable-final position in the orthography and in very careful styles of speech, in the casual style whose syllable structure we are examining here, these obstruents in syllable-final position are considerably weakened or lost entirely. The significant point for the SSC is that such weakening and loss does not apply to glides, liquids, or nasals. However, in many dialects we find a weakening of /s/ to [h], which is just a continuation of the general process creating open syllables. Typical syllable-final weakening and loss are represented in (5).

(5)

| Orthography | Phonetic Representations | |
| --- | --- | --- |
| *septiembre* | [seᵖtyembre] | [setyembre] |
| *octubre* | [oᵏtuβre] | [otuβre] |
| *absoluto* | [aβsoluto] | [asoluto] |
| *advertir* | [aðβertir] | [aβertir] |

Weakening in syllable-final position may be accounted for by the SSC. One condition that is a part of the SSC for Spanish is condition (6).

(6)    If a C is syllable-final, its strength may not exceed 5.

Or, more formally:

(6′)         I(C):      C$
              T(C):   [r strength],      where r ≤ 5.

The condition assigns a strength of 5 or less to any syllable-final C that is not already at [5 strength] or less. For the examples in (5), condition (6) reduces the voiceless stops to a very weak unreleased stop or deletes them entirely. Voiced spirants are also weakened or lost.

There are actually two ways the reduction of voiceless stops may be manifested phonetically. One way, as illustrated in (5), involves the retention of voicelessness but a reduction of the length of time the stop is held. The lack of sonority in the reduced stop accounts for its eventual deletion, as opposed to the alternate phonetic route to reduction. Some American dialects of Spanish do not drop the syllable-final stop, but rather reduce it to the weakest consonant, a glide (Malmberg, 1948).

(7)

| Orthography (standard) | | Dialectal |
| --- | --- | --- |
| *afecto* | 'emotion' | *afeuto* [afewto] |
| *caracter* | 'character' | *carauter* [karawter] |
| *satisfacción* | 'satisfaction' | *satisfaición* [satisfaysyon] |
| *cápsula* | 'capsule' | *cáusula* |
| *objeto* | 'object' | *oujeto* |
| *perfecto* | 'perfect' | *perfeito, perfeuto* |
| *actor* | 'actor' | *autor* |

The intermediate stages between the stop and the glide are:

(8)          1. voicing           aktor > agtor
             2. spirantization    aγtor
             3. vocalization      awtor

Stages 1 and 2 probably always take place together; *[agtor] is not attested, but [aytor] is (Malmberg, 1948:100,118; Navarro Tomás, 1957:137). It may seem odd to get a voiced C before a voiceless one; this example shows the dominance of the syllable-final weakening process (for more examples, see Navarro Tomás, 1957:87). Voicing is the most important stage for distinguishing between this path and the path that results in deletion. The sonority added by voicing makes the consonant more stable, and further reduction consists of making the articulation more vowel-like. For further details see Section 11.9.

## 11.6  The Voiceless Fricatives

Throughout the discussion of strength hierarchies, we have found the placement of voiceless fricatives to be somewhat problematical. This is particularly true for the Spanish strength scale, since each of the voiceless fricatives (/f/, /s/, and /x/) has different characteristics. They do, however, have in common the trait of appearing relatively weak for obstruents. Let us examine the characteristics of the voiceless fricatives.

In modern Spanish, /f/ may be the first member in a syllable-initial cluster:

(9)         *frío*          'cold'
            *frontera*      'border'
            *floja*         'limp'

But /f/ does not occur at the ends of syllables, except rarely in forms such as *afgano* 'Afghan'. These distributional facts may be accounted for by placing /f/ at 7 on the strength scale, equal to the voiced stops.

Distributionally, /s/ shows itself as weak. /s/ may occur in syllable-initial clusters only to the extent that the liquids and nasals can; /s/ occurs before glides but never before liquids. However, /s/ is very common in syllable-final position. The frequency is significant in that it shows the stability of /s/ in this position historically. While the other obstruents tend to be altered or lost from syllable-final position, /s/ quite consistently remains, which shows that /s/ has a strength that is compatible with syllable-final position. Of course, as I mentioned before, in some dialects (particularly Andalusian and American dialects), a syllable-final /s/ weakens to mere aspiration. But this cannot be evidence for the inherent weakness of /s/, because ALL obstruents weaken and/or drop in syllable-final position. The aspiration of /s/ in this position is evidence only of the weakness of syllable-final position.

The velar spirant /x/ does not participate in initial clusters and only rarely occurs in syllable-final position; the following is probably an exhaustive list of words with /x/ in final position (/x/ is usually spelled *j*): *reloj* 'watch', *boj* 'boxwood', *borraj* 'borax', *carcaj* 'rifle case'. Phonetically /x/ shows weakness: In many dialects it is pronounced as though it is only aspiration and not a fricative (Navarro Tomás, 1957:143).

The distributional properties of the voiceless fricatives may be schematized as follows:

$$
(10) \qquad \text{a.} \ \$ \ s \begin{Bmatrix} f \\ \ \\ x \end{Bmatrix} V \qquad \text{b.} \ \$ \ *s \begin{rcases} f \\ \ \\ *x \end{rcases} \begin{Bmatrix} r \\ l \end{Bmatrix} V \qquad \text{c.} \ V \begin{Bmatrix} *f \\ s \\ x \end{Bmatrix} \$
$$

In the framework developed above, such distributional properties may be accounted for by giving /f/ a different strength value from /s/ and /x/.

Since /f/ has the same distributional properties as the stronger obstruents, i.e., the stops (voiced and voiceless), that is, since /f/ occurs before /r/ and /l/ in syllable-initial position and is rare or unpronounced in syllable-final position, I have given /f/ the feature [7 strength]. Since /s/ and /x/ do not cluster with /r/ and /l/, and since /x/ shows additional characteristics of a weak C, I have given them the relative value [5 strength]. We have presented evidence that the coronal C's are weaker than the labials. The relation of /s/ to /f/, then, is part of a larger pattern.

The nonoccurrence of /x/ in some dialects in syllable-final position may also be accounted for in terms of strength. In those dialects in which /s/, but not /x/, occurs syllable-finally, /x/ will be ranked as stronger than /s/—too strong for syllable-final position. In the dialects in which both /s/ and /x/ are reduced to aspiration in syllable-final position, the strength values of /s/ and /x/ could be the same, but the strength value allowed in syllable-final position is very low, too low to allow /s/ or /x/.

The only evidence for the relative weakness of /s/ is its distributional properties. The lack of independent evidence regarding Spanish /s/ weakens our entire hypothesis about the relation of strength to syllable structure, particularly since /s/ in some languages (English, and for Icelandic, see Vennemann (1972d)) functions as a very strong C. It would be helpful to find some explanation for the different language-specific properties of /s/. Why is it that initial clusters of /sp/, /st/, and /sk/ are allowed in English but not in Spanish?

Why is it that in English there are syllable-final clusters in which /s/ may precede or follow a voiceless stop: *bask, backs, past, pats, clasp, claps*? The answer seems to be that /s/ is quite flexible; due to the combination of phonetic factors, /s/ may be syllabic. In English /s/ is allowed to be syllabic and may vary in degrees of syllabicity according to its position. This accounts for its ability to occur both before and after stops at the ends of syllables, as in *clasp, claps*. On the other hand, in Spanish /s/ is never syllabic. Historically, the syllabicity of /s/ is the source of the epenthetic vowel that appears before /s/ plus C clusters in word initial position, but currently /s/ itself is not syllabic in Spanish. The divergent language-specific behavior of /s/ is parallel to that of other consonants that may be syllabic. For instance, in languages that have syllabic nasals, nasal consonants may occur initially before obstruents and finally after obstruents, but in languages in which nasals are not syllabic, their distribution is much more limited; i.e., they generally do not occur in clusters. Thus the difference between /s/ in English and in Spanish is that in the former /s/ may be syllabic, and in the latter it may not.

## 11.7  Syllable-Final Consonant Clusters

The SSC as formulated in (2) has two C positions in syllable-final position, but the first can be filled only by a glide. Thus all sequences of two C's are ruled out in syllable-final position unless the first C is a glide. There are, however, some Spanish words that have syllable-final clusters of *rs$* and *ns$*. These clusters are found only in the prefix *trans-* and the combination of the prefixes *in-, con-,* and *per-* with a latinate stem beginning in /s/ plus C.

| (11) | | |
|---|---|---|
| | *instrucción* | 'instruction' |
| | *construcción* | 'construction' |
| | *transportar* | 'to transport' |
| | *perspectivo* | 'perspective' |
| | *perspicaz* | 'perspicacious' |

I did not formulate the SSC to encompass these clusters, because words of this type are relatively few and in casual speech such clusters are systematically simplified, and this simplification can be accounted for by the SSC. In very formal speech all the C's are pronounced. This style will require a more complex SSC. This is an example of the way borrowing may change the SSC.

The cluster Vns$ is simplified to Ṽs$ (Malmberg, 1948) and even the nasalization on the vowel is commonly lost. Historically, all nasalization was lost in such syllables. For instance, the Latin preposition *trans* 'across' gives Modern Spanish *tras* 'behind'. Modern Spanish forms with the Latin prefix *trans-* have an orthographic alternate with *tras:* *transportar, trasportar* 'to transport'; *transverso, trasverso* 'transverse';

*transformar, trasformar* 'transform'. But only in the most careful speech is the nasal ever pronounced. Similarly, *obscuro* is so regularly pronounced without the /b/ [oskuro] that *oscuro* is considered an acceptable spelling.

The cluster /rs/ was also simplified historically, even if the syllable division came between the two C's (Menéndez Pidal, 1968:136):

| Latin | | Medieval | | Modern |
|-------|---|----------|---|--------|
| *versura | > | *vassura* | > | *basura* |
| *ursu* | > | *osso* | > | *oso* |

The modern solution to the problem of the /rs/ cluster is similar. The /r/ is usually dropped; thus *perspectiva* is rendered [pespetiβa]. Pulgram (1970:98) also gives the following versions of the same word: *perpetiva* and *perespetiva*. In either case the result is an acceptable syllable structure, and that syllable structure does not include clusters in syllable-final position.

## 11.8   Syllable-Initial Strength

A further condition must be imposed on the syllable structure condition in order to ensure proper assignment of syllable boundaries and to account for some strengthening phenomena. This condition requires that a syllable-initial C be stronger than the immediately preceding syllable-final C:

(12)   If $XVC_r\$C_mV$, and there is no pause between $C_r$ and $C_m$, then $m > r$.

This condition is necessary to assign \$'s in the proper positions in Spanish in case a single C occurs between two V's: VCV. In this case the single C must be analyzed as occupying $C_m$ position; $C_r$ will be empty, making $r = 0$, and condition (12) will be met. Without (12) it would be possible for VC to be considered a possible syllable if the strength scale value of C is less than 5. Further, the single V also makes an acceptable syllable, but neither \$VC\$ nor \$V\$ is acceptable if the two are contiguous. The only possible syllabification of VCV is V\$CV. Condition (12) accounts for this syllabification.

This condition on contiguous syllables also accounts for some diachronic change in Spanish. The future and conditional forms of Modern Spanish were derived historically by combinations of the infinitive and the forms of the auxiliary *haber*: *amar + (h)a > amará*. Some infinitives underwent syncope of the pretonic vowel in the future and conditional forms:

> *venirá* > *venrá*     'he will come'
> *ponerá* > *ponrá*     'he will put'
> *salirá* > *salrá*     'he will leave'

The resulting forms were unacceptable because the /r/ in the sequence /nr/ and /lr/ was not strong enough to begin a syllable after /n/ and /l/, and /n/ and /l/ were not strong enough to begin a syllable with the second C as /r/. Menéndez Pidal (1968:323) reports several documented attempts to remedy this situation. Metathesis was tried: *verná, porná* (for *venrá* and *ponrá*); assimilation was also attempted: *verrá, porrá*. But the solution that was settled on in the standard dialect was to keep the existing segments in the same order and form and to make the second syllable acceptable by adding an obstruent to the initial position (for more on epenthesis, see Section 13.5):

(13)
> *venrá* > *vendrá*
> *ponrá* > *pondrá*
> *salrá* > *saldrá*

Condition (12) accounts for this change in a very natural and explanatory way.

The same problem finds a slightly different solution in the modern language. The single flap /r/ does not occur phonetically after /l/, /n/, or /s/. Instead, in syllable-initial position after one of these consonants, the strong trilled /r̄/ occurs:

(14)
| alrededor | [alr̄eðeðor] | 'around' |
| honra | [onr̄a] | 'honor' |
| Israel | [izr̄ael] | 'Israel' |

This alternation is necessary to satisfy condition (12). Notice that /r/ does not have to strengthen in syllable-initial position if the preceding segment is a V or glide:

(15)
| toro | [toro] | 'bull' |
| aire | [ayre] | 'air' |

## 11.9   The Feature Strength and the Generative Capacity of the SSC

In the foregoing discussion I have mentioned on several occasions that I expect the SSC to be able to automatically account for phonological phenomena conditioned by syllable structure. In this section I will present a specific proposal for the functioning of the SSC.

Every phonetic segment of the language, i.e., every possible phone, is assigned a numerical value for the feature strength. In large part the numerical values of the segments are universally determined. For example, on the Spanish strength scale every relation is universally predictable except for the values of the voiceless fricatives. Therefore there is very little "cost" in terms of language-specific grammar complication.[6]

As in TGP, each phone is characterized by a distinctive feature matrix filled out, for the most part, by + 's and − 's. The cover feature strength, however, always has a numerical value.[7] A sample matrix for some Spanish segments follows:

(16)

|  | m | β | b | p |
|---|---|---|---|---|
| consonantal | + | + | + | + |
| vocalic | − | − | − | − |
| coronal | − | − | − | − |
| anterior | + | + | + | + |
| voice | + | + | + | − |
| continuant | − | + | − | − |
| nasal | + | − | − | − |
| strength | 3 | 5 | 6 | 7 |

In the previous sections of this chapter I have claimed that the syllable structure condition for Spanish can explain certain phonological processes, such as syllable-final weakening and syllable-initial strengthening. In this section I will claim that the SSC can be made directly responsible for such processes. That is, I will show that the SSC not only explains these phenomena, it also can describe them by generating the feature changes conditioned by syllable structure.

Let us first consider syllable-final weakening of stop consonants. In Section 11.5, I described the two paths that a stop might follow in weakening to conformity with the SSC. A syllable-final stop can be weakened to a glide or dropped altogether: *concepto* [konsewto], [konseto].

---

[6] NGP does not rely on a simplicity metric to evaluate alternate analyses. Yet simplicity is highly valued in any science in the sense that the theory that accounts for the greatest number of phenomena with the fewest hypothetical constructs is to be preferred.

[7] In the Chomsky and Halle system, numerical values are absolute rather than relative and used with features that specify phonetic detail rather than with cover features.

Consider first the pronunciation of *concepto* in the most careful style of speech. The syllable-final /p/ may be fully enunciated, and yet it will never be as strong as a syllable-initial /p/. Harris (1969:42–45) describes the difference between syllable-initial [p] and its syllable-final cognate [p$^b$] with the features heightened subglottal pressure (hsp) and glottal constriction (gc):

$$
\begin{array}{ccc}
 & p & p^b \\
\text{hsp} & + & - \\
\text{gc} & + & -
\end{array}
$$

The cover feature strength assigns a higher numerical value to [p] than to [p$^b$]. Using the notation of Vennemann and Ladefoged (1973), we have the following feature redundancy rule (see Chapter 10):

$$
\text{strength}\left(\begin{bmatrix} A \\ +hsp \\ +gc \end{bmatrix}\right) > \text{strength}\left(\begin{bmatrix} A \\ -hsp \\ -gc \end{bmatrix}\right)
$$

In the most careful style of speech the SSC allows C's of strength equivalent to [p$^b$] in syllable-final position, but only syllable-initial position may tolerate a C as strong as [p]. Let us say arbitrarily that [p] is [8 strength] and [p$^b$] is [7 strength] and examine the exact workings of the SSC in this case.

As I explained in Chapter 9, the SSC has the ability to insert $'s and to alter C's to meet strength requirements. If the SSC is P(C): $C_mC_nC_pVC_qC_r$, and r $\geq$ 7 in the formal style of speech, then the /p/ in $C_r$ position is assigned the value [7 strength]. The redundancy rule given above then assigns /p/ the features [$-$gc] and [$-$hsp] producing the segment [p$^b$]. Therefore, the only choice is [w]. Given the following feature specification for [p] and [w], the features of [p] may be changed to the features of [w] by calling upon the universal redundancy rules discussed in Chapter 10:

|  | p | w |
|---|---|---|
| sonorant | − | + |
| voice | − | + |
| continuant | − | + |
| labial | + | + |

The particular redundancy rules that will be called into play depend upon the extent of the weakening, the phone inventory of the language, and the language-specific strength hierarchy.[8]

Thus in order to account for a process such as syllable-final weakening, very little extra machinery need be added to the grammar and no specific rule must be given. The entire process may be generated with only the SSC for that dialect, the strength scale values, the phonetic inventory, and the universal feature redundancy rules.

Such a treatment of syllable-final weakening achieves a higher degree of adequacy than an analysis requiring a separate rule to generate each case of syllable-final weakening, because the analysis with the SSC formally captures the relationship between all such processes of syllable-final weakening. Kisseberth (1970) has called processes such as syllable-final weakening, syllable-initial strengthening, epenthesis, and others "conspiracies," because they are rules that are related in their FUNCTION but not necessarily in their form. Kisseberth and others (notably Chen, 1972) have lamented the inability of TGP to describe formally conspiracies as related processes. The notion of SSC as developed here, a condition that may also be generative, along with the cover feature strength, make it possible in some cases to describe such conspiracies as unified processes. This ability to capture formally the notion conspiracy is another argument in favor of the devices described in this chapter. There are literally dozens of processes in Spanish that can be

---

[8] The language-specific strength hierarchy probably specifies the paths that a segment takes in strengthening or weakening. A strength scale for any language is actually more complex than the scale that I have given for Spanish. Theo Vennemann (personal communication) has suggested that a complete strength scale for any language is probably a multidimensional matrix in which all positional allophones of a given archisegment are related by strength to one another, and these scales for archisegments intersect to give a general scale. As a simple illustration, consider the following partial strength scale:

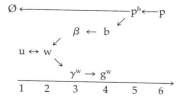

The right to left arrows indicate the path of weakening; the left to right arrows indicate strengthening. The particular example chosen for illustration shows that the paths need to be specified, because the strengthening does not necessarily retrace weakening. That is, [w] is the result of a weakened bilabial, but strengthened [w] is labiovelar, not bilabial. Professor Vennemann has also observed that with a completely specified strength hierarchy indicating paths of weakening and strengthening, one will never have to worry about an oral stop weakening to a nasal, since the scale for oral stops is partially independent of that for nasals.

automatically accounted for by the devices proposed here. Let us examine another such process.

The strengthening of /r/ in syllable-initial position after /n/, /l/, and /s/ may also be generated automatically by the SSC. Consider the word *alrededor* 'around'. The sequence /l\$r/ gives the numerical values $C_r = 3$, $C_m = 2$. Since condition (12) requires that if $XC_r\$C_mV$, then m > r, the strength value of r must be greater than 3. The strengthening in /r/ takes place by the same procedures outlined for weakening. If /r/ must have a strength greater than 3, then some features will have to be different in this position than in other positions. Again, the requirement is that /r/ in this position should differ from /r/ in other positions by as few features as possible while still attaining the required strength. Thus the allophone of /r/ in this position is the trilled [r̄]. According to Harris, the simple [r] is [ − tense] and [r̄] is [ + tense]. Therefore, in order for [r] to be strengthened, it must become [ + tense]. The universal feature redundancy rules given in Chapter 10 handle this change:

$$\text{strength}\left(\begin{bmatrix} A \\ +\text{tense} \end{bmatrix}\right) > \text{strength}\left(\begin{bmatrix} A \\ -\text{tense} \end{bmatrix}\right)$$

## 11.10   The Optimal Syllable Principle

The SSC for Spanish requires that certain consonants undergo weakening in syllable-final position and that a syllable-initial C be stronger than the preceding consonant. It does not require, however, that a syllable-initial C maintain any minimum strength level, because C's of all strengths may occur in syllable-initial position. The SSC itself does not automatically account for processes of syllable-initial strengthening. Yet syllable-initial strengthening is a common, natural process whose motivation is the intrinsic structure of the syllable—the fact that syllable-initial position is a strong position. Thus it seems that along with the SSC and strength scale proposed so far, we also need another principle, which I will call the Optimal Syllable Principle.

OPTIMAL SYLLABLE PRINCIPLE: The higher the strength scale value permitted in a given C position, the greater the likelihood that a C will occur in that position, and the higher the strength value for the C. Similarly, the lower the strength value permitted in a C position, the less likely that a C will occur in that position.

The Optimal Syllable Principle tells us that CV is the optimal syllable for Spanish, since the only C position with a high numerical value is syllable-initial position. This principle also explains why one of the favored possibilities for syllable-final position is complete deletion of the C. And this principle also states that a process such as glide strengthening in syllable-initial position, although not a completely necessary rule, is a highly favored rule, because its output is closer to the optimal syllable than its input. Thus a rule of strengthening in syllable-initial position is highly unmarked.

Glide strengthening is stated:

$$\begin{bmatrix} -\text{vocalic} \\ -\text{consonantal} \end{bmatrix} \longrightarrow [+\text{consonantal}] / \$ \underline{\qquad}$$

A change from [−consonantal] to [+consonantal] is a strengthening process.

I have illustrated only a few of the syllable-related processes that can be accounted for by the SSC and the strength scale. The SSC stated in terms of strength, besides having great explanatory power, achieves a maximum economy. This simple statement (whose basic form is universal; see Chapter 12) and the cover feature strength, whose assignment is largely universal and independently motivated, can account for the majority of the constraints on sequence structure and all allophonic variation that is conditioned by syllable position. When we consider that all segments show some phonetic variation between syllable-initial and final position and when we realize that none of these rules will have to be stated separately, we see that the SSC and strength hierarchy represent major economy and highly significant generalizations.

# 12

# Further Implications
# of the Theory
# of Syllable Structure

## 12.1 Syllable Structure Conditions in Synchronic Grammers

In most languages SSC's cannot be viewed as absolute constraints on phonetic structure. The interaction of SSC's with other phonological processes, notably deletion processes, produces a very interesting, but somewhat complex picture. In this section we will discuss some typical examples of the complexities arising due to the interaction of conflicting processes.

Vowel deletion processes are common in stress languages, and at times these deletions are blocked if the result would be an unacceptable syllable, as in the Spanish apocope example discussed in Section 6.4. But in many cases vowel deletions take place even where unacceptable syllables result. Consider the example from Brazilian Portuguese, discussed briefly in Section 7.1. In the careful styles of speech, no syllable may end in a stop or affricate. Borrowed words are modified by vowel epenthesis if they are in violation of this SSC. Thus *tecnico* 'technician' is [tekiniko] in Largo speech, *ritmico* 'rhythmic' is [hičimiko], *etnico*

227

'ethnic' is [ečiniko]. In the latter two examples the epenthetic vowel conditions palatalization of the preceding /t/. In Allegretto speech, where an [i] occurs after [č], the [i] is deleted giving, e.g., [hičmiku] and [ečniku]. These forms have a syllable-final affricate. In a synchronic grammar of Brazilian Portuguese, it is necessary to give a strong SSC for Largo speech and a different, somewhat weaker condition for Allegretto speech. Or the SSC for Largo speech could be given as the only SSC, with the proviso that violations of it are allowed in Allegretto speech.

Examples of this type abound. In English, initial clusters of two obstruents are restricted to /s/ followed by /p, t, k, f/ in careful speech. However, in casual speech many other obstruent clusters are created by the deletion of schwa. Thus *pecan* and *potato* may be pronounced as [pkán] and [ptéyɾo], again in violation of the conditions for careful speech (Hooper 1976a).

In other cases, careful speech allows more complex syllable structure than casual speech. In Spanish, loan words introduced from Latin violate the casual speech SSC: e.g., *septiembre, perspectiva, obscuro, instrucción*. These complex syllable codas are tolerated in careful speech, for a while at least, but in casual speech they are altered to conform to the preferred syllable structure, giving [setyembre], [pespetiβa], [oskuro], [istruksión]. In this case it would appear that the casual style has a strong SSC, but violations of it are allowed in careful speech.

French offers another example. Final schwa deletion in French takes place in spite of the creation of highly marked syllables such as those ending in an obstruent followed by a liquid: *pauvre* [povr] 'poor', *théâtre* [teatr] 'theater', *ministre* [ministr] 'minister'. The current trend in casual speech in the dialects spoken in Montreal, is to drop off the final consonants until a syllable ending in a single consonant or a cluster of a sonorant plus obstruent is achieved (Tranel, 1974a:181).

(1)

|  |  | Standard | Quebecois |  |
| --- | --- | --- | --- | --- |
|  | *pauvre* | [povr] | [pov] | 'poor' |
|  | *théâtre* | [teatr] | [teat] | 'theater' |
|  | *contact* | [kɔ̃takt] | [kɔ̃tak] | 'contact' |
|  | *ministre* | [ministr] | [minis] | 'minister' |
| but | *calme* | [kalm] | [kalm]*[kal] | 'calm' |

That is, there is now a trend back toward the universally preferred syllable structure.

Diachronically, the progression is quite transparent: A deletion process or a large influx of loan words may override the SSC for the language, but after a time certain changes will take place, and the preferred SSC will be reinstated. This progression implies that a preferred SSC remains part of the system, part of the speakers' competence, in the face of violations of it. The synchronic representation of the state of affairs in these cases is not so transparent. It appears that two or more SSC's are needed for the various styles of speech, but one SSC must be designated as preferred so that the direction of change can be predicted. The preferred syllable structure can be determined on a universal basis, as we shall see in the next section.

## 12.2 Universal Conditions for Preferred Syllable Structure

The intrinsic structure of the syllable described in Chapter 10 is universally applicable. In the few cases of languages that allow syllables that violate these general principles, these violations arose as historical by-products of some other process that had some distinct motivation. Thus the final clusters in French *pauvre, ministre,* etc., arose because of the deletion of the final vowel, whose motivation was, not to create bad syllable structure, but to eliminate unstressed vowels and, if Schane (1972) is correct, to regularize stress placement. All processes whose sole raison d'être is to alter syllable structure—i.e., consonant weakening, strengthening, insertion and deletion rules, and vowel insertion rules—create syllable structure that conforms to the principles outlined in Chapter 10. Therefore, these principles should be included in the metatheory as a characterization of preferred syllable structure and as a constraint on syllabically motivated processes.

The general form of the universal SSC should be as follows:

(2)     Universal condition on preferred syllable structure:

$$P(C): \; \$C_m C_n C_p C_q V C_r C_s C_t \$$$

where $m > n > p > q$

$r > s > t$

$m > t$

$m \neq \emptyset$

This condition somewhat arbitrarily shows four C positions at the beginning of the syllable and three at the end. It is possible that more positions would be necessary to encompass the syllable structure of every language. For the purpose of illustration, (2) will suffice as stated.

The condition states that the SSC for any given language has a uniform shape: The C's are on the margins, and an obligatory V (or

[+syllabic] segment) makes up the nucleus. The strength scale values for the various C positions should descend from syllable-initial position inward toward the nucleus and also descend from syllable-final position inward toward the nucleus.

The condition m > t means, in this context, that for the SSC of any given language, the strongest C permitted in syllable-initial position must be stronger than the strongest C permitted in syllable-final position. (It does NOT mean that, for a particular syllable of a particular language, the syllable-initial C must be stronger than the syllable-final C, e.g., that a syllable such as $yan$ would be ruled out. This would clearly be wrong.) The universal SSC is a condition on preferred language-specific SSC's.

One must bear in mind that the strength requirements refer to the particular phonetic realization of a C in a particular position. Thus English allows /t/ in syllable-initial and syllable-final position. In syllable-initial position the strongest allophone occurs: [tʰ]; in syllable-final position the weakest occurs: unreleased [t'] or glottal stop. The claim that for any language-specific SSC, m > t, implies that syllable-initial allophones will always be stronger than the syllable-final allophones.

The condition m ≠ Ø means that a given language may not have an SSC that does not permit $CV$ syllables. In other words, every language must allow CV syllables. Any of the other C positions may be obligatorily empty in the SSC of a specific language.

The universal syllable structure condition in conjunction with a universal strength hierarchy can account for some implicational universals of the type proposed originally by Jakobson (1941 [1972]). The particular implicational universals to be discussed here were discovered by Greenberg (1965). Cairns (1969) accounted for them by marking conventions or universal neutralization rules.[1]

The first implicational law accounted for by the universal SSC is that if a language allows syllable-initial clusters of $CNV (where N = nasal consonant), it must also have syllable-initial clusters of $CLV (where L = liquid). We have been claiming that nasals are universally stronger than liquids. Therefore, if the strength value of the C in second position is high enough to allow nasals, it must also be high enough to allow liquids:

---

[1] Greenberg gives a few more implicational laws that I will not account for. He was using stem-initial clusters rather than syllable-initial, so that some of the clusters he accounts for may actually be bisyllabic, e.g., clusters of +NCV. Another law deals with voicing assimilation in clusters; the SSC is not intended to account for such phenomena.

(3)    $\dfrac{L\quad N\quad K}{1\quad 2\quad 3}$,    where K = obstruent

(4)    $\$C_m C_n VC\$$

Conditions:    $n \leq 2$

The $C_n$ position must allow both nasal and liquid consonants.

Second, if the claims made here are correct, we can predict that if a language allows syllable-initial obstruent clusters, it must also allow obstruent-nasal clusters. This prediction seems to be true, for example, in English, which has two-obstruent clusters with /s/ as the first member and, furthermore, has obstruent + nasal clusters where /s/ is the first member. Classical Greek had two-obstruent clusters such as /pt/ in syllable-initial position and also allowed obstruent nasal clusters such as /pn/.

Third, if a language allows the syllable-initial cluster $\$cNV$ (where c = voiced consonant), then it must also allow clusters of $\$CNV$ (where C = voiceless consonant). This automatically follows from the fact that voiceless consonants are stronger than voiced ones. If a cluster is allowed with as little difference in strength as between c and N, then a cluster with a greater difference in strength must also be allowed.

Fourth, if a language allows an initial sequence of $\$NLV$, then it must also allow $\$CLV$. In the SSC for Spanish, we ruled out clusters of $\$NLV$ by stipulating that the C that precedes an L must be at least three points stronger than the liquid. A language that allows $\$NLV$ obviously does not have this stronger restriction, but only the universal condition that $m > n$. Thus if this is the only condition, then $\$CLV$ must also be allowed.

Finally, the nonexistence of clusters of two liquids in syllable-initial position is ruled out by the requirement that $m > n$ and the condition that there by some minimum difference in strength between the first and second C in the cluster.

The theory of syllable structure presented here also makes some claims regarding possible syllable-final clusters. In many languages (e.g., English) syllable-final clustering is much freer than syllable-initial clustering. Still, a universal concerning preferred syllable codas has been discovered by Guile (1973). Guile states that "if a language allows obstruents in the environment $C_0V\underline{\quad}C_0$, then it must also allow non-obstruents in the same environment" [p. 147]. The stated environment includes all positions after the nucleus: $V\underline{\quad}$, $V\underline{\quad}C$, $V\underline{\quad}CC$, etc. This condition is automatically accounted for by our statement of SSC's in terms of a maximum strength value for each position. For if obstruents are allowed, all weaker C's must be allowed. Our universal condition also predicts a relation among syllable-final C's, but these predictions have not been tested.

Cairns (1969) has proposed that these implicational laws be accounted for by U's and M's in lexical entries. I do not intend to give a full comparison of the two methods, but to see the value of the theory proposed here, it is important to note two things. First, the universal SSC, which is independently necessary and which is based on a general hypothesis about the relation between consonantal strength and syllable structure, automatically, without any additional devices, accounts for the implicational laws and offers an explanation for them. Second, for those laws that state that certain clusters are universally nonoccurring, Cairns must posit an additional set of rules, the universal neutralization rules, in order to exclude these clusters. On the other hand, our SSC and strength hierarchy automatically exclude some of the nonoccurring clusters. Finally, we should note that the universal SSC, unlike any other universal markedness proposal, also attempts to account for conditions on the consonant sequences at the ENDS of syllables.

The universal condition on preferred syllable structure also serves as a constraint on possible syllabically motivated processes. If a natural process is conditioned by position in the syllable, it will not produce a structure that violates this universal condition. As we have mentioned, processes motivated by other phonetic factors, such as vowel deletion, may be constrained by condition (2) so as not to apply if an unacceptable syllable would result, or such processes may themselves be strong enough to apply even in cases in which violations of (2) result. Violations of the universal SSC in particular languages are always the result of conflicting natural processes, and I would claim that there is always a tendency to correct these violations by changes in the direction of the universal SSC.

# 13

# Natural Insertion
# and Deletion Rules

The purpose of this final chapter is two-fold. One goal is to explain how insertion and deletion rules are handled in natural generative phonology since, as I will demonstrate below, the strong constraints on NGP preclude any obligatory rules that insert or delete segments. This goal is only secondary, however, to the larger goal of developing a set of universal constraints on natural processes that insert and delete vowels and consonants. This chapter, then, is intended as a contribution to a general theory of natural rules; the constraints proposed here will become a part of the metatheoretical specification of "possible P-rule."

## 13.1 The Problem

In NGP there can be no synchronic rules of phonetically motivated insertion or deletion unless such insertions and deletions take place in environments created by derivation and not present in the lexicon.[1] Be-

[1] Recall that in morphosyntactically conditioned "insertions" and "deletions," the segment that alternates with "Ø" is represented lexically.

cause every P-rule in NGP represents a true generalization about surface phonological structure, every form must comply with every rule.
With the True Generalization Condition, a grammar of Spanish cannot
have an epenthesis rule of the type postulated for Spanish by Harris
(1969):

(1)     $\emptyset \longrightarrow$ e / # ____s [+consonantal]

This rule was discussed in Chapter 9. There I explained that such a rule
could be used to derive the following Spanish words from foreign loan
words.

(2)     *esnob*      'snob'
        *esmoking*   'tuxedo (smoking jacket)'
        *eslavo*     'Slav'

In TGP rule (1) is permissible but in NGP it is not, because the rule requires that ALL sequences of /s/ + C have to be preceded by /e/. There
are many Spanish words that have other vowels before /s/ + C clusters:

(3)     *hospital*   [ospital]   'hospital'
        *historia*   [istorya]   'history'
        *astro*      [astro]     'star'
        *usted*      [usteð]     'you'

In an NGP all words with initial /esC/ are entered in the lexicon with the
/e/ present; rule (1) is not necessary for ordinary derivations. Yet the
generalization expressed by rule (1) cannot be ignored: It is a very
striking fact about Spanish that this epenthetic V consistently appears
in loan adaptation and, furthermore, frequently appears in a Spanish
speaker's pronunciation of English and other languages (i.e., it is, like
all natural processes, very difficult for the speaker to suppress). Thus
even though no synchronic derivations require rule (1), this rule is obviously a part of a native speaker's competence. In the next section, I
will describe how the phenomenon represented by rule (1) and illustrated in (2) can be handled by the SSC proposed in Chapter 11 for
Spanish and by a few universal principles governing vowel insertion.

## 13.2   The Role of the SSC

The motivation behind the epenthesis rule (1) is the constraint on syllable structure extensively discussed in Chapter 11. It is not possible for
a Spanish syllable to begin with a cluster of /s/ + C. The effect of (1) is to
create an extra syllable so that the /s/ and the following C may be sepa-

rated by a $. The /s/, then, is in syllable-final position, a position in which it is favored, and the following consonant begins the next syllable. Given that the function of (1) is to create acceptable syllable structure, we might expect that the effects of (1) could be generated by the SSC for Spanish proposed in Chapter 11. Indeed, this is possible.

The SSC is an abbreviation for several if–then conditions, one of which inserts $'s between appropriate segments. The syllabification of the foreign word *slavo* procedes as follows. (i) $'s are inserted at the beginning and end of the word: $slabo$. (ii) $'s are inserted before any C or cluster that may be syllable-initial. The division $sla$bo$ is not problematical, since in a -VCV-sequence the C always begins the syllable. But another division must also be made, because /sl/ is not a possible syllable-initial sequence. The /s/ is not sufficiently strong to precede a liquid. The /l/ must be analyzed as syllable-initial: $s$la$bo$. (iii) The syllabification has been accomplished, but the result is that the first "syllable" is not an acceptable syllable because it does not contain a V. The SSC may also remedy this situation, as explained in Chapter 9, by inserting a vowel:

(4)                             $Vs$la$bo$

The position of the inserted vowel is not automatically predicted by the SSC. An acceptable syllable could be derived by inserting the V after the /s/: $sV$la$bo$. However, the order $Vs$ is preferred because it allows the original order of C's to remain, thereby hispanicizing the word with the minimum amount of change from its original form. Once the foreign word has been adjusted to fit native syllable structure, the nativized form with the epenthetic V is listed in the lexicon.

To arrive at (4) it has not been necessary to add any rules to the grammar of Spanish. The independently motivated SSC for Spanish has adjusted the foreign word to fit Spanish. The analysis of epenthesis using the SSC is more highly valued than one that attributes the process to an isolated rule such as (1), because it captures the significant relationship between phonotactic constraints and loan word treatment. In the next section I will explain how the quality of the inserted V is predictable on universal grounds.

## 13.3 Vowel Insertion

In Hooper (1972a,b) I claimed that all V's that are inserted or deleted in purely phonetic environments are predictable on the basis of two universal principles: The epenthetic V must always be the minimal V or a V whose features are copied from a nearby segment; usually this V is identical to a nearby V, although in some cases surrounding C's have an effect. Stress languages, which usually have vowel reduction processes, insert or delete the minimal vowel. Many tone languages and all vowel harmony languages insert and delete V's that are identical to some nearby V.

An obvious example of insertion and deletion of the minimal vowel is found in English. In English the minimal vowel is schwa, [ə]. The following are examples of insertion: *athlete* is often pronounced *ath* [ə]*lete*, and *arthritis* is sometimes *arth*[ə]*ritis*. Deletions are numerous: *camera* [kæmrə], *chocolate* [čoklət], *separate* [seprət], *reasoning* [riyznin]. (See Zwicky (1972) and Hooper (1976a) for more examples.)

In Brazilian Portuguese the high vowels are the weak vowels. In the last syllable of a word the mid vowels are reduced to high vowels.

(5)

| Orthographic | Phonetic | |
|---|---|---|
| *pronto* | [prontu] | 'ready' |
| *carro* | [kaxu] | 'car' |
| *fome* | [fomi] | 'hunger' |
| *sabe* | [sabi] | 'he knows' |

Brazilian Portuguese has a rule of epenthesis that inserts /i/ to avoid certain syllable-final obstruents, as pointed out in Sections 7.1 and 12.1.

(6)

| Portugal | Brazil | |
|---|---|---|
| [substituysão] | [subistituysão] | 'substitution' |
| [advokadu] | [aǰivokadu] | 'lawyer' |
| [futbol] | [fuǰbol] | 'soccer' |
| [admiravel] | [aǰimiravew] | 'admirable' |

The epenthetic /i/, like other instances of /i/, conditions palatalization in coronal consonants. Both /i/ and /u/ appear as reduced vowels, but only /i/ acts as an epenthetic vowel. This is probably due to the added strength the back vowel gets from the feature of roundness, which makes it stronger than the front vowel, leaving the front vowel as the weakest and thus the natural choice for insertion rules.

This suggestion gains plausibility if we consider Japanese where we find, as in Portuguese, the high vowels are the weakest. In Japanese, /i/ and /u/ are the only vowels that devoice in voiceless environments.

(7)  ikimasita  [ikimasIta]  'go (past)'
     ikimasuka  [ikimasUka]  'go (interrogative)'

The high back vowel in Japanese has little or no lip rounding, and although both high vowels can be used epenthetically, the back vowel is by far the most common. Since Japanese has a very restricted set of possibilities for syllable structures, vowels are inserted in foreign words to achieve the permissible structures. The following examples are representative of the treatment of loan words.

(8)  huransugo  France + go 'language', i.e., 'French'
     supeingo   Spain + go 'language', i.e., 'Spanish'
     bureeki    'brakes'
     biiru      'beer'
     napukin    'napkin'

(The inserted vowels are boldface.) There are some consonantal factors at work in determining the quality of the inserted vowel, but in the majority of cases it will be the high back vowel. The back vowel is the weakest in this case because it lacks rounding.

Languages that have no vowel reduction, typically tone languages or vowel harmony languages, insert or delete vowels that are predictable from their environments, that is, vowels identical in feature composition to some nearby vowel. For example, Ga, a Niger–Congo language, has alternate forms for a few words:

(9)  abele   able   'corn'
     hɔlɔ    hlɔ    'shade'
     dzʷere  dzʷre  'to congratulate'
     tele    tre    'to carry on one's head'

It is not clear whether insertion or deletion is involved here, but it is clear that the process depends on the vowel being identical to the following vowel. Such alternates do not exist for words with nonidentical vowels, such as pila 'to wound'.

In early Latin an epenthetic vowel identical to the following vowel developed between certain consonant clusters (Buck, 1933:98):

(10)  *pōclom > pōcolom > pōculum  'cup'
      *faclis > facilis  'easy'
      *stablis > stabilis  'stable'

Similar examples can be found in almost every language.

Given that all phonetically motivated vowel insertions are accounted for by SSC's that insert unspecified vowels, we can account for the quality of the inserted vowel by two universal principles for the interpretation of unspecified vowels, (11) and (12):

(11)
$$\begin{bmatrix} V \\ 0 \text{ features} \end{bmatrix} \longrightarrow \begin{bmatrix} V \\ \alpha\text{features} \end{bmatrix} / \begin{bmatrix} V \\ \alpha\text{features} \end{bmatrix}$$

The environment after the slash line designates a nearby vowel, either before or after the unspecified vowel. The other choice for the features of the inserted vowel is the minimal or weak vowel. A cover feature strength may be applied to vowels as well as to consonants:

(12)
$$\begin{bmatrix} V \\ 0 \text{ features} \end{bmatrix} \longrightarrow \begin{bmatrix} V \\ 1 \text{ strength} \end{bmatrix}$$

Rules (11) and (12) are meant to be universal rules. Which rule the language uses is determined by other factors, particularly the prosodic characteristics of the language. It is also possible for a language to make use of both rule types (see Hooper, 1972b).

Rule (12) presupposes a strength scale for vowels that varies from language to language but that can be determined on the basis of synchronic and diachronic processes of vowel reduction. For example, in Spanish, historical processes of vowel reduction lowered high vowels in unstressed weak syllables, particularly word-final syllables and pretonic syllables:

(13)
|  |  |  |
|---|---|---|
| *dixi* | > *dije* | 'I said' |
| *lacus* | > *lagos* | 'lakes' |
| *plicare* | > *llegar* | 'to arrive' |
| *lucrare* | > *lograr* | 'to succeed' |

This means that, in Spanish, high vowels are stronger than mid vowels. The low vowel /a/ is the strongest of the lot; /a/ has never undergone reduction or deletion, while all other vowels have been deleted in posttonic position: *órfano* > *huérfano* 'orphan', *sábana* > *sábana* 'sheet'. The front vowels are in general weaker than the back vowels if the back vowels are reinforced by the redundant feature round. Thus the vowels of Spanish may be ranked as follows:

(14)
$$\overrightarrow{\begin{array}{ccccc} e & o & i & u & a \\ 1 & 2 & 3 & 4 & 5 \end{array}}$$

Further evidence that /e/ is the weakest of the group is that /e/ has been deleted in word-final position after certain single consonants, while /o/ and /a/ remain.

Given the SSC for Spanish, the strength scale (14), and the universal rule (12), there is no language-specific, ad hoc rule needed to generate the epenthetic vowel in new loan words. All of these mechanisms are independently motivated. Notice, however, that in an NGP all of these rules come into play in a generative capacity only when the language is faced with a new loan word that needs to be nativized. Once the loan word is adapted by syllabification and vowel insertion, the restructured word is entered in the lexicon.

The diachronic explanation for epenthesis, rule (1), in Spanish is not that a new rule was simply added to the grammar, but rather that the SSC for Spanish changed. In the earliest stages, the SSC allowed syllable-initial clusters of /s/ + C, but a simplification of the SSC made the insertion of a V necessary.

Comparing once again the TGP treatment of epenthesis, recall that in Chapter 9 I pointed out that the TGP analysis allows lexical entries that begin with a cluster of /s/ + C. The MSC's of Spanish would have to allow such a cluster, even though native speakers feel them to be non-Spanish. In the NGP treatment, these epenthetic vowels appear in the lexicon. The constraint that requires the addition of a vowel to nonnative forms that begin /s/ + C is not an ad hoc rule, but a part of the entire phenomenon of syllable structure in general. In fact, all cases of phonetically motivated insertion can be accounted for by the SSC of the language, and the motivation for all vowel insertion is the prevailing SSC of the language.

Deleted vowels are phonologically predictable on the basis of universal principles in the same way that inserted vowels are. A vowel deleted between two C's is always either the minimal vowel or a vowel with features identical to those of a nearby segment. (In this discussion I exclude from consideration V-elision that affects one of two contiguous V's. Such processes are more complex than the cases treated here; however, the result of V-elision may also be governed by hierarchical strength relations among V's (see Sanders, 1974).) The SSC also plays a role in deletion processes. A deletion is sometimes blocked if an unacceptable syllable would result. Also an NGP may not contain synchronic rules of deletion unless a surface alternation exists. Because of constraints on underlying forms in NGP, if a vowel is deleted in all surface allomorphs, the lexical form is automatically changed.

## 13.4 Consonant Insertion and Deletion

For vowels I have claimed that only an identical or minimal vowel may be deleted. This is because deletion of a minimal or identical V represents a minimal loss of nonredundant features. The claim entails that all deletions are obligatorily preceded by vowel reduction. The nonredundant features of the segment are lost first, which decreases the functional load of the segment to the point that it is practically useless and may be deleted because it has no distinguishing function. The same claim holds for vowel insertion for similar reasons. Since insertions are always motivated by phonotactic constraints, the inserted vowel does not have a distinguishing function and therefore does not need to have nonredundant features.

Exactly the same claims may be made concerning consonant insertion and deletion. Weakening or reduction must be chronologically prior to deletion of C's, and the only C's that are subject to deletion are the very weak C's or C's whose features have been assimilated to surrounding segments. Although C insertion is somewhat rarer than deletion, the principle of identity of features applies to insertion and, to a lesser extent, the requirement that the inserted C be minimal (or weak) applies. There is a difference between the way these principles apply to V's and the way they apply to C's. In general, a language will systematically choose one principle or the other to apply to inserted or deleted vowels; either the minimal V will be consistently inserted and deleted or an identical V will be used. The choice depends on typology. Stress languages usually have V reduction and will use the minimal V; vowel harmony languages will usually take an identical vowel. For C insertion and deletion it is possible for a language to apply either principle, depending on the context for the insertion or deletion, and in some cases it appears that both principles are at work. The important point here is that insertion and deletion of C's and V's are never random or arbitrary but are always governed by strict principles.

First consider the consonant shift that took place in the history of Spanish, the one Foley (1970) described as weakening. The following chart summarizes the changes:

(15)  a.  tt ⟶ t
      b.  t ⟶ d
      c.  d ⟶ ð
      d.  ð ⟶ θ

This weakening is still going on in modern Spanish. In many dialects [ð], which is considered to be an allophonic variant of /d/, falls out intervocalically, as shown in (16). The important point here is that it is the minimal obstruent [ð] that deletes, not [d] or [t] or some other segment; in fact, [d] or [t] could not delete until first undergoing a weakening. We saw similar examples in the discussion of syllable-final weakening in Chapter 11. In these cases, too, weakening was a prelude to deletion.

(16)

| Orthography | Standard | Dialectal | |
|---|---|---|---|
| soldado | [soldaðo] | [soldao] | 'soldier' |
| venido | [beniðo] | [benio] | past participle of venir 'to come' |

Assimilation is also a weakening (Vennemann, 1972d:15). There are two respects in which assimilation can be considered a weakening. (i) The acquisition of feature values from surrounding segments reduces the distinctive function of the assimilated C, and (ii) assimilation is always the precursor of deletion. Consider the case of a syllable-final nasal. Such nasals usually assimilate to the following consonant. All point of articulation features are redundant. The assimilated nasal is weak in that its only nonredundant feature is nasality. A condition on deletion of the nasal C is the transfer of the one distinctive feature, nasality, to the preceding V: VN $\longrightarrow$ ṼN. Once this process is accomplished, the nasal C carries no distinctive information of its own. It is entirely redundant and this subject to deletion. (The claim that assimilation to the following consonant, if there is one, and nasalization of the preceding V are necessary conditions for the deletion of a nasal C is an empirical claim.)

Assimilation must also be considered a weakening process even when the result of the assimilation is, according to the strength hierarchy, stronger than the original C. For instance, Malmberg (1948:102) cites the following examples as cases of syllable-final weakening. Spanish *verde* is in some dialects *vedde* [bedde] 'green', *carga, cagga* [kagga] 'charge', and *alma, amma* [amma] 'soul'. In each case the result of the assimilation is a C stronger than the original but, in context, weaker, because all features are redundant. Thus it is important to distinguish context-free weakening from context-sensitive weakening, which is assimilation.

A similar pattern is found in insertion rules. In Chapter 11 we discussed the Spanish future and conditional forms that went through the following development:

(17)     *venirá > venrá > vendrá*
         *salirá > salrá > saldrá*

The same type of process applied in the history of the word *hombre*.

Latin:  *hominem > homne > homre > hombre*

The inserted C in these cases is entirely predictable from surrounding segments; it took on the features of the preceding segment. Although the inserted C is strong (an obstruent, but notice that it is voiced, not voiceless), it brings a minimum of new features into the form, and, as we have pointed out, the result of the insertion is an improved syllable structure. Not all C insertion is motivated by the SSC, but C insertion is certainly constrained by the SSC; i.e., a C will not be inserted if its insertion would produce a violation of the SSC.

Consonantal insertion between vowels always involves a minimal segment, usually a glide. Sometimes an epenthetic glide develops between two contiguous vowels, as in these dialectal forms for the first singular of the present tense (Menéndez Pidal, 1968:189):

(18)

| Standard | Dialectal (Astorga) | |
|---|---|---|
| *veo* | *veyo* | 'I see' |
| *leo* | *leyo* | 'I read' |
| *creo* | *creyo* | 'I believe' |

The quality of the glide is determined by the preceding vowel. Thus the examples in (18) have a front glide; variant Old Spanish forms show the insertion of the labial fricative after a back vowel: *juicio, juvizio* 'justice'; *juez, juvez* 'judge'. This fricative is only a little stronger than the back glide [w]. (In fact the spelling *v* may have actually represented this glide.) A C inserted between two V's is never a strong segment ([t], [b], etc.).

The source of the inserted glide is the transition between the articulation of the two V's. The motivation for the development of a full glide here is the Optimal Syllable Principle; a CV syllable replaces a V syllable. Glide epenthesis does not occur in word-initial position because there is no source for a glide. Instead, in word-initial position the epenthetic C, if one develops at all, is the glottal stop (the minimal stop), as found in English before initial V's.

The purpose of this chapter has been to show how segmental insertions and deletions are handled in NGP, since most insertion and deletion rules are not possible P-rules. We have seen that isolated rules of insertion and deletion are usually not necessary in NGP, because SSC's and a few universal principles can account for all the facts. The superiority of the methods for accounting for insertions proposed here over the methods involving stating insertions in individual P-rules is that the NGP method captures the significant relation between these insertions and the constraints on syllable structure of the language.

# References

Abaurre, M. B. (1974). Some problems of Portuguese phonology in the light of NGP and the revised Strong Naturalness Condition. Ms. Buffalo, New York: State University of New York.

Alonso, D., Vicente, A. Z., and Canellada de Zamora, M. J. (1950). Vocales Andaluzas. *Nueva Revista de Filología Hispánica,* **4**(3), 209–230.

Andersen, H. (1973). Abductive and deductive change. *Language,* **49,** 765–793.

Anderson, J., and Jones, C. (Eds.) (1974). *Proceeding of the First International Conference on Historical Linguistics, Volume II.* Amsterdam: North Holland.

Anderson, S. (1974). *The organization of phonology.* New York: Academic Press.

Anderson, S., and Kiparsky, P. (Eds.) (1973). *A Festschrift for Morris Halle.* New York: Holt.

Bach, E., and Harms, R. (Eds.) (1968). *Universals in linguistic theory.* New York: Holt.

Bach, E., and Harms, R. (1972). How do languages get crazy rules? In R. P. Stockwell and R. K. S. Macaulay (Eds.), *Linguistic change and generative theory.* Bloomington: Indiana University Press.

Bloomfield, L. (1933). *Language.* New York: Holt.

Botha, R. P. (1971). *Methodological aspects of transformational generative phonology.* The Hague: Mouton.

Bowen, J. D. (1952). *The Spanish of Santa Antonito.* Dissertation. Albuquerque, New Mexico: University of New Mexico.

Boyd-Bowman, P. (1960). *El habla de Guanajuato.* Mexico City, Mexico: Imprenta Universitaria.

Brame, M. K. (1974). The cycle in phonology: Stress in Palestinian, Maltese and Spanish. *Linguistic Inquiry,* **5,** 39–60.

Brame, M. K., and Bordelois, I. (1973). Vocalic alternations in Spanish. *Linguistic Inquiry,* **4,** 111–168.

Brame, M. K., and Bordelois, I. (1974). Some controversial questions in Spanish phonology. *Linguistic Inquiry,* **5,** 282–298.

Bruck, A., Fox, R. A., and LaGaly, M. W. (1974). *Natural phonology.* Chicago: Chicago Linguistic Society.

Buck, C. D. (1933). *Comparative grammar of Greek and Latin.* Chicago: University of Chicago Press.

Cairns, C. E. (1969). Markedness and universal redundancy rules. *Language,* **45**(4), 863–885.

Campbell, L. (1973). Extrinsic ordering lives. Ms. Bloomington: Indiana University Linguistics Club.

Chen, M. (1972). Cross dialectal comparison: A case study and some theoretical considerations. *Journal of Chinese Linguistics,* 1(1), 38–63.

Chen, M. (1973). On the formal expression of natural rules in phonology. *Journal of Linguistics,* **9,** 223–249.

Chen, M. (1974). Natural phonology from a diachronic viewpoint. *Natural Phonology Parasession,* pp. 43–80. Chicago: Chicago Linguistic Society.

Chen, M., and Wang, W. S.-Y. (1975). Sound change: actuation and implementation. *Language,* **51,** 255–281.

Chomsky, N. (1964). Current issues in linguistic theory. In J. A. Fodor and J. J. Katz (Eds.), *The structure of language.* Englewood Cliffs, New Jersey: Prentice-Hall.

Chomsky, N., and Halle, M. (1968). *The sound pattern of English.* New York: Harper and Row.

Clayton, M. (1976). The redundance of morpheme structure conditions. *Language,* **52,** 295–313.

Crothers, J. (1971). On the abstractness controversy. *Project on Linguistic Analysis,* 11–12, CR1–CR–29. Berkeley: University of California.

Dingwall, W. O. (Ed.) (1971). *A survey of linguistic science.* College Park, Maryland: University of Maryland Press.

Entwistle, W. (1937). *The Spanish language.* London: Faber and Faber.

Espinosa, A. M. (1946). Estudios sobre el español de Nuevo Méjico, Parte II: Morfología. In A. Rosenblat (Ed.), *Biblioteca de dialectología hispano americano, II.* Facultad de Filosofía y Letras de la Universidad de Buenos Aires, Instituto de Filología. Buenos Aires.

Fidelholtz, J. L. (1975). Word frequency and vowel reduction in English. Papers from the Eleventh Meeting of the Chicago Linguistic Society.

Fodor, J. A., and Katz, J. J. (1964). *The structure of language.* Englewood Cliffs, New Jersey: Prentice-Hall.

Foley, J. (1965). Spanish morphology. Unpublished doctoral dissertation. Cambridge, Massachusetts: Massachusetts Institute of Technology.

Foley, J. (1970). Phonological distinctive features. *Folia Linguistica,* **4,** 87–92.

Foley, J. (1972). Rule precursors and phonological change by metarule. In R. P. Stockwell and R. K. S. Macaulay (Eds.), *Linguistic change and generative theory,* pp. 96–100. Bloomington: Indiana University Press.

Fudge, E. (1969). Syllables. *Journal of Linguistics,* **5,** 253–286.

Fujimura, O. (Ed.) (1973). *Three dimensions of linguistic theory.* Tokyo: TEC Company.

Greenberg, J. (1965). Some generalizations concerning initial and final consonant sequences. *Linguistics,* **18,** 5–34.

Guile, T. (1973). Glide-obstruentization and the syllable coda hierarchy. Papers from the Ninth Regional Meeting of the Chicago Linguistic Society, pp. 139–156.

Hale, K. (1971). Deep-surface canonical disparities in relation to analysis and change: An Australian example. In T. Sebeok, H. Hoenigswald, and R. Longacre (Eds.), Current trends in linguistics, II. The Hague: Mouton.

Halle, M. (1962). Phonology in generative grammar. Word, 18, 54–72. Reprinted in J. A. Fodor and J. J. Katz (Eds.) (1964), The structure of language. Englewood Cliffs, New Jersey: Prentice-Hall.

Halle, M. (1964). On the basis of phonology. In J. A. Fodor and J. J. Katz (Eds.), The structure of language, pp. 324–333. Englewood Cliffs, New Jersey: Prentice-Hall.

Halle, M. (1973). Prolegomena to a theory of word formation. Linguistic Inquiry, 4(1), 3–16.

Hankamer, J., and Aissen, J. (1974). The sonority hierarchy. Natural Phonology Parasession, pp. 131–145. Chicago: Chicago Linguistic Society.

Harms, R. (1973). How abstract is Nupe? Language, 49, 439–446.

Harris, J. W. (1969). Spanish phonology. Cambridge, Massachusetts: MIT Press.

Harris, H. W. (1972). Five classes of irregular verbs in Spanish. In J. Casagrande and B. Saciuk (Eds.), Generative studies in Romance Languages, pp. 247–271. Rowley, Massachusetts: Newbury House.

Harris, J. W. (1973a). Morphologization of phonological rules: An example from Chicano Spanish. In R. J. Campbell, M. G. Goldin, and M. C. Wang (Eds.), Linguistic studies in Romance Languages. Washington: Georgetown Press.

Harris, J. W. (1973b). On the ordering of certain phonological rules. In S. Anderson and P. Kiparsky (Eds.), Festschrift for Morris Halle. New York: Holt.

Harris, J. W. (1974a). On certain claims concerning Spanish phonology. Linguistic Inquiry, 5, 271–281.

Harris, J. W. (1974b). Stress assignment rules in Spanish. Paper read at the Texas Symposium on Romance Linguistics, Austin, Texas.

Harris, J. W. (1975). Morphology is generative grammar: vowel alternations in Spanish verb forms. In J. Guitart and J. Roy (Eds.), El español y la lingüística generativo-transformacional. Barcelona: Edicions 62, Península. In press.

Hoard, J. E. (1971). Aspiration, tenseness, and syllabication in English. Language, 47(1), 133–140.

Hooper, J. B. (1972a). Constraints on vowel insertion and deletion. Paper read at the summer LSA meeting, Chapel Hill, North Carolina.

Hooper, J. B. (1972b). A note on inserted and deleted vowels. Stanford Working Papers on Language Universals, 10, 141–144.

Hooper, J. B. (1972c). The syllable in phonological theory. Language, 48(3), 525–540.

Hooper, J. B. (1975). The archisegment in natural generative phonology. Language, 51(3), 536–560.

Hooper, J. B. (1976a). Constraints on schwa-deletion in American English. Read at the International Conference on Historical Phonology, Ustronie, Poland. To appear in the Proceedings. The Hague: Mouton.

Hooper, J. B. (1976b). Word frequency in lexical diffusion and the source of morphophonological change. In W. Christie (Ed.), Proceedings of the Second International Conference on Historical Linguistics. Amsterdam: North Holland.

Hooper, J. B., and Terrell, T. (1976). Stress assignment in Spanish: A natural generative analysis. Glossa, 10(1).

Hudson, G. (1974a). The representation of non-productive alternations. In J. Anderson and C. Jones (Eds.), Preceedings of the First International Conference on Historical Linguistics, Volume II, pp. 203–229. Amsterdam: North Holland.

Hudson, G. (1974b). The role of surface phonetic constraints in natural generative phonology. *Natural Phonology Parasession*. Chicago: Chicago Linguistic Society.

Hudson, G. (1975a). Formal and functional explanation of diachronic evidence for phonemics. In R. Grossman, J. San, and T. Vance (Eds.), *Papers from the parasession on functionalism*. Chicago: Chicago Linguistic Society.

Hudson, G. (1975b). Suppletion in the representation of alternations. Doctoral dissertation. Los Angeles: University of California.

Hyman, L. (1970). How concrete is phonology? *Language*, **46**, 58–76.

Hyman, L. (1973a). Nupe three years later. *Language*, **49**, 447–452.

Hyman, L. (1973b). Synchronic and diachronic naturalness. Unpublished paper. Los Angeles: University of Southern California.

Hyman, L. (1974). How do natural rules become unnatural? Project on Linguistic Analysis. Berkeley: University of California.

Jakobson, R. (1941[1972]). *Child language, aphasia and phonological universals*. The Hague: Mouton.

Jakobson, R., and Halle, M. (1956). *Fundamentals of language*. The Hague: Mouton.

Kachru, B. (Ed.) (1973). *Issues in linguistics: Papers in honor of Henry and Renee Kahane*. Urbana, Illinois: University of Illinois Press.

Kahane, H., and Pietrangelo, A. (Eds.) (1959). *Structural studies on Spanish themes*. Salamanca: Acta Salamanticensia, XII.

Kaye, J. (1971). Nasal harmony in Desano. *Linguistic Inquiry*, **2**, 36–56.

Kaye, J., and Piggot, G. (1973). On the cyclic nature of Ojibwa T-palatalization. *Linguistic Inquiry* **4**, 345–362.

Kenstowicz, M. J., and Kisseberth, C. W. (1971). Unmarked bleeding orders. In C. W. Kisseberth (Ed.), *Studies in generative phonology*. Edmonton, Alberta: Linguistic Research, Inc.

Kenstowicz, M. J., and Kisseberth, C. W. (Eds.) (1973). *Issues in phonological theory*. The Hague: Mouton.

Kettunen, L. (1940). *Suomen murrekartasto (Suomen murteet, III: A. murrekartasto)*. Helsinki: Suomalaisen Kirjallisuuden Seura.

King, R. D. (1969). *Historical linguistics and generative grammar*. Englewood Cliffs, New Jersey: Prentice-Hall.

King, R. D. (1973). Rule insertion. *Language*, **49**, 551–578.

Kiparsky, P. (1965). Phonological change. Dissertation. Massachusetts Institute of Technology. Available from the Indiana University Linguistics Club, Bloomington, Indiana.

Kiparsky, P. (1968). Linguistic universals and linguistic change. In E. Bach and R. Harms (Eds.), *Universals in linguistic theory*. New York: Holt.

Kiparsky, P. (1968[1973]). How abstract is phonology? In O. Fujimura (Ed.), *Three dimensions of linguistic theory*, pp. 5–56. Tokyo: TEC Company.

Kiparsky, P. (1971). Historical Linguistics. In W. O. Dingwall (Ed.), *A survey of linguistic science*, pp. 577–649. College Park, Maryland: University of Maryland Press.

Kiparsky, P. (1973a). Elsewhere in phonology. In S. Anderson and P. Kiparsky (Eds.), *A Festschrift for Morris Halle*. New York: Holt.

Kiparsky, P. (1973b). Phonological representations. In O. Fujimura (Ed.), *Three dimensions of linguistic theory*. Tokyo: TEC Company.

Kiparsky, P. (1974). On the evaluation measure. *Natural Phonology Parasession*, pp. 328–337. Chicago: Chicago Linguistic Society.

Kisseberth, C. (1970). On the functional unity of phonological rules. *Linguistic Inquiry*, **1**(3), 291–306.

Kisseberth, C. (1973). Is rule ordering necessary in phonology? In B. Kachru (Ed.), *Issues in linguistics: Papers in honor of Henry and Renee Kahane*, pp. 418–441. Urbana, Illinois: University of Illinois Press.

Koutsoudas, A., Sanders, G., and Noll, C. (1974). On the application of phonological rules. *Language*, **50**, 1–28.

Kučera, H. (1973). Language variability, rule interdependency, and the grammar of Czech. *Linguistic Inquiry*, **4**, 499–521.

Labov, W. (1972). The internal evolution of linguistic rules. In R. P. Stockwell and R. K. S. Macaulay (Eds.), *Linguistic change and generative theory*, pp. 101–171. Bloomington: Indiana University Press.

Ladefoged, P. (1971). *Preliminaries to linguistic phonetics*. Chicago: University of Chicago Press.

Malmberg, B. (1948). La structure syllabique de l'espagnol: étude phonétique. *Boletím de filologia*, **9**, 99–120.

Malmberg, B. (1963). *Phonetics*. New York: Dover Publications.

Martinet, A. (1952). Function, structure and sound change. *Word*, **8**, 1–32.

Menéndez Pidal, R. (1968). *Manual de gramática histórica española*. Madrid: Espasa-Calpe.

Mondéjar, J. (1970). El verbo andaluz. *Revista de filología española*, anejo 90.

Mowrey, R. A. (1975). Descriptive parameters and the notation of diachronic change in phonology. Ms. Buffalo, New York: State University of New York.

Navarro Tomás, T. (1957). *Manual de pronunciación española*. New York: Hafner.

Norman, L. J. (1973). Rule addition and intrinsic order. University of Minnesota Working Papers in Philosophy and Linguistics.

Otero, C. P. (1971). *Evolución y revolución en romance*. Barcelona: Editorial Seix Barral.

Picard, M. (1974). Re-examining phonological rules: Examples from French. *Montreal Working Papers in Linguistics*, **1**, 123–132.

Postal, P. (1968). *Aspects of phonological theory*. New York: Harper and Row.

Pulgram, E. (1970). *Syllable, word, nexus, cursus*. The Hague: Mouton.

Pyle, C. (1974). Why a conspiracy? *Natural Phonology Parasession*, pp. 275–284. Chicago: Chicago Linguistic Society.

Rapola, M. (1966). *Suomen Kielen äännehistorian luennot*. Helsinki: Suomalaisen Kirjallisuuden Seura.

Reyes, R. (1972). Studies in Chicano Spanish. Doctoral dissertation. Cambridge, Massachusetts: Harvard University.

Rosenblat, A. (1946). *Biblioteca de dialectología hispano americano, II*. Facultad de Filosofía y Letras de la Universidad de Buenos Aires, Instituto de Filología. Buenos Aires.

Rudes, B. (1976). Lexical representations and variable rules in natural generative phonology. *Glossa* **10,1**.

Sanders, G. A. (1974). Precedence relations in language. *Foundations of Language*, **11**, 361–400.

Saporta, S. (1959). Morpheme alternants in Spanish. In H. Kahane and A. Pietrangelo (Eds.), *Structural studies on Spanish themes*, pp. 15–162. Salamanca: Acta Salmanticensia, XII.

Saporta, S. (1965). Ordered rules, dialect differences and historical processes. *Language*, **41**, 218–224.

Saussure, F. de. (1915[1959]). *Course in general linguistics*. New York: Philosophical Library.

Schachter, P., and Fromkin, V. (1968). A phonology of Akan: Akuapem, Asante, & Fante. *Working Papers in Phonetics*, No. 9. Los Angeles: University of California Press.

Schane, S. (1968). *French phonology and morphology*. Cambridge, Massachusetts: MIT Press.

Schane, S. (1971). The phoneme revisited. *Language*, **47**, 503–521.

Schane, S. (1972). Natural rules in phonology. In R. P. Stockwell and R. K. S. Macauley (Eds.), *Linguistic change and generative theory*. Bloomington: Indiana University Press.

Schane, S. (1973). *Generative phonology*. Englewood Cliffs, New Jersey: Prentice-Hall.

Schane, S. (1974). How abstract is abstract? *Natural Phonology Parasession*, pp. 297–317. Chicago: Chicago Linguistic Society.

Schuchardt, H. (1885[1972]). On sound laws: Against the neogrammarians. In T. Vennemann and T. H. Wilbur (Eds.) (1972), *Schuchardt, the neogrammarians, and the transformational theory of phonological change* (*Linguistische Forschungen 26*), pp. 39–72, Frankfurt am Main: Athenäum Verlag.

Schuh, R. G. (1972). Rule inversion in Chadic. *Studies in African Linguistics*, **3**(3), 379–397.

Sebeok, T., Hoenigswald, H., and Longacre, R. (1971). *Current trends in linguistics, II*. The Hague: Mouton.

Shibatani, M. (1973). The role of surface phonetic constraints in generative phonology. *Language*, **49**(1), 87–106.

Shopen, T. (1971). Caught in the act. Papers from the Seventh Regional Meeting of the Chicago Linguistics Society, pp. 254–263.

Shuy, R., and Bailey, C. J. (1974). *Toward tomorrow's linguistics*. Washington, D. C.: Georgetown University Press.

Skousen, R. (1972). On capturing regularities. Papers from the Eighth Regional Meeting of the Chicago Linguistic Society, pp. 567–577. Chicago: Chicago Linguistic Society.

Smith, N. V. (1967). The phonology of Nupe. *Journal of African Languages* **6**, 153–169.

Sommer, B. (1970). An Australian language without CV syllables. *International Journal of American Linguistics*, **36**, 57–58.

Stampe, D. (1969). On the acquisition of phonetic representation. Papers from the Fifth Regional Meeting of the Chicago Linguistic Society, pp. 443–454. Chicago: Chicago Linguistic Society.

Stampe, D. (1973a). A dissertation on natural phonology. Doctoral dissertation. University of Chicago.

Stampe, D. (1973b). On chapter nine. In M. J. Kenstowicz and C. W. Kisseberth (Eds.), *Issues in phonological theory*. The Hague: Mouton.

Stanley, R. (1967). Redundancy rules in phonology. *Language*, **43**, 393–436.

Stockwell, R. P., and Macaulay, R. K. S. (1972). *Linguistic change and generative theory*. Bloomington: Indiana University Press.

Thompson, S. A. (1974). On the issue of productivity in the lexicon. In S. A. Thompson and C. Lord (Eds.), *Approaches to the lexicon*, pp. 1–25. Papers in Syntax, No. 6. Los Angeles: University of California.

Tranel, B. (1974a). A note on final consonant deletion, the pronunciation of cardinal numbers, and linguistic changes in progress in modern French. *Montreal Working Papers in Linguistics*, **3**, 173–189.

Tranel, B. (1974b). The phonology of nasal vowels in modern French. Ph.D. Dissertation. San Diego: University of California.

Truitner, K., and Dunnigan, T. (1975). Palatalization in Ojibwa. *Linguistic Inquiry*, **4**, 301–316.

Vásquez, W. (1953). El fonema /s/ en el español del Uruguay. *Revista de la facultad de humanidades y ciencias*, **10**, 87–94.

Vennemann, T. (1971). Natural generative phonology. Paper read at annual meeting of the Linguistic Society of America, St. Louis, Missouri.

Vennemann, T. (1972a). Phonetic analogy and conceptual analogy. In T. Vennemann and T. H. Wilbur (Eds.), *Schuchardt, the neogrammarians, and the transformational theory of phonological change (Linguistische Forschungen 26)*, pp. 181–204. Frankfurt am Main: Athenäum Verlag.

Vennemann, T. (1972b). Phonetic detail in assimilation: Problems in Germanic phonology. *Language*, **48**(4), 863–892.

Vennemann, T. (1972c). Phonological uniqueness in natural generative grammar. *Glossa*, **6**, 105–116.

Vennemann, T. (1972d). On the theory of syllabic phonology. *Linguistische Berichte*, **18**, 1–18.

Venneman, T. (1972e). Rule inversion. *Lingua*, **29**, 209–242.

Vennemann, T. (1972f). Sound change and markedness theory: On the history of the German consonant system. In R. P. Stockwell and R. K. S. Macaulay (Eds.), *Linguistic change and generative theory*, pp. 230–274. Bloomington: Indiana University Press.

Vennemann, T. (1974a). Phonological concreteness in natural generative grammar. In R. Shuy and C. J. Bailey (Eds.), *Toward tomorrow's linguistics*. Washington, D.C.: Georgetown University Press.

Vennemann, T. (1974b). Words and syllables in natural generative grammar. *Natural Phonology Parasession*, pp. 346–374. Chicago: Chicago Linguistic Society.

Vennemann, T., and Ladefoged, P. (1973). Phonetic features and phonological features. *Lingua*, **32**, 61–74.

Vennemann, T., and Wilbur, T. H. (1972). *Schuchardt, the neogrammarians, and the transformational theory of phonological change (Linguistische Forschungen 26)*. Frankfurt am Main: Athenäum Verlag.

Wang, W. S.-Y. (1969). Competing changes as a cause of residue. *Language*, **45**, 9–25.

Williamson, K. (1972). Consonant distribution in Ijo. *Archibald Hill Festschrift*, Polomé et al. (Eds.).

Zwicky, A. (1972). A Note on a phonological hierarchy in English. In R. P. Stockwell and R. K. S. Macaulay (Eds.), *Linguistic change and generative theory*. Bloomington: Indiana University Press.

# Index

251

A 6
B 7
C 8
D 9
E 0
F 1
G 2
H 3
I 4
J 5